Networking and Kubernetes
A Layered Approach

James Strong and Vallery Lancey

Beijing · Boston · Farnham · Sebastopol · Tokyo

Networking and Kubernetes

by James Strong and Vallery Lancey

Published by O'Reilly Media, Inc., 1005 Gravenstein Highway North, Sebastopol, CA 95472.

O'Reilly books may be purchased for educational, business, or sales promotional use. Online editions are also available for most titles (*http://oreilly.com*). For more information, contact our corporate/institutional sales department: 800-998-9938 or *corporate@oreilly.com*.

Acquisitions Editor: John Devins
Development Editor: Melissa Potter
Production Editor: Beth Kelly
Copyeditor: Kim Wimpsett
Proofreader: Piper Editorial Consulting, LLC

Indexer: Sam Arnold-Boyd
Interior Designer: David Futato
Cover Designer: Karen Montgomery
Illustrator: Kate Dullea

September 2021:   First Edition

Revision History for the First Edition
2021-09-07:   First Release

See *http://oreilly.com/catalog/errata.csp?isbn=9781492081654* for release details.

978-1-492-08165-4

[LSI]

Table of Contents

Preface

Just Another Packet

Since the first two computers were joined together over a cable, networking has been a crucial part of our infrastructure. Networks now have layers and layers of complexity to support a multitude of use cases, and the advent of containers and projects like Mesosphere and Kubernetes have not changed that. While the contributors of Kubernetes have attempted to abstract away this networking complexity for developers, computer science is just that, abstraction upon abstraction. Kubernetes, and its networking API, is another abstraction that makes it easier and faster to deploy applications for consumption. What about the administrator who has to manage Kubernetes? This book intends to dispel the mysticism around the abstractions Kubernetes puts in place, guide administrators through the layers of complexity, and help you realize Kubernetes is not just another packet.

Who This Book Is For

According to 451 Research (*https://oreil.ly/2SlsD*), the global application container market is expected to grow from USD 2.1 billion in 2019 to USD 4.2 billion by 2022 . This explosive growth in the container market underscores the need for IT professionals to be knowledgeable in deploying, managing, and troubleshooting containers.

This book is intended to be read from beginning to end by new network, Linux, or cluster administrators, and it can be used by more experienced DevOps engineers to jump to specific topics for which they find themselves needing to be upskilled. Network, Linux, and cluster administrators need to be familiar with how to operate Kubernetes at scale.

In this book, readers will find the information required to navigate the layers of complexity that come with running a Kubernetes network. This book will peel back the abstractions that Kubernetes puts in place so that developers have a similar experience across deployments on-premises, in the cloud, and with managed services.

Engineers responsible for production cluster operations and network uptime can use this book to bridge the gap in their knowledge of those abstractions.

What You Will Learn

By the end of this book, the reader will understand the following:

- The Kubernetes networking model
- The Container Network Interface (CNI) project and how to choose a CNI project for their clusters
- Networking and Linux primitives that power Kubernetes
- The relationship between the abstractions powering the Kubernetes network

Also, the reader will be able to do the following:

- Deploy and manage a production-scale network for Kubernetes clusters
- Troubleshoot underlying network-related application issues inside a Kubernetes cluster

Conventions Used in This Book

The following typographical conventions are used in this book:

Italic
: Indicates new terms, URLs, email addresses, filenames, and file extensions.

`Constant width`
: Used for program listings, as well as within paragraphs to refer to program elements such as variable or function names, databases, data types, environment variables, statements, and keywords.

`Constant width bold`
: Shows commands or other text that should be typed literally by the user.

`Constant width italic`
: Shows text that should be replaced with user-supplied values or by values determined by context.

 This element signifies a tip or suggestion.

This element signifies a general note.

 This element indicates a warning or caution.

Using Code Examples

Supplemental material (code examples, exercises, etc.) is available for download at *https://github.com/strongjz/Networking-and-Kubernetes*.

If you have a technical question, or a problem using the code examples, please send email to *bookquestions@oreilly.com*.

This book is here to help you get your job done. In general, if example code is offered with this book, you may use it in your programs and documentation. You do not need to contact us for permission unless you're reproducing a significant portion of the code. For example, writing a program that uses several chunks of code from this book does not require permission. Selling or distributing examples from O'Reilly books does require permission. Answering a question by citing this book and quoting example code does not require permission. Incorporating a significant amount of example code from this book into your product's documentation does require permission.

We appreciate, but generally do not require, attribution. An attribution usually includes the title, author, publisher, and ISBN. For example: "*Networking and Kubernetes* by James Strong and Vallery Lancey (O'Reilly). Copyright 2021 Strongjz tech and Vallery Lancey, 978-1-492-08165-4.*"

If you feel your use of code examples falls outside fair use or the permission given above, feel free to contact us at *permissions@oreilly.com*.

O'Reilly Online Learning

 For more than 40 years, *O'Reilly Media* has provided technology and business training, knowledge, and insight to help companies succeed.

Our unique network of experts and innovators share their knowledge and expertise through books, articles, and our online learning platform. O'Reilly's online learning platform gives you on-demand access to live training courses, in-depth learning paths, interactive coding environments, and a vast collection of text and video from O'Reilly and 200+ other publishers. For more information, visit *http://oreilly.com*.

How to Contact Us

Please address comments and questions concerning this book to the publisher:

O'Reilly Media, Inc.
1005 Gravenstein Highway North
Sebastopol, CA 95472
800-998-9938 (in the United States or Canada)
707-829-0515 (international or local)
707-829-0104 (fax)

We have a web page for this book, where we list errata, examples, and any additional information. You can access this page at *https://oreil.ly/NetKubernetes*.

Email *bookquestions@oreilly.com* to comment or ask technical questions about this book.

For news and information about our books and courses, visit *http://oreilly.com*.

Find us on Facebook: *http://facebook.com/oreilly*.

Follow us on Twitter: *http://twitter.com/oreillymedia*.

Watch us on YouTube: *http://youtube.com/oreillymedia*.

Acknowledgments

The authors would like to thank the team at O'Reilly Media for helping them through the process of writing their first book. Melissa Potter was instrumental in getting this across the finish line. We would also like to recognize Thomas Behnken for aiding us with his Azure expertise.

James: Karen, thank you for all your faith in me and for helping him believe in himself even when he didn't. Wink, you are the reason I started working in this field, and I am forever grateful. Ann, I have come a long way since learning English is supposed to be capitalized. James would also like to thank all the other teachers and coaches in his life who supported him.

Vallery: I'd like to thank the friendly faces in SIG-Network for helping me get started in upstream Kubernetes.

Finally, the authors would like to thank the Kubernetes community; this book wouldn't exist without them. We hope it helps further the knowledge for all engineers looking to adopt Kubernetes.

## CHAPTER 1

Networking Introduction

"Guilty until proven innocent." That's the mantra of networks and the engineers who supervise them. In this opening chapter, we will wade through the development of networking technologies and standards, give a brief overview of the dominant theory of networking, and introduce our Golang web server that will be the basis of the networking examples in Kubernetes and the cloud throughout the book.

Let's begin…at the beginning.

Networking History

The internet we know today is vast, with cables spanning oceans and mountains and connecting cities with lower latency than ever before. Barrett Lyon's "Mapping the Internet," shown in Figure 1-1, shows just how vast it truly is. That image illustrates all the connections between the networks of networks that make up the internet. The purpose of a network is to exchange information from one system to another system. That is an enormous ask of a distributed global system, but the internet was not always global; it started as a conceptual model and slowly was built up over time, to the behemoth in Lyon's visually stunning artwork. There are many factors to consider when learning about networking, such as the last mile, the connectivity between a customer's home and their internet service provider's network—all the way to scaling up to the geopolitical landscape of the internet. The internet is integrated into the fabric of our society. In this book, we will discuss how networks operate and how Kubernetes abstracts them for us.

Figure 1-1. Barrett Lyon, "Mapping the Internet," 2003

Table 1-1 briefly outlines the history of networking before we dive into a few of the important details.

Table 1-1. A brief history of networking

Year	Event
1969	ARPANET's first connection test
1969	Telnet 1969 Request for Comments (RFC) 15 drafted
1971	FTP RFC 114 drafted
1973	FTP RFC 354 drafted
1974	TCP RFC 675 by Vint Cerf, Yogen Dalal, and Carl Sunshine drafted
1980	Development of Open Systems Interconnection model begins
1981	IP RFC 760 drafted
1982	NORSAR and University College London left the ARPANET and began using TCP/IP over SATNET
1984	ISO 7498 Open Systems Interconnection (OSI) model published
1991	National Information Infrastructure (NII) Bill passed with Al Gore's help
1991	First version of Linux released
2015	First version of Kubernetes released

In its earliest forms, networking was government run or sponsored; in the United States, the Department of Defense (DOD) sponsored the Advanced Research Projects Agency Network (ARPANET), well before Al Gore's time in politics, which will be relevant in a moment. In 1969, ARPANET was deployed at the University of California–Los Angeles, the Augmentation Research Center at Stanford Research Institute, the University of California–Santa Barbara, and the University of Utah School of Computing. Communication between these nodes was not completed until 1970, when they began using the Network Control Protocol (NCP). NCP led to the development and use of the first computer-to-computer protocols like Telnet and File Transfer Protocol (FTP).

The success of ARPANET and NCP, the first protocol to power ARPANET, led to NCP's downfall. It could not keep up with the demands of the network and the variety of networks connected. In 1974, Vint Cerf, Yogen Dalal, and Carl Sunshine began drafting RFC 675 for Transmission Control Protocol (TCP). (You'll learn more about RFCs in a few paragraphs.) TCP would go on to become the standard for network connectivity. TCP allowed for exchanging packets across different types of networks. In 1981, the Internet Protocol (IP), defined in RFC 791, helped break out the responsibilities of TCP into a separate protocol, increasing the modularity of the network. In the following years, many organizations, including the DOD, adopted TCP as the standard. By January 1983, TCP/IP had become the only approved protocol on ARPANET, replacing the earlier NCP because of its versatility and modularity.

A competing standards organization, the International Organization for Standardization (ISO), developed and published ISO 7498, "Open Systems Interconnection Reference Model," which detailed the OSI model. With its publication also came the protocols to support it. Unfortunately, the OSI model protocols never gained traction and lost out to the popularity of TCP/IP. The OSI model is still an excellent learning tool for understanding the layered approach to networking, however.

In 1991, Al Gore invented the internet (well, really he helped pass the National Information Infrastructure [NII] Bill), which helped lead to the creation of the Internet Engineering Task Force (IETF). Nowadays standards for the internet are under the management of the IETF, an open consortium of leading experts and companies in the field of networking, like Cisco and Juniper. RFCs are published by the Internet Society and the Internet Engineering Task Force. RFCs are prominently authored by individuals or groups of engineers and computer scientists, and they detail their processes, operations, and applications for the internet's functioning.

An IETF RFC has two states:

Proposed Standard
> A protocol specification has reached enough community support to be considered a standard. The designs are stable and well understood. A proposed standard can be deployed, implemented, and tested. It may be withdrawn from further consideration, however.

Internet Standard
> Per RFC 2026: "In general, an internet standard is a stable specification and well understood, technically competent, has multiple, independent, and interoperable implementations with substantial operational experience, enjoys significant public support, and is recognizably useful in some parts of the internet."

 Draft standard is a third classification that was discontinued in 2011.

There are thousands of internet standards defining how to implement protocols for all facets of networking, including wireless, encryption, and data formats, among others. Each one is implemented by contributors of open source projects and privately by large organizations like Cisco.

A lot has happened in the nearly 50 years since those first connectivity tests. Networks have grown in complexity and abstractions, so let's start with the OSI model.

OSI Model

The OSI model is a conceptual framework for describing how two systems communicate over a network. The OSI model breaks down the responsibility of sending data across networks into layers. This works well for educational purposes to describe the relationships between each layer's responsibility and how data gets sent over networks. Interestingly enough, it was meant to be a protocol suite to power networks but lost to TCP/IP.

Here are the ISO standards that outline the OSI model and protocols:

- ISO/IEC 7498-1, "The Basic Model"
- ISO/IEC 7498-2, "Security Architecture"
- ISO/IEC 7498-3, "Naming and Addressing"
- ISO/IEC 7498-4, "Management Framework"

The ISO/IEC 7498-1 describes what the OSI model attempts to convey:

> 5.2.2.1 The basic structuring technique in the Reference Model of Open Systems Inter-connection is layering. According to this technique, each open system is viewed as logically composed of an ordered set of (N)-subsystems…Adjacent (N)-subsystems communicate through their common boundary. (N)-subsystems of the same rank (N) collectively form the (N)-layer of the Reference Model of Open Systems Interconnection. There is one and only one (N)-subsystem in an open system for layer N. An (N)-subsystem consists of one or several (N)-entities. Entities exist in each (N)-layer. Entities in the same (N)-layer are termed peer-(N)-entities. Note that the highest layer does not have an (N+l)-layer above it, and the lowest layer does not have an (N-1)-layer below it.

The OSI model description is a complex and exact way of saying networks have layers like cakes or onions. The OSI model breaks the responsibilities of the network into seven distinct layers, each with different functions to aid in transmitting information from one system to another, as shown in Figure 1-2. The layers encapsulate information from the layer below it; these layers are Application, Presentation, Session, Transport, Network, Data Link, and Physical. Over the next few pages, we will go over each layer's functionality and how it sends data between two systems.

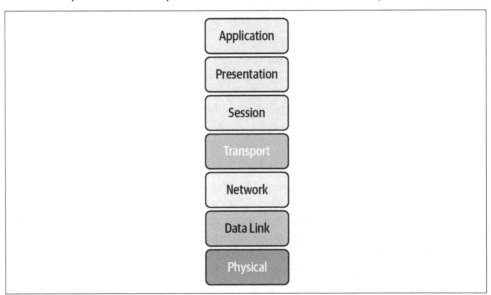

Figure 1-2. OSI model layers

Each layer takes data from the previous layer and encapsulates it to make its Protocol Data Unit (PDU). The PDU is used to describe the data at each layer. PDUs are also part of TCP/IP. The applications of the Session layer are considered "data" for the PDU, preparing the application information for communication. Transport uses ports to distinguish what process on the local system is responsible for the data. The

Network layer PDU is the packet. Packets are distinct pieces of data routed between networks. The Data Link layer is the frame or segment. Each packet is broken up into frames, checked for errors, and sent out on the local network. The Physical layer transmits the frame in bits over the medium. Next we will outline each layer in detail:

Application

The Application layer is the top layer of the OSI model and is the one the end user interacts with every day. This layer is not where actual applications live, but it provides the interface for applications that use it like a web browser or Office 365. The single biggest interface is HTTP; you are probably reading this book on a web page hosted by an O'Reilly web server. Other examples of the Application layer that we use daily are DNS, SSH, and SMTP. Those applications are responsible for displaying and arranging data requested and sent over the network.

Presentation

This layer provides independence from data representation by translating between application and network formats. It can be referred to as the *syntax layer*. This layer allows two systems to use different encodings for data and still pass data between them. Encryption is also done at this layer, but that is a more complicated story we'll save for "TLS" on page 25.

Session

The Session layer is responsible for the duplex of the connection, in other words, whether sending and receiving data at the same time. It also establishes procedures for performing checkpointing, suspending, restarting, and terminating a session. It builds, manages, and terminates the connections between the local and remote applications.

Transport

The Transport layer transfers data between applications, providing reliable data transfer services to the upper layers. The Transport layer controls a given connection's reliability through flow control, segmentation and desegmentation, and error control. Some protocols are state- and connection-oriented. This layer tracks the segments and retransmits those that fail. It also provides the acknowledgment of successful data transmission and sends the next data if no errors occurred. TCP/IP has two protocols at this layer: TCP and User Datagram Protocol (UDP).

Network

The Network layer implements a means of transferring variable-length data flows from a host on one network to a host on another network while sustaining service quality. The Network layer performs routing functions and might also perform fragmentation and reassembly while reporting delivery errors. Routers operate at this layer, sending data throughout the neighboring networks. Several management protocols belong to the Network layer, including routing protocols, multicast group management, network-layer information, error handling, and network-layer address assignment, which we will discuss further in "TCP/IP" on page 8.

Data Link

This layer is responsible for the host-to-host transfers on the same network. It defines the protocols to create and terminate the connections between two devices. The Data Link layer transfers data between network hosts and provides the means to detect and possibly correct errors from the Physical layer. Data Link frames, the PDU for layer 2, do not cross the boundaries of a local network.

Physical

The Physical layer is represented visually by an Ethernet cord plugged into a switch. This layer converts data in the form of digital bits into electrical, radio, or optical signals. Think of this layer as the physical devices, like cables, switches, and wireless access points. The wire signaling protocols are also defined at this layer.

 There are many mnemonics to remember the layers of the OSI model; our favorite is All People Seem To Need Data Processing.

Table 1-2 summarizes the OSI layers.

Table 1-2. OSI layer details

Layer number	Layer name	Protocol data unit	Function overview
7	Application	Data	High-level APIs and application protocols like HTTP, DNS, and SSH.
6	Presentation	Data	Character encoding, data compression, and encryption/decryption.
5	Session	Data	Continuous data exchanges between nodes are managed here: how much data to send, when to send more.
4	Transport	Segment, datagram	Transmission of data segments between endpoints on a network, including segmentation, acknowledgment, and multiplexing.
3	Network	Packet	Structuring and managing addressing, routing, and traffic control for all endpoints on the network.
2	Data Link	Frame	Transmission of data frames between two nodes connected by a Physical layer.
1	Physical	Bit	Sending and receiving of bitstreams over the medium.

The OSI model breaks down all the necessary functions to send a data packet over a network between two hosts. In the late 1980s and early 1990s, it lost out to TCP/IP as the standard adopted by the DOD and all other major players in networking. The standard defined in ISO 7498 gives a brief glimpse into the implementation details that were considered by most at the time to be complicated, inefficient, and to an extent unimplementable. The OSI model at a high level still allows those learning networking to comprehend the basic concepts and challenges in networking. In addition, these terms and functions are used in the TCP/IP model covered in the next section and ultimately in Kubernetes abstractions. Kubernetes services break out each function depending on the layer it is operating at, for example, a layer 3 IP address or a layer 4 port; you will learn more about that in Chapter 4. Next, we will do a deep dive into the TCP/IP suite with an example walk-through.

TCP/IP

TCP/IP creates a heterogeneous network with open protocols that are independent of the operating system and architectural differences. Whether the hosts are running Windows, Linux, or another OS, TCP/IP allows them to communicate; TCP/IP does not care if you are running Apache or Nginx for your web server at the Application layer. The separation of responsibilities similar to the OSI model makes that possible. In Figure 1-3, we compare the OSI model to TCP/IP.

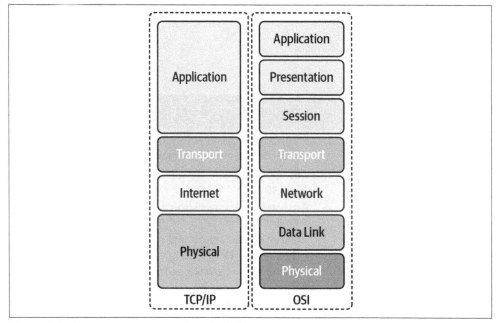

Figure 1-3. OSI model compared to TCP/IP

Here we expand on the differences between the OSI model and the TCP/IP:

Application

In TCP/IP, the Application layer comprises the communications protocols used in process-to-process communications across an IP network. The Application layer standardizes communication and depends upon the underlying Transport layer protocols to establish the host-to-host data transfer. The lower Transport layer also manages the data exchange in network communications. Applications at this layer are defined in RFCs; in this book, we will continue to use HTTP, RFC 7231 as our example for the Application layer.

Transport

TCP and UDP are the primary protocols of the Transport layer that provide host-to-host communication services for applications. Transport protocols are responsible for connection-oriented communication, reliability, flow control, and multiplexing. In TCP, the window size manages flow control, while UDP does not manage the congestion flow and is considered unreliable; you'll learn more about that in "UDP" on page 28. Each port identifies the host process responsible for processing the information from the network communication. HTTP uses the well-known port 80 for nonsecure communication and 443 for secure communication. Each port on the server identifies its traffic, and the sender generates a random port locally to identify itself. The governing body that manages port number assignments is the Internet Assigned Number Authority (IANA); there are 65,535 ports.

Internet

The Internet, or Network layer, is responsible for transmitting data between networks. For an outgoing packet, it selects the next-hop host and transmits it to that host by passing it to the appropriate link-layer. Once the packet is received by the destination, the Internet layer will pass the packet payload up to the appropriate Transport layer protocol.

IP provides the fragmentation or defragmentation of packets based on the maximum transmission unit (MTU); this is the maximum size of the IP packet. IP makes no guarantees about packets' proper arrival. Since packet delivery across diverse networks is inherently unreliable and failure-prone, that burden is with the endpoints of a communication path, rather than on the network. The function of providing service reliability is in the Transport layer. A checksum ensures that the information in a received packet is accurate, but this layer does not validate data integrity. The IP address identifies packets on the network.

Link

The Link layer in the TCP/IP model comprises networking protocols that operate only on the local network that a host connects to. Packets are not routed to non-local networks; that is the Internet layer's role. Ethernet is the dominant protocol at this layer, and hosts are identified by the link-layer address or commonly their Media Access Control addresses on their network interface cards. Once determined by the host using Address Resolution Protocol 9 (ARP), data sent off the local network is processed by the Internet layer. This layer also includes protocols for moving packets between two Internet layer hosts.

Physical layer

The Physical layer defines the components of the hardware to use for the network. For example, the Physical network layer stipulates the physical characteristics of the communications media. The Physical layer of TCP/IP details hardware standards such as IEEE 802.3, the specification for Ethernet network media. Several interpretations of RFC 1122 for the Physical layer are included with the other layers; we have added this for completeness.

Throughout this book, we will use the minimal Golang web server (also called Go) from Example 1-1 to show various levels of networking components from `tcpdump`, a Linux syscall, to show how Kubernetes abstracts the syscalls. This section will use it to demonstrate what is happening at the Application, Transport, Network, and Data Link layers.

Application

As mentioned, Application is the highest layer in the TCP/IP stack; it is where the user interacts with data before it gets sent over the network. In our example walkthrough, we are going to use Hypertext Transfer Protocol (HTTP) and a simple HTTP transaction to demonstrate what happens at each layer in the TCP/IP stack.

HTTP

HTTP is responsible for sending and receiving Hypertext Markup Language (HTML) documents—you know, a web page. A vast majority of what we see and do on the internet is over HTTP: Amazon purchases, Reddit posts, and tweets all use HTTP. A client will make an HTTP request to our minimal Golang web server from Example 1-1, and it will send an HTTP response with "Hello" text. The web server runs locally in an Ubuntu virtual machine to test the full TCP/IP stack.

 See the example code repository (*https://oreil.ly/Jan5M*) for full instructions.

Example 1-1. Minimal web server in Go

```
package main

import (
        "fmt"
        "net/http"
)

func hello(w http.ResponseWriter, _ *http.Request) {
        fmt.Fprintf(w, "Hello")
}

func main() {
        http.HandleFunc("/", hello)
        http.ListenAndServe("0.0.0.0:8080", nil)
}
```

In our Ubuntu virtual machine we need to start our minimal web server, or if you have Golang installed locally, you can just run this:

```
go run web-server.go
```

Let's break down the request for each layer of the TPC/IP stack.

cURL is the requesting client for our HTTP request example. Generally, for a web page, the client would be a web browser, but we're using cURL to simplify and show the command line.

cURL (*https://curl.haxx.se*) is meant for uploading and downloading data specified with a URL. It is a client-side program (the *c*) to request data from a URL and return the response.

In Example 1-2, we can see each part of the HTTP request that the cURL client is making and the response. Let's review what all those options and outputs are.

Example 1-2. Client request

```
○ → curl localhost:8080 -vvv  ❶
*   Trying ::1...
* TCP_NODELAY set
* Connected to localhost (::1) port 8080  ❷
> GET / HTTP/1.1  ❸
> Host: localhost:8080  ❹
> User-Agent: curl/7.64.1  ❺
> Accept: */*  ❻
>
< HTTP/1.1 200 OK  ❼
```

```
< Date: Sat, 25 Jul 2020 14:57:46 GMT ❽
< Content-Length: 5 ❾
< Content-Type: text/plain; charset=utf-8 ❿
<
* Connection #0 to host localhost left intact
Hello* Closing connection 0 ⓫
```

❶ curl localhost:8080 -vvv: This is the curl command that opens a connection to the locally running web server, localhost on TCP port 8080. -vvv sets the verbosity of the output so we can see everything happening with the request. Also, TCP_NODELAY instructs the TCP connection to send the data without delay, one of many options available to the client to set.

❷ Connected to localhost (::1) port 8080: It worked! cURL connected to the web server on localhost and over port 8080.

❸ Get / HTTP/1.1: HTTP has several methods for retrieving or updating information. In our request, we are performing an HTTP GET to retrieve our "Hello" response. The forward slash is the next part, a Uniform Resource Locator (URL), which indicates where we are sending the client request to the server. The last section of this header is the version of HTTP the server is using, 1.1.

❹ Host: localhost:8080: HTTP has several options for sending information about the request. In our request, the cURL process has set the HTTP Host header. The client and server can transmit information with an HTTP request or response. An HTTP header contains its name followed by a colon (:) and then its value.

❺ User-Agent: cURL/7.64.1: The user agent is a string that indicates the computer program making the HTTP request on behalf of the end user; it is cURL in our context. This string often identifies the browser, its version number, and its host operating system.

❻ Accept: */*: This header instructs the web server what content types the client understands. Table 1-3 shows examples of common content types that can be sent.

❼ HTTP/1.1 200 OK: This is the server response to our request. The server responds with the HTTP version and the response status code. There are several possible responses from the server. A status code of 200 indicates the response was successful. 1XX means informational, 2XX means successful, 3XX means redirects, 4XX responses indicate there are issues with the requests, and 5XX generally refers to issues from the server.

8 `Date: Sat, July 25, 2020, 14:57:46 GMT`: The `Date` header field represents the date and time at which the message originated. The sender generates the value as the approximate date and time of message generation.

9 `Content-Length: 5`: The `Content-Length` header indicates the size of the message body, in bytes, sent to the recipient; in our case, the message is 5 bytes.

10 `Content-Type: text/plain; charset=utf-8`: The `Content-Type` entity header is used to indicate the resource's media type. Our response is indicating that it is returning a plain-text file that is UTF-8 encoded.

11 `Hello* Closing connection 0`: This prints out the response from our web server and closes out the HTTP connection.

Table 1-3. Common content types for HTTP data

Type	Description
application	Any kind of binary data that doesn't fall explicitly into one of the other types. Common examples include application/json, application/pdf, application/pkcs8, and application/zip.
audio	Audio or music data. Examples include audio/mpeg and audio/vorbis.
font	Font/typeface data. Common examples include font/woff, font/ttf, and font/otf.
image	Image or graphical data including both bitmap and vector such as animated GIF or APNG. Common examples are image/jpg, image/png, and image/svg+xml.
model	Model data for a 3D object or scene. Examples include model/3mf and model/vrml.
text	Text-only data including human-readable content, source code, or text data. Examples include text/plain, text/csv, and text/html.
video	Video data or files, such as video/mp4.

This is a simplistic view that happens with every HTTP request. Today, a single web page makes an exorbitant number of requests with one load of a page, and in just a matter of seconds! This is a brief example for cluster administrators of how HTTP (and for that matter, the other seven layers' applications) operate. We will continue to build our knowledge of how this request is completed at each layer of the TCP/IP stack and then how Kubernetes completes those same requests. All this data is formatted and options are set at layer 7, but the real heavy lifting is done at the lower layers of the TCP/IP stack, which we will go over in the next sections.

Transport

The Transport layer protocols are responsible for connection-oriented communication, reliability, flow control, and multiplexing; this is mostly true of TCP. We'll describe the differences in the following sections. Our Golang web server is a layer 7 application using HTTP; the Transport layer that HTTP relies on is TCP.

TCP

As already mentioned, TCP is a connection-oriented, reliable protocol, and it provides flow control and multiplexing. TCP is considered connection-oriented because it manages the connection state through the life cycle of the connection. In TCP, the window size manages flow control, unlike UDP, which does not manage the congestion flow. In addition, UDP is unreliable, and data may arrive out of sequence. Each port identifies the host process responsible for processing the information from the network communication. TCP is known as a host-to-host layer protocol. To identify the process on the host responsible for the connection, TCP identifies the segments with a 16-bit port number. HTTP servers use the well-known port of 80 for nonsecure communication and 443 for secure communication using Transport Layer Security (TLS). Clients requesting a new connection create a source port local in the range of 0–65534.

To understand how TCP performs multiplexing, let's review a simple HTML page retrieval:

1. In a web browser, type in a web page address.
2. The browser opens a connection to transfer the page.
3. The browser opens connections for each image on the page.
4. The browser opens another connection for the external CSS.
5. Each of these connections uses a different set of virtual ports.
6. All the page's assets download simultaneously.
7. The browser reconstructs the page.

Let's walk through how TCP manages multiplexing with the information provided in the TCP segment headers:

Source port *(16 bits)*
: This identifies the sending port.

Destination port *(16 bits)*
: This identifies the receiving port.

Sequence number *(32 bits)*
: If the SYN flag is set, this is the initial sequence number. The sequence number of the first data byte and the acknowledged number in the corresponding ACK is this sequence number plus 1. It is also used to reassemble data if it arrives out of order.

Acknowledgment number *(32 bits)*

If the ACK flag is set, then this field's value is the next sequence number of the ACK the sender is expecting. This acknowledges receipt of all preceding bytes (if any). Each end's first ACK acknowledges the other end's initial sequence number itself, but no data has been sent.

Data offset *(4 bits)*

This specifies the size of the TCP header in 32-bit words.

Reserved *(3 bits)*

This is for future use and should be set to zero.

Flags *(9 bits)*

There are nine 1-bit fields defined for the TCP header:

- NS–ECN-nonce: Concealment protection.
- CWR: Congestion Window Reduced; the sender reduced its sending rate.
- ECE: ECN Echo; the sender received an earlier congestion notification.
- URG: Urgent; the Urgent Pointer field is valid, but this is rarely used.
- ACK: Acknowledgment; the Acknowledgment Number field is valid and is always on after a connection is established.
- PSH: Push; the receiver should pass this data to the application as soon as possible.
- RST: Reset the connection or connection abort, usually because of an error.
- SYN: Synchronize sequence numbers to initiate a connection.
- FIN: The sender of the segment is finished sending data to its peer.

 The NS bit field is further explained in RFC 3540, "Robust Explicit Congestion Notification (ECN) Signaling with Nonces." This specification describes an optional addition to ECN improving robustness against malicious or accidental concealment of marked packets.

Window size *(16 bits)*

This is the size of the receive window.

Checksum *(16 bits)*

The checksum field is used for error checking of the TCP header.

Urgent pointer *(16 bits)*
This is an offset from the sequence number indicating the last urgent data byte.

Options
Variable 0–320 bits, in units of 32 bits.

Padding
The TCP header padding is used to ensure that the TCP header ends, and data begins on a 32-bit boundary.

Data
This is the piece of application data being sent in this segment.

In Figure 1-4, we can see all the TCP segment headers that provide metadata about the TCP streams.

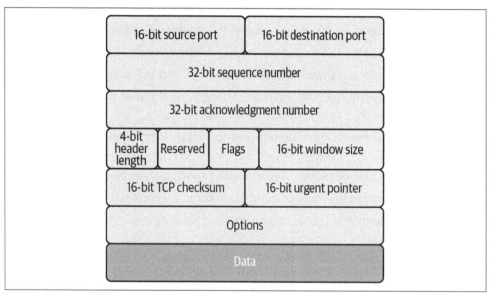

Figure 1-4. TCP segment header

These fields help manage the flow of data between two systems. Figure 1-5 shows how each step of the TCP/IP stack sends data from one application on one host, through a network communicating at layers 1 and 2, to get data to the destination host.

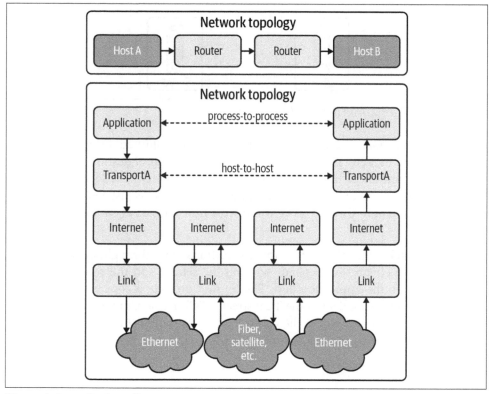

Figure 1-5. tcp/ip data flow

In the next section, we will show how TCP uses these fields to initiate a connection through the three-way handshake.

TCP handshake

TCP uses a three-way handshake, pictured in Figure 1-6, to create a connection by exchanging information along the way with various options and flags:

1. The requesting node sends a connection request via a SYN packet to get the transmission started.

2. If the receiving node is listening on the port the sender requests, the receiving node replies with a SYN-ACK, acknowledging that it has heard the requesting node.

3. The requesting node returns an ACK packet, exchanging information and letting them know the nodes are good to send each other information.

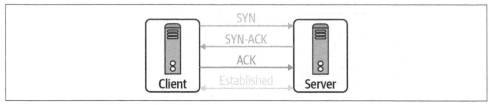

Figure 1-6. TCP three-way handshake

Now the connection is established. Data can be transmitted over the physical medium, routed between networks, to find its way to the local destination—but how does the endpoint know how to handle the information? On the local and remote hosts, a socket gets created to track this connection. A socket is just a logical endpoint for communication. In Chapter 2, we will discuss how a Linux client and server handle sockets.

TCP is a stateful protocol, tracking the connection's state throughout its life cycle. The state of the connection depends on both the sender and the receiver agreeing where they are in the connection flow. The connection state is concerned about who is sending and receiving data in the TCP stream. TCP has a complex state transition for explaining when and where the connection is, using the 9-bit TCP flags in the TCP segment header, as you can see in Figure 1-7.

The TCP connection states are:

LISTEN *(server)*
: Represents waiting for a connection request from any remote TCP and port

SYN-SENT *(client)*
: Represents waiting for a matching connection request after sending a connection request

SYN-RECEIVED *(server)*
: Represents waiting for a confirming connection request acknowledgment after having both received and sent a connection request

ESTABLISHED *(both server and client)*
: Represents an open connection; data received can be delivered to the user—the intermediate state for the data transfer phase of the connection

FIN-WAIT-1 *(both server and client)*
: Represents waiting for a connection termination request from the remote host

FIN-WAIT-2 *(both server and client)*
: Represents waiting for a connection termination request from the remote TCP

CLOSE-WAIT *(both server and client)*
> Represents waiting for a local user's connection termination request

CLOSING *(both server and client)*
> Represents waiting for a connection termination request acknowledgment from the remote TCP

LAST-ACK *(both server and client)*
> Represents waiting for an acknowledgment of the connection termination request previously sent to the remote host

TIME-WAIT *(either server or client)*
> Represents waiting for enough time to pass to ensure the remote host received the acknowledgment of its connection termination request

CLOSED *(both server and client)*
> Represents no connection state at all

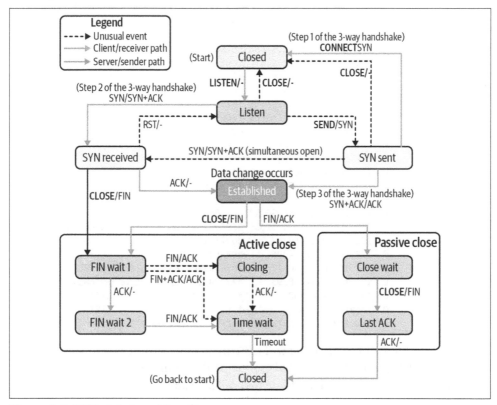

Figure 1-7. TCP state transition diagram

Example 1-3 is a sample of a Mac's TCP connections, their state, and the addresses for both ends of the connection.

Example 1-3. TCP connection states

```
○ → netstat -ap TCP
Active internet connections (including servers)
Proto Recv-Q Send-Q  Local Address          Foreign Address          (state)
tcp6      0      0    2607:fcc8:a205:c.53606 g2600-1407-2800-.https ESTABLISHED
tcp6      0      0    2607:fcc8:a205:c.53603 g2600-1408-5c00-.https ESTABLISHED
tcp4      0      0    192.168.0.17.53602      ec2-3-22-64-157..https ESTABLISHED
tcp6      0      0    2607:fcc8:a205:c.53600 g2600-1408-5c00-.https ESTABLISHED
tcp4      0      0    192.168.0.17.53598      164.196.102.34.b.https ESTABLISHED
tcp4      0      0    192.168.0.17.53597      server-99-84-217.https ESTABLISHED
tcp4      0      0    192.168.0.17.53596      151.101.194.137.https  ESTABLISHED
tcp4      0      0    192.168.0.17.53587      ec2-52-27-83-248.https ESTABLISHED
tcp6      0      0    2607:fcc8:a205:c.53586 iad23s61-in-x04..https ESTABLISHED
tcp6      0      0    2607:fcc8:a205:c.53542 iad23s61-in-x04..https ESTABLISHED
tcp4      0      0    192.168.0.17.53536      ec2-52-10-162-14.https ESTABLISHED
tcp4      0      0    192.168.0.17.53530      server-99-84-178.https ESTABLISHED
tcp4      0      0    192.168.0.17.53525      ec2-52-70-63-25..https ESTABLISHED
tcp6      0      0    2607:fcc8:a205:c.53480 upload-lb.eqiad..https ESTABLISHED
tcp6      0      0    2607:fcc8:a205:c.53477 text-lb.eqiad.wi.https ESTABLISHED
tcp4      0      0    192.168.0.17.53466      151.101.1.132.https    ESTABLISHED
tcp4      0      0    192.168.0.17.53420      ec2-52-0-84-183..https ESTABLISHED
tcp4      0      0    192.168.0.17.53410      192.168.0.18.8060      CLOSE_WAIT
tcp6      0      0    2607:fcc8:a205:c.53408 2600:1901:1:c36:.https ESTABLISHED
tcp4      0      0    192.168.0.17.53067      ec2-52-40-198-7..https ESTABLISHED
tcp4      0      0    192.168.0.17.53066      ec2-52-40-198-7..https ESTABLISHED
tcp4      0      0    192.168.0.17.53055      ec2-54-186-46-24.https ESTABLISHED
tcp4      0      0    localhost.16587         localhost.53029        ESTABLISHED
tcp4      0      0    localhost.53029         localhost.16587        ESTABLISHED
tcp46     0      0    *.16587                 *.*                    LISTEN
tcp6     56      0    2607:fcc8:a205:c.56210 ord38s08-in-x0a..https CLOSE_WAIT
tcp6      0      0    2607:fcc8:a205:c.51699 2606:4700::6810:.https ESTABLISHED
tcp4      0      0    192.168.0.17.64407      do-77.lastpass.c.https ESTABLISHED
tcp4      0      0    192.168.0.17.64396      ec2-54-70-97-159.https ESTABLISHED
tcp4      0      0    192.168.0.17.60612      ac88393aca5853df.https ESTABLISHED
tcp4      0      0    192.168.0.17.58193      47.224.186.35.bc.https ESTABLISHED
tcp4      0      0    localhost.63342         *.*                    LISTEN
tcp4      0      0    localhost.6942          *.*                    LISTEN
tcp4      0      0    192.168.0.17.55273      ec2-50-16-251-20.https ESTABLISHED
```

Now that we know more about how TCP constructs and tracks connections, let's review the HTTP request for our web server at the Transport layer using TCP. To accomplish this, we use a command-line tool called tcpdump.

tcpdump

> tcpdump prints out a description of the contents of packets on a network interface that matches the boolean expression.

—tcpdump man page

tcpdump allows administrators and users to display all the packets processed on the system and filter them out based on many TCP segment header details. In the request, we filter all packets with the destination port 8080 on the network interface labeled lo0; this is the local loopback interface on the Mac. Our web server is running on 0.0.0.0:8080. Figure 1-8 shows where tcpdump is collecting data in reference to the full TCP/IP stack, between the network interface card (NIC) driver and layer 2.

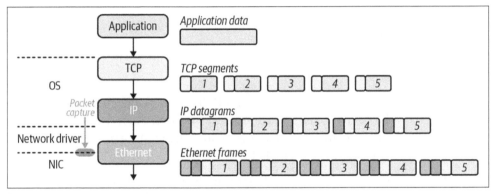

Figure 1-8. tcpdump packet capture

A loopback interface is a logical, virtual interface on a device. A loopback interface is not a physical interface like Ethernet interface. Loopback interfaces are always up and running and always available, even if other interfaces are down on the host.

The general format of a tcpdump output will contain the following fields: tos, TTL, id, offset, flags, proto, length, and options. Let's review these:

tos
    The type of service field.

TTL
    The time to live; it is not reported if it is zero.

id
    The IP identification field.

offset
> The fragment offset field; it is printed whether this is part of a fragmented datagram or not.

flags
> The DF, Don't Fragment, flag, which indicates that the packet cannot be fragmented for transmission. When unset, it indicates that the packet can be fragmented. The MF, More Fragments, flag indicates there are packets that contain more fragments and when unset, it indicates that no more fragments remain.

proto
> The protocol ID field.

length
> The total length field.

options
> The IP options.

Systems that support checksum offloading and IP, TCP, and UDP checksums are calculated on the NIC before being transmitted on the wire. Since we are running a tcpdump packet capture before the NIC, errors like cksum 0xfe34 (incorrect -> 0xb4c1) appear in the output of Example 1-4.

To produce the output for Example 1-4, open another terminal and start a tcpdump trace on the loopback for only TCP and port 8080; otherwise, you will see a lot of other packets not relevant to our example. You'll need to use escalated privileges to trace packets, so that means using sudo in this case.

Example 1-4. tcpdump

```
○ → sudo tcpdump -i lo0 tcp port 8080 -vvv   ❶

tcpdump: listening on lo0, link-type NULL (BSD loopback),
capture size 262144 bytes   ❷

08:13:55.009899 localhost.50399 > localhost.http-alt: Flags [S],
cksum 0x0034 (incorrect -> 0x1bd9), seq 2784345138,
win 65535, options [mss 16324,nop,wscale 6,nop,nop,TS val 587364215 ecr 0,
sackOK,eol], length 0   ❸

08:13:55.009997 localhost.http-alt > localhost.50399: Flags [S.],
cksum 0x0034 (incorrect -> 0xbe5a), seq 195606347,
ack 2784345139, win 65535, options [mss 16324,nop,wscale 6,nop,nop,
TS val 587364215 ecr 587364215,sackOK,eol], length 0   ❹

08:13:55.010012 localhost.50399 > localhost.http-alt: Flags [.],
cksum 0x0028 (incorrect -> 0x1f58), seq 1, ack 1,
```

win 6371, options [nop,nop,TS val 587364215 ecr 587364215],
length 0 ❺

v 08:13:55.010021 localhost.http-alt > localhost.50399: Flags [.],
cksum 0x0028 (incorrect -> 0x1f58), seq 1, ack
1, win 6371, options [nop,nop,TS val 587364215 ecr 587364215],
length 0 ❻

08:13:55.010079 localhost.50399 > localhost.http-alt: Flags [P.],
cksum 0x0076 (incorrect -> 0x78b2), seq 1:79,
ack 1, win 6371, options [nop,nop,TS val 587364215 ecr 587364215],
length 78: HTTP, length: 78 ❼
GET / HTTP/1.1
Host: localhost:8080
User-Agent: curl/7.64.1
Accept: */*
08:13:55.010102 localhost.http-alt > localhost.50399: Flags [.],
cksum 0x0028 (incorrect -> 0x1f0b), seq 1,
ack 79, win 6370, options [nop,nop,TS val 587364215 ecr 587364215],
length 0 ❽

08:13:55.010198 localhost.http-alt > localhost.50399: Flags [P.],
cksum 0x00a1 (incorrect -> 0x05d7), seq 1:122,
ack 79, win 6370, options [nop,nop,TS val 587364215 ecr 587364215],
length 121: HTTP, length: 121 ❾
HTTP/1.1 200 OK
Date: Wed, 19 Aug 2020 12:13:55 GMT
Content-Length: 5
Content-Type: text/plain; charset=utf-8
Hello[!http]

08:13:55.010219 localhost.50399 > localhost.http-alt: Flags [.], cksum 0x0028
(incorrect -> 0x1e93), seq 79,
ack 122, win 6369, options [nop,nop,TS val 587364215 ecr 587364215], length 0 ❿

08:13:55.010324 localhost.50399 > localhost.http-alt: Flags [F.],
cksum 0x0028 (incorrect -> 0x1e92), seq 79,
ack 122, win 6369, options [nop,nop,TS val 587364215 ecr 587364215],
length 0 ⓫

08:13:55.010343 localhost.http-alt > localhost.50399: Flags [.],
cksum 0x0028 (incorrect -> 0x1e91), seq 122,
\ack 80, win 6370, options [nop,nop,TS val 587364215 ecr 587364215],
length 0 ⓬

08:13:55.010379 localhost.http-alt > localhost.50399: Flags [F.],
cksum 0x0028 (incorrect -> 0x1e90), seq 122,
ack 80, win 6370, options [nop,nop,TS val 587364215 ecr 587364215],
length 0 ⓭

08:13:55.010403 localhost.50399 > localhost.http-alt: Flags [.],
cksum 0x0028 (incorrect -> 0x1e91), seq 80, ack

```
123, win 6369, options [nop,nop,TS val 587364215 ecr 587364215],
length 0  ⓮

 12 packets captured, 12062 packets received by filter
 0 packets dropped by kernel.  ⓯
```

❶ This is the start of the tcpdump collection with its command and all of its options. The sudo packet captures the required escalated privileges. tcpdump is the tcpdump binary. -i lo0 is the interface from which we want to capture packets. dst port 8080 is the matching expression that the man page discussed; here we are matching on all packets destined for TCP port 8080, which is the port the web service is listening to for requests. -v is the verbose option, which allows us to see more details from the tcpdump capture.

❷ Feedback from tcpdump letting us know about the tcpdump filter running.

❸ This is the first packet in the TCP handshake. We can tell it's the SYN because the flags bit is set with [S], and the sequence number is set to 2784345138 by cURL, with the localhost process number being 50399.

❹ The SYN-ACK packet is the the one filtered by tcpdump from the localhost.http-alt process, the Golang web server. The flag is to [S.], so it is a SYN-ACK. The packet sends 195606347 as the next sequence number, and ACK 2784345139 is set to acknowledge the previous packet.

❺ The acknowledgment packet from cURL is now sent back to the server with the ACK flag set, [.], with the ACK and SYN numbers set to 1, indicating it is ready to send data.

❻ The acknowledgment number is set to 1 to indicate the client's SYN flag's receipt in the opening data push.

❼ The TCP connection is established; both the client and server are ready for data transmission. The next packets are our data transmissions of the HTTP request with the flag set to a data push and ACK, [P.]. The previous packets had a length of zero, but the HTTP request is 78 bytes long, with a sequence number of 1:79.

❽ The server acknowledges the receipt of the data transmission, with the ACK flag set, [.], by sending the acknowledgment number of 79.

❾ This packet is the HTTP server's response to the cURL request. The data push flag is set, [P.], and it acknowledges the previous packet with an ACK number of

79. A new sequence number is set with the data transmission, 122, and the data length is 121 bytes.

⑩ The cURL client acknowledges the receipt of the packet with the ACK flag set, sets the acknowledgment number to 122, and sets the sequence number to 79.

⑪ The start of closing the TCP connection, with the client sending the FIN-ACK packet, the [F.], acknowledging the receipt of the previous packet, number 122, and a new sequence number to 80.

⑫ The server increments the acknowledgment number to 80 and sets the ACK flag.

⑬ TCP requires that both the sender and the receiver set the FIN packet for closing the connection. This is the packet where the FIN and ACK flags are set.

⑭ This is the final ACK from the client, with acknowledgment number 123. The connection is closed now.

⑮ tcpdump on exit lets us know the number of packets in this capture, the total number of the packets captured during the tcpdump, and how many packets were dropped by the operating system.

tcpdump is an excellent troubleshooting application for network engineers as well as cluster administrators. Being able to verify connectivity at many levels in the cluster and the network are valuable skills to have. You will see in Chapter 6 how useful tcpdump can be.

Our example was a simple HTTP application using TCP. All of this data was sent over the network in plain text. While this example was a simple Hello World, other requests like our bank logins need to have some security. The Transport layer does not offer any security protection for data transiting the network. TLS adds additional security on top of TCP. Let's dive into that in our next section.

TLS

TLS adds encryption to TCP. TLS is an add-on to the TCP/IP suite and is not considered to be part of the base operation for TCP. HTTP transactions can be completed without TLS but are not secure from eavesdroppers on the wire. TLS is a combination of protocols used to ensure traffic is seen between the sender and the intended recipient. TLS, much like TCP, uses a handshake to establish encryption capabilities and exchange keys for encryption. The following steps detail the TLS handshake between the client and the server, which can also be seen in Figure 1-9:

1. ClientHello: This contains the cipher suites supported by the client and a random number.

2. ServerHello: This message contains the cipher it supports and a random number.

3. ServerCertificate: This contains the server's certificate and its server public key.

4. ServerHelloDone: This is the end of the ServerHello. If the client receives a request for its certificate, it sends a ClientCertificate message.

5. ClientKeyExchange: Based on the server's random number, our client generates a random premaster secret, encrypts it with the server's public key certificate, and sends it to the server.

6. Key Generation: The client and server generate a master secret from the premaster secret and exchange random values.

7. ChangeCipherSpec: Now the client and server swap their ChangeCipherSpec to begin using the new keys for encryption.

8. Finished Client: The client sends the finished message to confirm that the key exchange and authentication were successful.

9. Finished Server: Now, the server sends the finished message to the client to end the handshake.

Kubernetes applications and components will manage TLS for developers, so a basic introduction is required; Chapter 5 reviews more about TLS and Kubernetes.

As demonstrated with our web server, cURL, and `tcpdump`, TCP is a stateful and reliable protocol for sending data between hosts. Its use of flags, combined with the sequence and acknowledgment number dance it performs, delivers thousands of messages over unreliable networks across the globe. That reliability comes at a cost, however. Of the 12 packets we set, only two were real data transfers. For applications that do not need reliability such as voice, the overhead that comes with UDP offers an alternative. Now that we understand how TCP works as a reliable connection-oriented protocol, let's review how UDP differs from TCP.

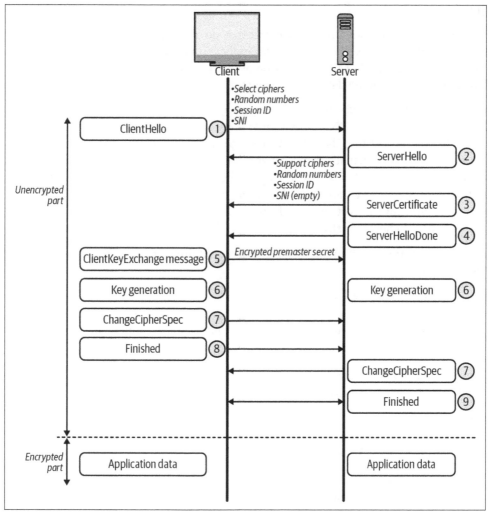

Figure 1-9. TLS handshake

UDP

UDP offers an alternative to applications that do not need the reliability that TCP provides. UDP is an excellent choice for applications that can withstand packet loss such as voice and DNS. UDP offers little overhead from a network perspective, only having four fields and no data acknowledgment, unlike its verbose brother TCP.

It is transaction-oriented, suitable for simple query and response protocols like the Domain Name System (DNS) and Simple Network Management Protocol (SNMP). UDP slices a request into datagrams, making it capable for use with other protocols for tunneling like a virtual private network (VPN). It is lightweight and straightforward, making it great for bootstrapping application data in the case of DHCP. The stateless nature of data transfer makes UDP perfect for applications, such as voice, that can withstand packet loss—did you hear that? UDP's lack of retransmit also makes it an apt choice for streaming video.

Let's look at the small number of headers required in a UDP datagram (see Figure 1-10):

Source port number *(2 bytes)*
> Identifies the sender's port. The source host is the client; the port number is ephemeral. UDP ports have well-known numbers like DNS on 53 or DHCP 67/68.

Destination port number *(2 bytes)*
> Identifies the receiver's port and is required.

Length *(2 bytes)*
> Specifies the length in bytes of the UDP header and UDP data. The minimum length is 8 bytes, the length of the header.

Checksum *(2 bytes)*
> Used for error checking of the header and data. It is optional in IPv4, but mandatory in IPv6, and is all zeros if unused.

UDP and TCP are general transport protocols that help ship and receive data between hosts. Kubernetes supports both protocols on the network, and services allow users to load balance many pods using services. Also important to note is that in each service, developers must define the transport protocol; if they do not TCP is the default used.

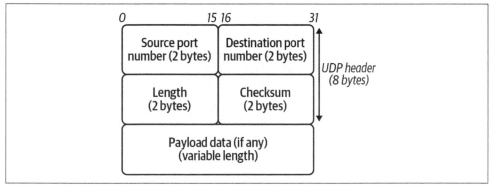

Figure 1-10. UDP header

The next layer in the TCP/IP stack is the Internetworking layer—these are packets that can get sent across the globe on the vast networks that make up the internet. Let's review how that gets completed.

Network

All TCP and UDP data gets transmitted as IP packets in TCP/IP in the Network layer. The Internet or Network layer is responsible for transferring data between networks. Outgoing packets select the next-hop host and send the data to that host by passing it the appropriate Link layer details; packets are received by a host, de-encapsulated, and sent up to the proper Transport layer protocol. In IPv4, both transmit and receive, IP provides fragmentation or defragmentation of packets based on the MTU; this is the maximum size of the IP packet.

IP makes no guarantees about packets' proper arrival; since packet delivery across diverse networks is inherently unreliable and failure-prone, that burden is with the endpoints of a communication path, rather than on the network. As discussed in the previous section, providing service reliability is a function of the Transport layer. Each packet has a checksum to ensure that the received packet's information is accurate, but this layer does not validate data integrity. Source and destination IP addresses identify packets on the network, which we'll address next.

Internet Protocol

This almighty packet is defined in RFC 791 and is used for sending data across networks. Figure 1-11 shows the IPv4 header format.

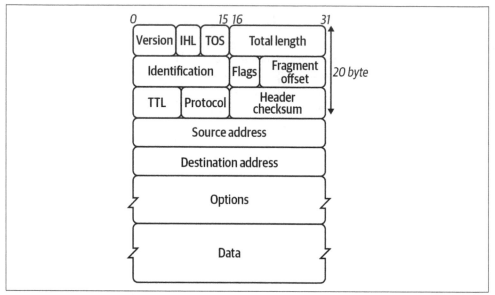

Figure 1-11. IPv4 header format

Let's look at the header fields in more detail:

Version
:   The first header field in the IP packet is the four-bit version field. For IPv4, this is always equal to four.

Internet Header Length *(IHL)*
:   The IPv4 header has a variable size due to the optional 14th field option.

Type of Service
:   Originally defined as the type of service (ToS), now Differentiated Services Code Point (DSCP), this field specifies differentiated services. DSC Pallows for routers and networks to make decisions on packet priority during times of congestion. Technologies such as Voice over IP use DSCP to ensure calls take precedence over other traffic.

Total Length
:   This is the entire packet size in bytes.

Identification
:   This is the identification field and is used for uniquely identifying the group of fragments of a single IP datagram.

Flags

This is used to control or identify fragments. In order from most significant to least:

- bit 0: Reserved, set to zero
- bit 1: Do not Fragment
- bit 2: More Fragments

Fragment Offset

This specifies the offset of a distinct fragment relative to the first unfragmented IP packet. The first fragment always has an offset of zero.

Time To Live (TTL)

An 8-bit time to live field helps prevent datagrams from going in circles on a network.

Protocol

This is used in the data section of the IP packet. IANA has a list of IP protocol numbers in RFC 790; some well-known protocols are also detailed in Table 1-4.

Table 1-4. IP protocol numbers

Protocol number	Protocol name	Abbreviation
1	Internet Control Message Protocol	ICMP
2	Internet Group Management Protocol	IGMP
6	Transmission Control Protocol	TCP
17	User Datagram Protocol	UDP
41	IPv6 Encapsulation	ENCAP
89	Open Shortest Path First	OSPF
132	Stream Control Transmission Protocol	SCTP

Header Checksum *(16-bit)*

The IPv4 header checksum field is used for error checking. When a packet arrives, a router computes the header's checksum; the router drops the packet if the two values do not match. The encapsulated protocol must handle errors in the data field. Both UDP and TCP have checksum fields.

When the router receives a packet, it lowers the TTL field by one. As a consequence, the router must compute a new checksum.

Source address

This is the IPv4 address of the sender of the packet.

 The source address may be changed in transit by a network address translation device; NAT will be discussed later in this chapter and extensively in Chapter 3.

Destination address

This is the IPv4 address of the receiver of the packet. As with the source address, a NAT device can change the destination IP address.

Options

The possible options in the header are Copied, Option Class, Option Number, Option Length, and Option Data.

The crucial component here is the address; it's how networks are identified. They simultaneously identify the host on the network and the whole network itself (more on that in "Getting round the network" on page 35). Understanding how to identify an IP address is critical for an engineer. First, we will review IPv4 and then understand the drastic changes in IPv6.

IPv4 addresses are in the dotted-decimal notation for us humans; computers read them out as binary strings. Figure 1-12 details the dotted-decimal notation and binary. Each section is 8 bits in length, with four sections, making the complete length 32 bits. IPv4 addresses have two sections: the first part is the network, and the second is the host's unique identifier on the network.

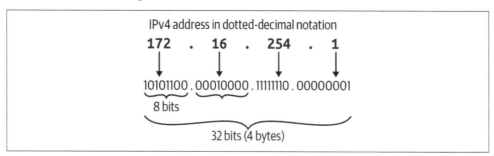

Figure 1-12. IPv4 address

In Example 1-5, we have the output of a computer's IP address for its network interface card and we can see its IPv4 address is 192.168.1.2. The IP address also has a subnet mask or netmask associated with it to make out what network it is assigned. The example's subnet is netmask 0xffffff00 in dotted-decimal, which is 255.255.255.0.

Example 1-5. IP address

```
○ → ifconfig en0
en0: flags=8863<UP,BROADCAST,SMART,RUNNING,SIMPLEX,MULTICAST> mtu 1500
        options=400<CHANNEL_IO>
        ether 38:f9:d3:bc:8a:51
        inet6 fe80::8f4:bb53:e500:9557%en0 prefixlen 64 secured scopeid 0x6
        inet 192.168.1.2 netmask 0xffffff00 broadcast 192.168.1.255
        nd6 options=201<PERFORMNUD,DAD>
        media: autoselect
        status: active
```

The subnet brings up the idea of classful addressing. Initially, when an IP address range was assigned, a range was considered to be the combination of an 8-, 16-, or 24-bit network prefix along with a 24-, 16-, or 8-bit host identifier, respectively. Class A had 8 bits for the host, Class B 16, and Class C 24. Following that, Class A had 2 to the power of 16 hosts available, 16,777,216; Class B had 65,536; and Class C had 256. Each class had a host address, the first one in its boundary, and the last one was designated as the broadcast address. Figure 1-13 demonstrates this for us.

 There are two other classes, but they are not generally used in IP addressing. Class D addresses are used for IP multicasting, and Class E addresses are reserved for experimental use.

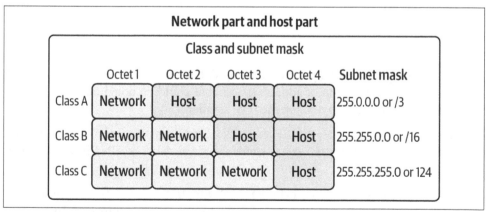

Network part and host part				
Class and subnet mask				
	Octet 1	Octet 2	Octet 3	Octet 4	Subnet mask
Class A	Network	Host	Host	Host	255.0.0.0 or /3
Class B	Network	Network	Host	Host	255.255.0.0 or /16
Class C	Network	Network	Network	Host	255.255.255.0 or 124

Figure 1-13. IP class

Classful addressing was not scalable on the internet, so to help alleviate that scale issue, we began breaking up the class boundaries using Classless Inter-Domain Routing (CIDR) ranges. Instead of having the full 16 million-plus addresses in a class address range, an internet entity gives only a subsection of that range. This effectively allows network engineers to move the subnet boundary to anywhere inside the class range, giving them more flexibility with CIDR ranges, and helping to scale IP address ranges.

In Figure 1-14, we can see the breakdown of the 208.130.29.33 IPv4 address and the hierarchy that it creates. The 208.128.0.0/11 CIDR range is assigned to ARIN from IANA. ARIN further breaks down the subnet to smaller and smaller subnets for its purposes, leading to the single host on the network 208.130.29.33/32.

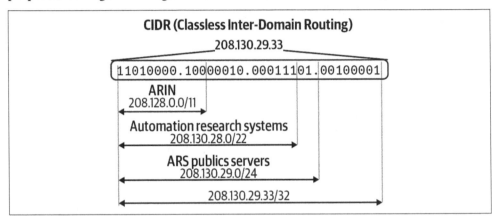

Figure 1-14. CIDR example

The global coordination of the DNS root, IP addressing, and other internet protocol resources is performed by IANA.

Eventually, though, even this practice of using CIDR to extend the range of an IPv4 address led to an exhaustion of address spaces that could be doled out, leading network engineers and IETF to develop the IPv6 standard.

In Figure 1-15, we can see that IPv6, unlike IPv4, uses hexadecimal to shorten addresses for writing purposes. It has similar characteristics to IPv4 in that it has a host and network prefix.

The most significant difference between IPv4 and IPv6 is the size of the address space. IPv4 has 32 bits, while IPv6 has 128 bits to produce its addresses. To put that size differential in perspective, here are those numbers:

IPv4 has 4,294,967,296.

IPv6 has 340,282,366,920,938,463,463,374,607,431,768,211,456.

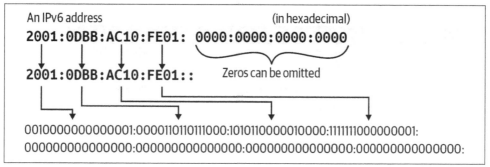

Figure 1-15. IPv6 address

Now that we understand how an individual host on the network is identified and what network it belongs to, we will explore how those networks exchange information between themselves using routing protocols.

Getting round the network

Packets are addressed, and data is ready to be sent, but how do our packets get from our host on our network to the intended hosted on another network halfway around the world? That is the job of routing. There are several routing protocols, but the internet relies on Border Gateway Protocol (BGP), a dynamic routing protocol used to manage how packets get routed between edge routers on the internet. It is relevant for us because some Kubernetes network implementations use BGP to route cluster network traffic between nodes. Between each node on separate networks is a series of routers.

If we refer to the map of the internet in Figure 1-1, each network on the internet is assigned a BGP autonomous system number (ASN) to designate a single administrative entity or corporation that represents a common and clearly defined routing policy on the internet. BGP and ASNs allows network administrators to maintain control of their internal network routing while announcing and summarizing their routes on the internet. Table 1-5 lists the available ASNs managed by IANA and other regional entities.[1]

---

1 "Autonomous System (AS) Numbers". (*https://oreil.ly/Jgi2c*) IANA.org. 2018-12-07. Retrieved 2018-12-31.

Table 1-5. ASNs available

Number	Bits	Description	Reference
0	16	Reserved	RFC 1930, RFC 7607
1–23455	16	Public ASNs	
23456	16	Reserved for AS Pool Transition	RFC 6793
23457–64495	16	Public ASNs	
64496–64511	16	Reserved for use in documentation/sample code	RFC 5398
64512–65534	16	Reserved for private use	RFC 1930, RFC 6996
65535	16	Reserved	RFC 7300
65536–65551	32	Reserved for use in documentation and sample code	RFC 4893, RFC 5398
65552–131071	32	Reserved	
131072–4199999999	32	Public 32-bit ASNs	
4200000000–4294967294	32	Reserved for private use	RFC 6996
4294967295	32	Reserved	RFC 7300

In Figure 1-16 ,we have five ASNs, 100–500. A host on `130.10.1.200` wants to reach a host destined on `150.10.2.300`. Once the local router or default gateway for the host `130.10.1.200` receives the packet, it will look for the interface and path for `150.10.2.300` that BGP has determined for that route.

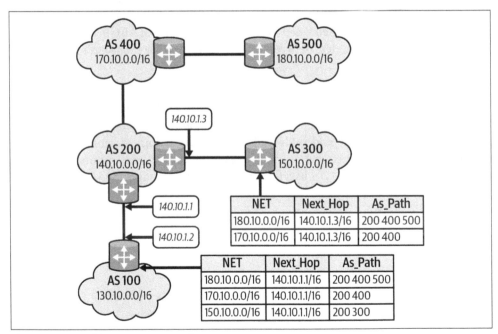

Figure 1-16. BGP routing example

Based on the routing table in Figure 1-17, the router for AS 100 determined the packet belongs to AS 300, and the preferred path is out interface `140.10.1.1`. Rinse and repeat on AS 200 until the local router for `150.10.2.300` on AS 300 receives that packet. The flow here is described in Figure 1-6, which shows the TCP/IP data flow between networks. A basic understanding of BGP is needed because some container networking projects, like Calico, use it for routing between nodes; you'll learn more about this in Chapter 3.

```
o → netstat -nr
Routing tables

Internet:
Destination          Gateway              Flags       Netif Expire
default              192.168.1.254        UGSc        en8
127                  127.0.0.1            UCS         lo0
127.0.0.1            127.0.0.1            UH          lo0
169.254              link#11              UCS         en8     !
192.168.1            link#11              UCS         en8     !
192.168.1.153/32     link#11              UCS         en8     !
192.168.1.254/32     link#11              UCS         en8     !
192.168.1.254        10:93:97:6e:6b:60    UHLWIir     en8    1186
224.0.0/4            link#11              UmCS        en8     !
224.0.0.251          1:0:5e:0:0:fb        UHmLWI      en8
239.255.255.250      1:0:5e:7f:ff:fa      UHmLWI      en8
255.255.255.255/32   link#11              UCS         en8     !
```

Figure 1-17. Local routing table

Figure 1-17 displays a local route table. In the route table, we can see the interface that a packet will be sent out is based on the destination IP address. For example, a packet destined for `192.168.1.153` will be sent out the `link#11` gateway, which is local to the network, and no routing is needed. `192.168.1.254` is the router on the network attached to our internet connection. If the destination network is unknown, it is sent out the default route.

> Like all Linux and BSD OSs, you can find more information on `net stat`'s man page (`man netstat`). Apple's `netstat` is derived from the BSD version. More information can be found in the FreeBSD Handbook (*https://oreil.ly/YM0eQ*).

Routers continuously communicate on the internet, exchanging route information and informing each other of changes on their respective networks. BGP takes care of a lot of that data exchange, but network engineers and system administrators can use the ICMP protocol and `ping` command line tools to test connectivity between hosts and routers.

ICMP

`ping` is a network utility that uses ICMP for testing connectivity between hosts on the network. In Example 1-6, we see a successful `ping` test to `192.168.1.2`, with five packets all returning an ICMP echo reply.

Example 1-6. ICMP echo request

```
○ → ping 192.168.1.2 -c 5
PING 192.168.1.2 (192.168.1.2): 56 data bytes
64 bytes from 192.168.1.2: icmp_seq=0 ttl=64 time=0.052 ms
64 bytes from 192.168.1.2: icmp_seq=1 ttl=64 time=0.089 ms
64 bytes from 192.168.1.2: icmp_seq=2 ttl=64 time=0.142 ms
64 bytes from 192.168.1.2: icmp_seq=3 ttl=64 time=0.050 ms
64 bytes from 192.168.1.2: icmp_seq=4 ttl=64 time=0.050 ms
--- 192.168.1.2 ping statistics ---
5 packets transmitted, 5 packets received, 0.0% packet loss
round-trip min/avg/max/stddev = 0.050/0.077/0.142/0.036 ms
```

Example 1-7 shows a failed ping attempt that times out trying to reach host `1.2.3.4`. Routers and administrators will use `ping` for testing connections, and it is useful in testing container connectivity as well. You'll learn more about this in Chapters 2 and 3 as we deploy our minimal Golang web server into a container and a pod.

Example 1-7. ICMP echo request failed

```
○ → ping 1.2.3.4 -c 4
PING 1.2.3.4 (1.2.3.4): 56 data bytes
Request timeout for icmp_seq 0
Request timeout for icmp_seq 1
Request timeout for icmp_seq 2
--- 1.2.3.4 ping statistics ---
4 packets transmitted, 0 packets received, 100.0% packet loss
```

As with TCP and UDP, there are headers, data, and options in ICMP packets; they are reviewed here and shown in Figure 1-18:

Type
   ICMP type.

Code
   ICMP subtype.

Checksum
> Internet checksum for error checking, calculated from the ICMP header and data with value 0 substitutes for this field.

Rest of Header *(4-byte field)*
> Contents vary based on the ICMP type and code.

Data
> ICMP error messages contain a data section that includes a copy of the entire IPv4 header.

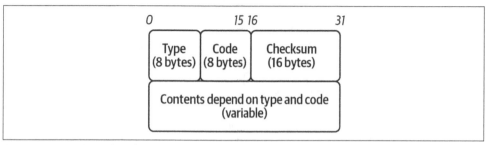

Figure 1-18. ICMP header

 Some consider ICMP a Transport layer protocol since it does not use TCP or UDP. Per RFC 792, it defines ICMP, which provides routing, diagnostic, and error functionality for IP. Although ICMP messages are encapsulated within IP datagrams, ICMP processing is considered and is typically implemented as part of the IP layer. ICMP is IP protocol 1, while TCP is 6, and UDP is 17.

The value identifies control messages in the Type field. The code field gives additional context information for the message. You can find some standard ICMP type numbers in Table 1-6.

Table 1-6. Common ICMP type numbers

Number	Name	Reference
0	Echo reply	RFC 792
3	Destination unreachable	RFC 792
5	Redirect	RFC 792
8	Echo	RFC 792

Now that our packets know which networks they are being sourced and destined to, it is time to start physically sending this data request across the network; this is the responsibility of the Link layer.

Link Layer

The HTTP request has been broken up into segments, addressed for routing across the internet, and now all that is left is to send the data across the wire. The Link layer of the TCP/IP stack comprises two sublayers: the Media Access Control (MAC) sublayer and the Logical Link Control (LLC) sublayer. Together, they perform OSI layers 1 and 2, Data Link and Physical. The Link layer is responsible for connectivity to the local network. The first sublayer, MAC, is responsible for access to the physical medium. The LLC layer has the privilege of managing flow control and multiplexing protocols over the MAC layer to transmit and demultiplexing when receiving, as shown in Figure 1-19. IEEE standard 802.3, Ethernet, defines the protocols for sending and receiving frames to encapsulate IP packets. IEEE 802 is the overarching standard for LLC (802.2), wireless (802.11), and Ethernet/MAC (802.3).

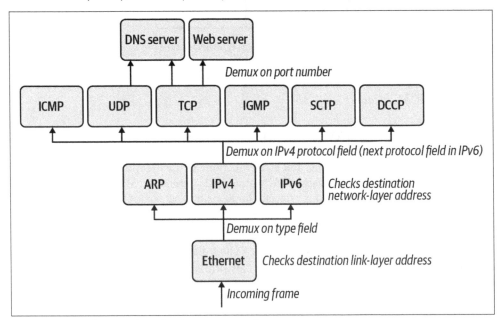

Figure 1-19. Ethernet demultiplexing example

As with the other PDUs, Ethernet has a header and footers, as shown in Figure 1-20.

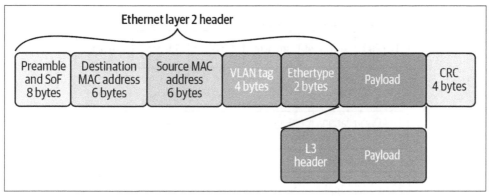

Figure 1-20. Ethernet header and footer

Let's review these in detail:

Preamble *(8 bytes)*
   Alternating string of ones and zeros indicate to the receiving host that a frame is incoming.

Destination MAC Address *(6 bytes)*
   MAC destination address; the Ethernet frame recipient.

Source MAC Address *(6 bytes)*
   MAC source address; the Ethernet frame source.

VLAN tag *(4 bytes)*
   Optional 802.1Q tag to differentiate traffic on the network segments.

Ether-type *(2 bytes)*
   Indicates which protocol is encapsulated in the payload of the frame.

Payload *(variable length)*
   The encapsulated IP packet.

Frame Check Sequence (FCS) *or* Cycle Redundancy Check (CRC) *(4 bytes)*
   The frame check sequence (FCS) is a four-octet cyclic redundancy check (CRC) that allows the detection of corrupted data within the entire frame as received on the receiver side. The CRC is part of the Ethernet frame footer.

Figure 1-21 shows that MAC addresses get assigned to network interface hardware at the time of manufacture. MAC addresses have two parts: the organization unit identifier (OUI) and the NIC-specific parts.

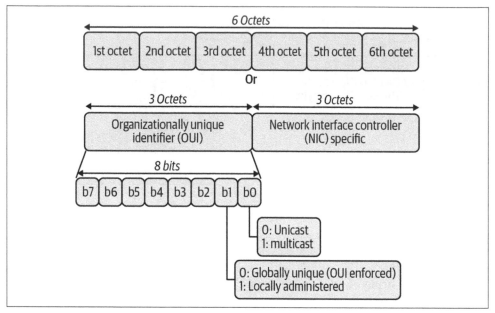

Figure 1-21. MAC address

The frame indicates to the recipient of the Network layer packet type. Table 1-7 details the common protocols handled. In Kubernetes, we are mostly interested in IPv4 and ARP packets. IPv6 has recently been introduced to Kubernetes in the 1.19 release.

Table 1-7. Common EtherType protocols

EtherType	Protocol
0x0800	Internet Protocol version 4 (IPv4)
0x0806	Address Resolution Protocol (ARP)
0x8035	Reverse Address Resolution Protocol (RARP)
0x86DD	Internet Protocol version 6 (IPv6)
0x88E5	MAC security (IEEE 802.1AE)
0x9100	VLAN-tagged (IEEE 802.1Q) frame with double tagging

When an IP packet reaches its destination network, the destination IP address is resolved with the Address Resolution Protocol for IPv4 (Neighbor Discovery Protocol in the case of IPv6) into the destination host's MAC address. The Address Resolution Protocol must manage address translation from internet addresses to Link layer addresses on Ethernet networks. The ARP table is for fast lookups for those known hosts, so it does not have to send an ARP request for every frame the host wants to send out. Example 1-8 shows the output of a local ARP table. All devices on the network keep a cache of ARP addresses for this purpose.

Example 1-8. ARP table

```
○ → arp -a
? (192.168.0.1) at bc:a5:11:f1:5d:be on en0 ifscope [ethernet]
? (192.168.0.17) at 38:f9:d3:bc:8a:51 on en0 ifscope permanent [ethernet]
? (192.168.0.255) at ff:ff:ff:ff:ff:ff on en0 ifscope [ethernet]
? (224.0.0.251) at 1:0:5e:0:0:fb on en0 ifscope permanent [ethernet]
? (239.255.255.250) at 1:0:5e:7f:ff:fa on en0 ifscope permanent [ethernet]
```

Figure 1-22 shows the exchange between hosts on the local network. The browser makes an HTTP request for a website hosted by the target server. Through DNS, it determines that the server has the IP address 10.0.0.1. To continue to send the HTTP request, it also requires the server's MAC address. First, the requesting computer consults a cached ARP table to look up 10.0.0.1 for any existing records of the server's MAC address. If the MAC address is found, it sends an Ethernet frame with the destination address of the server's MAC address, containing the IP packet addressed to 10.0.0.1 onto the link. If the cache did not produce a hit for 10.0.0.2, the requesting computer must send a broadcast ARP request message with a destination MAC address of FF:FF:FF:FF:FF:FF, which is accepted by all hosts on the local network, requesting an answer for 10.0.0.1. The server responds with an ARP response message containing its MAC and IP address. As part of answering the request, the server may insert an entry for requesting the computer's MAC address into its ARP table for future use. The requesting computer receives and caches the response information in its ARP table and can now send the HTTP packets.

This also brings up a crucial concept on the local networks, broadcast domains. All packets on the broadcast domain receive all the ARP messages from hosts. In addition, all frames are sent all nodes on the broadcast, and the host compares the destination MAC address to its own. It will discard frames not destined for itself. As hosts on the network grow, so too does the broadcast traffic.

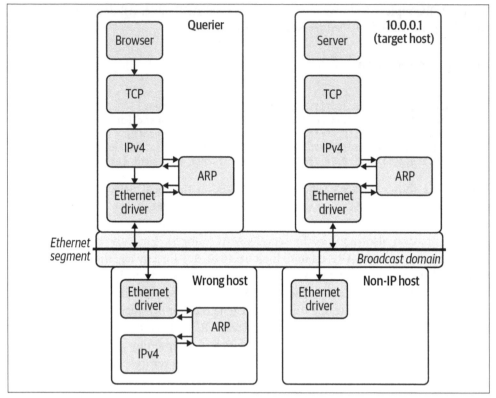

Figure 1-22. ARP request

We can use `tcpdump` to view all the ARP requests happening on the local network as in Example 1-9. The packet capture details the ARP packets; the Ethernet type used, `Ethernet (len 6)`; and the higher-level protocol, `IPv4`. It also includes who is requesting the MAC address of the IP address, `Request who-has 192.168.0.1 tell 192.168.0.12`.

Example 1-9. ARP tcpdump

```
○ → sudo tcpdump -i en0 arp -vvv
tcpdump: listening on en0, link-type EN10MB (Ethernet), capture size 262144 bytes
17:26:25.906401 ARP, Ethernet (len 6), IPv4 (len 4),
Request who-has 192.168.0.1 tell 192.168.0.12, length 46
17:26:27.954867 ARP, Ethernet (len 6), IPv4 (len 4),
Request who-has 192.168.0.1 tell 192.168.0.12, length 46
17:26:29.797714 ARP, Ethernet (len 6), IPv4 (len 4),
Request who-has 192.168.0.1 tell 192.168.0.12, length 46
17:26:31.845838 ARP, Ethernet (len 6), IPv4 (len 4),
Request who-has 192.168.0.1 tell 192.168.0.12, length 46
17:26:33.897299 ARP, Ethernet (len 6), IPv4 (len 4),
```

```
Request who-has 192.168.0.1 tell 192.168.0.12, length 46
17:26:35.942221 ARP, Ethernet (len 6), IPv4 (len 4),
Request who-has 192.168.0.1 tell 192.168.0.12, length 46
17:26:37.785585 ARP, Ethernet (len 6), IPv4 (len 4),
Request who-has 192.168.0.1 tell 192.168.0.12, length 46
17:26:39.628958 ARP, Ethernet (len 6), IPv4 (len 4),
Request who-has 192.168.0.1 tell 192.168.0.13, length 28
17:26:39.833697 ARP, Ethernet (len 6), IPv4 (len 4),
Request who-has 192.168.0.1 tell 192.168.0.12, length 46
17:26:41.881322 ARP, Ethernet (len 6), IPv4 (len 4),
Request who-has 192.168.0.1 tell 192.168.0.12, length 46
17:26:43.929320 ARP, Ethernet (len 6), IPv4 (len 4),
Request who-has 192.168.0.1 tell 192.168.0.12, length 46
17:26:45.977691 ARP, Ethernet (len 6), IPv4 (len 4),
Request who-has 192.168.0.1 tell 192.168.0.12, length 46
17:26:47.820597 ARP, Ethernet (len 6), IPv4 (len 4),
Request who-has 192.168.0.1 tell 192.168.0.12, length 46
^C
13 packets captured
233 packets received by filter
0 packets dropped by kernel
```

To further segment the layer 2 network, network engineers can use virtual local area network (VLAN) tagging. Inside the Ethernet frame header is an optional VLAN tag that differentiates traffic on the LAN. It is useful to use VLANs to break up LANs and manage networks on the same switch or different ones across the network campus. Routers between VLANs filter broadcast traffic, enable network security, and alleviate network congestion. They are useful to the network administrator for those purposes, but Kubernetes network administrators can use the extended version of the VLAN technology known as a *virtual extensible LAN* (VXLAN).

Figure 1-23 shows how a VXLAN is an extension of a VLAN that allows network engineers to encapsulate layer 2 frames into layer 4 UDP packets. A VXLAN increases scalability up to 16 million logical networks and allows for layer 2 adjacency across IP networks. This technology is used in Kubernetes networks to produce overlay networks, which you'll learn more about in later chapters.

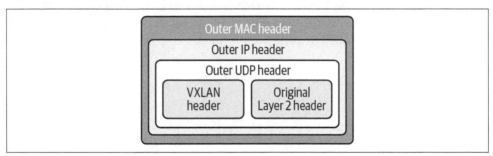

Figure 1-23. VXLAN packet

Ethernet also details the specifications for the medium to transmit frames on, such as twisted pair, coaxial cable, optical fiber, wireless, or other transmission media yet to be invented, such as the gamma-ray network that powers the Philotic Parallax Instantaneous Communicator.[2] Ethernet even defines the encoding and signaling protocols used on the wire; this is out of scope for our proposes.

The Link layer has multiple other protocols involved from a network perspective. Like the layers discussed previously, we have only touched the surface of the Link layer. We constrained this book to those details needed for a base understanding of the Link layer for the Kubernetes networking model.

Revisiting Our Web Server

Our journey through all the layers of TCP/IP is complete. Figure 1-24 outlines all the headers and footers each layer of the TCP/IP model produces to send data across the internet.

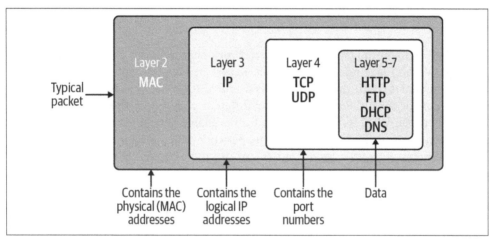

Figure 1-24. TCP/IP PDU full view

Let's review the journey and remind ourselves again what is going on now that we understand each layer in detail. Example 1-10 shows our web server again, and Example 1-11 shows the cURL request for it from earlier in the chapter.

---

2 In the movie *Ender's Game*, they use the Ansible network to communicate across the galaxy instantly. Philotic Parallax Instantaneous Communicator is the official name of the Ansible network.

Example 1-10. Minimal web server in Go

```go
package main

import (
        "fmt"
        "net/http"
)

func hello(w http.ResponseWriter, _ *http.Request) {
        fmt.Fprintf(w, "Hello")
}

func main() {
        http.HandleFunc("/", hello)
        http.ListenAndServe("0.0.0.0:8080", nil)
}
```

Example 1-11. Client request

```
○ → curl localhost:8080 -vvv
*   Trying ::1...
* TCP_NODELAY set
* Connected to localhost (::1) port 8080
> GET / HTTP/1.1
> Host: localhost:8080
> User-Agent: curl/7.64.1
> Accept: */*
>
< HTTP/1.1 200 OK
< Date: Sat, 25 Jul 2020 14:57:46 GMT
< Content-Length: 5
< Content-Type: text/plain; charset=utf-8
<
* Connection #0 to host localhost left intact
Hello* Closing connection 0
```

We begin with the web server waiting for a connection in Example 1-10. cURL requests the HTTP server at 0.0.0.0 on port 8080. cURL determines the IP address and port number from the URL and proceeds to establish a TCP connection to the server. Once the connection is set up, via a TCP handshake, cURL sends the HTTP request. When the web server starts up, a socket of 8080 is created on the HTTP server, which matches TCP port 8080; the same is done on the cURL client side with a random port number. Next, this information is sent to the Network layer, where the source and destination IP addresses are attached to the packet's IP header. At the client's Data Link layer, the source MAC address of the NIC is added to the Ethernet frame. If the destination MAC address is unknown, an ARP request is made to find it. Next, the NIC is used to transmit the Ethernet frames to the web server.

When the web server receives the request, it creates packets of data that contain the HTTP response. The packets are sent back to the cURL process by routing them through the internet using the source IP address on the request packet. Once received by the cURL process, the packet is sent from the device to the drivers. At the Data Link layer, the MAC address is removed. At the Network Protocol layer, the IP address is verified and then removed from the packet. For this reason, if an application requires access to the client IP, it needs to be stored at the Application layer; the best example here is in HTTP requests and the X-Forwarded-For header. Now the socket is determined from the TCP data and removed. The packet is then forwarded to the client application that creates that socket. The client reads it and processes the response data. In this case, the socket ID was random, corresponding to the cURL process. All packets are sent to cURL and pieced together into one HTTP response. If we were to use the -O output option, it would have been saved to a file; otherwise, cURL outputs the response to the terminal's standard out.

Whew, that is a mouthful, 50 pages and 50 years of networking condensed into two paragraphs! The basics of networking we have reviewed are just the beginning but are required knowledge if you want to run Kubernetes clusters and networks at scale.

Conclusion

The HTTP transactions modeled in this chapter happen every millisecond, globally, all day on the internet and data center network. This is the type of scale that the Kubernetes networks' APIs help developers abstract away into simple YAML. Understanding the scale of the problem is our first in step in mastering the management of a Kubernetes network. By taking our simple example of the Golang web server and learning the first principles of networking, you can begin to wrangle the packets flowing into and out of your clusters.

So far, we have covered the following:

- History of networking
- OSI model
- TCP/IP

Throughout this chapter, we discussed many things related to networks but only those needed to learn about using the Kubernetes abstractions. There are several O'Reilly books about TCP/IP; *TCP/IP Network Administration* (*https://oreil.ly/UIP62*) by Craig Hunt (O'Reilly) is a great in-depth read on all aspects of TCP.

We discussed how networking evolved, walked through the OSI model, translated it to the TCP/IP stack, and with that stack completed an example HTTP request. In the next chapter, we will walk through how this is implemented for the client and server with Linux networking.

## CHAPTER 2

Linux Networking

To understand the implementation of networking in Kubernetes, we will need to understand the fundamentals of networking in Linux. Ultimately, Kubernetes is a complex management tool for Linux (or Windows!) machines, and this is hard to ignore while working with the Kubernetes network stack. This chapter will provide an overview of the Linux networking stack, with a focus on areas of note in Kubernetes. If you are highly familiar with Linux networking and network management, you may want to skim or skip this chapter.

 This chapter introduces many Linux programs. Manual, or *man*, pages, accessible with `man <program>`, will provide more detail.

Basics

Let's revisit our Go web server, which we used in Chapter 1. This web server listens on port 8080 and returns "Hello" for HTTP requests to / (see Example 2-1).

Example 2-1. Minimal web server in Go

```
package main

import (
        "fmt"
        "net/http"
)

func hello(w http.ResponseWriter, _ *http.Request) {
        fmt.Fprintf(w, "Hello")
```

```
}
func main() {
        http.HandleFunc("/", hello)
        http.ListenAndServe("0.0.0.0:8080", nil)
}
```

> Ports 1–1023 (also known as *well-known ports*) require root per-
> mission to bind to.
>
> Programs should always be given the least permissions necessary to
> function, which means that a typical web service should not be run
> as the root user. Because of this, many programs will listen on port
> 1024 or higher (in particular, port 8080 is a common choice for
> HTTP services). When possible, listen on a nonprivileged port, and
> use infrastructure redirects (load balancer forwarding, Kubernetes
> services, etc.) to forward an externally visible privileged port to a
> program listening on a nonprivileged port.
>
> This way, an attacker exploiting a possible vulnerability in your ser-
> vice will not have overly broad permissions available to them.

Suppose this program is running on a Linux server machine and an external client
makes a request to /. What happens on the server? To start off, our program needs to
listen to an address and port. Our program creates a socket for that address and port
and binds to it. The socket will receive requests addressed to both the specified
address and port - 8080 with any IP address in our case.

> 0.0.0.0 in IPv4 and [::] in IPv6 are wildcard addresses. They
> match all addresses of their respective protocol and, as such, listen
> on all available IP addresses when used for a socket binding.
>
> This is useful to expose a service, without prior knowledge of what
> IP addresses the machines running it will have. Most network-
> exposed services bind this way.

There are multiple ways to inspect sockets. For example, ls -lah /proc/<server
proc>/fd will list the sockets. We will discuss some programs that can inspect sockets
at the end of this chapter.

The kernel maps a given packet to a specific connection and uses an internal state
machine to manage the connection state. Like sockets, connections can be inspected
through various tools, which we will discuss later in this chapter. Linux represents
each connection with a file. Accepting a connection entails a notification from the
kernel to our program, which is then able to stream content to and from the file.

Going back to our Golang web server, we can use `strace` to show what the server is doing:

```
$ strace ./main
execve("./main", ["./main"], 0x7ebf2700 /* 21 vars */) = 0
brk(NULL)                               = 0x78e000
uname({sysname="Linux", nodename="raspberrypi", ...}) = 0
mmap2(NULL, 8192, PROT_READ|PROT_WRITE, MAP_PRIVATE|MAP_ANONYMOUS, -1, 0)
= 0x76f1d000
[Content cut]
```

Because `strace` captures all the system calls made by our server, there is a *lot* of output. Let's reduce it somewhat to the relevant network syscalls. Key points are highlighted, as the Go HTTP server performs many syscalls during startup:

```
openat(AT_FDCWD, "/proc/sys/net/core/somaxconn",
O_RDONLY|O_LARGEFILE|O_CLOEXEC) = 3
epoll_create1(EPOLL_CLOEXEC)            = 4 ❶
epoll_ctl(4, EPOLL_CTL_ADD, 3, {EPOLLIN|EPOLLOUT|EPOLLRDHUP|EPOLLET,
    {u32=1714573248, u64=1714573248}}) = 0
fcntl(3, F_GETFL)                       = 0x20000 (flags O_RDONLY|O_LARGEFILE)
fcntl(3, F_SETFL, O_RDONLY|O_NONBLOCK|O_LARGEFILE) = 0
read(3, "128\n", 65536)                 = 4
read(3, "", 65532)                      = 0
epoll_ctl(4, EPOLL_CTL_DEL, 3, 0x20245b0) = 0
close(3)                                = 0
socket(AF_INET, SOCK_STREAM|SOCK_CLOEXEC|SOCK_NONBLOCK, IPPROTO_TCP) = 3
close(3)                                = 0
socket(AF_INET6, SOCK_STREAM|SOCK_CLOEXEC|SOCK_NONBLOCK, IPPROTO_TCP) = 3 ❷
setsockopt(3, SOL_IPV6, IPV6_V6ONLY, [1], 4) = 0 ❸
bind(3, {sa_family=AF_INET6, sin6_port=htons(0),
inet_pton(AF_INET6, "::1", &sin6_addr),
    sin6_flowinfo=htonl(0), sin6_scope_id=0}, 28) = 0
socket(AF_INET6, SOCK_STREAM|SOCK_CLOEXEC|SOCK_NONBLOCK, IPPROTO_TCP) = 5
setsockopt(5, SOL_IPV6, IPV6_V6ONLY, [0], 4) = 0
bind(5, {sa_family=AF_INET6,
sin6_port=htons(0), inet_pton(AF_INET6,
    "::ffff:127.0.0.1", &sin6_addr), sin6_flowinfo=htonl(0),
sin6_scope_id=0}, 28) = 0
close(5)                                = 0
close(3)                                = 0
socket(AF_INET6, SOCK_STREAM|SOCK_CLOEXEC|SOCK_NONBLOCK, IPPROTO_IP) = 3
setsockopt(3, SOL_IPV6, IPV6_V6ONLY, [0], 4) = 0
setsockopt(3, SOL_SOCKET, SO_BROADCAST, [1], 4) = 0
setsockopt(3, SOL_SOCKET, SO_REUSEADDR, [1], 4) = 0
bind(3, {sa_family=AF_INET6, sin6_port=htons(8080),
inet_pton(AF_INET6, "::", &sin6_addr),
    sin6_flowinfo=htonl(0), sin6_scope_id=0}, 28) = 0 ❹
listen(3, 128)                          = 0
epoll_ctl(4, EPOLL_CTL_ADD, 3,
{EPOLLIN|EPOLLOUT|EPOLLRDHUP|EPOLLET, {u32=1714573248,
    u64=1714573248}}) = 0
```

```
getsockname(3, {sa_family=AF_INET6, sin6_port=htons(8080),

inet_pton(AF_INET6, "::", &sin6_addr), sin6_flowinfo=htonl(0),
sin6_scope_id=0},
    [112->28]) = 0
accept4(3, 0x2032d70, [112], SOCK_CLOEXEC|SOCK_NONBLOCK) = -1 EAGAIN
    (Resource temporarily unavailable)
epoll_wait(4, [], 128, 0)                = 0
epoll_wait(4, ❺
```

❶ Open a file descriptor.

❷ Create a TCP socket for IPv6 connections.

❸ Disable IPV6_V6ONLY on the socket. Now, it can listen on IPv4 and IPv6.

❹ Bind the IPv6 socket to listen on port 8080 (all addresses).

❺ Wait for a request.

Once the server has started, we see the output from strace pause on epoll_wait.

At this point, the server is listening on its socket and waiting for the kernel to notify it about packets. When we make a request to our listening server, we see the "Hello" message:

```
$ curl <ip>:8080/
Hello
```

 If you are trying to debug the fundamentals of a web server with strace, you will probably not want to use a web browser. Additional requests or metadata sent to the server may result in additional work for the server, or the browser may not make expected requests. For example, many browsers try to request a favicon file automatically. They will also attempt to cache files, reuse connections, and do other things that make it harder to predict the exact network interaction. When simple or minimal reproduction matters, try using a tool like curl or telnet.

In strace, we see the following from our server process:

```
[{EPOLLIN, {u32=1714573248, u64=1714573248}}], 128, -1) = 1
accept4(3, {sa_family=AF_INET6, sin6_port=htons(54202), inet_pton(AF_INET6,
    "::ffff:10.0.0.57", &sin6_addr), sin6_flowinfo=htonl(0), sin6_scope_id=0},
    [112->28], SOCK_CLOEXEC|SOCK_NONBLOCK) = 5
epoll_ctl(4, EPOLL_CTL_ADD, 5, {EPOLLIN|EPOLLOUT|EPOLLRDHUP|EPOLLET,
    {u32=1714573120, u64=1714573120}}) = 0
getsockname(5, {sa_family=AF_INET6, sin6_port=htons(8080),
    inet_pton(AF_INET6, "::ffff:10.0.0.30", &sin6_addr), sin6_flowinfo=htonl(0),
```

```
    sin6_scope_id=0}, [112->28]) = 0
setsockopt(5, SOL_TCP, TCP_NODELAY, [1], 4) = 0
setsockopt(5, SOL_SOCKET, SO_KEEPALIVE, [1], 4) = 0
setsockopt(5, SOL_TCP, TCP_KEEPINTVL, [180], 4) = 0
setsockopt(5, SOL_TCP, TCP_KEEPIDLE, [180], 4) = 0
accept4(3, 0x2032d70, [112], SOCK_CLOEXEC|SOCK_NONBLOCK) = -1 EAGAIN
    (Resource temporarily unavailable)
```

After inspecting the socket, our server writes response data ("Hello" wrapped in the HTTP protocol) to the file descriptor. From there, the Linux kernel (and some other userspace systems) translates the request into packets and transmits those packets back to our cURL client.

To summarize what the server is doing when it receives a request:

1. Epoll returns and causes the program to resume.

2. The server sees a connection from `::ffff:10.0.0.57`, the client IP address in this example.

3. The server inspects the socket.

4. The server changes `KEEPALIVE` options: it turns `KEEPALIVE` on, and sets a 180-second interval between `KEEPALIVE` probes.

This is a bird's-eye view of networking in Linux, from an application developer's point of view. There's a lot more going on to make everything work. We'll look in more detail at parts of the networking stack that are particularly relevant for Kubernetes users.

The Network Interface

Computers use a *network interface* to communicate with the outside world. Network interfaces can be physical (e.g., an Ethernet network controller) or virtual. Virtual network interfaces do not correspond to physical hardware; they are abstract interfaces provided by the host or hypervisor.

IP addresses are assigned to network interfaces. A typical interface may have one IPv4 address and one IPv6 address, but multiple addresses can be assigned to the same interface.

Linux itself has a concept of a network interface, which can be physical (such as an Ethernet card and port) or virtual. If you run `ifconfig`, you will see a list of all network interfaces and their configurations (including IP addresses).

The *loopback interface* is a special interface for same-host communication. `127.0.0.1` is the standard IP address for the loopback interface. Packets sent to the loopback interface will not leave the host, and processes listening on `127.0.0.1` will be accessible only to other processes on the same host. Note that making a process listen on 127.0.0.1 is not a security boundary. CVE-2020-8558 was a past Kubernetes vulnerability, in which kube-proxy rules allowed some remote systems to reach 127.0.0.1. The loopback interface is commonly abbreviated as lo.

 The ip command can also be used to inspect network interfaces.

Let's look at a typical ifconfig output; see Example 2-2.

Example 2-2. Output from ifconfig on a machine with one pysical network interface (ens4), and the loopback interface

```
$ ifconfig
ens4: flags=4163<UP,BROADCAST,RUNNING,MULTICAST>  mtu 1460
        inet 10.138.0.4  netmask 255.255.255.255  broadcast 0.0.0.0
        inet6 fe80::4001:aff:fe8a:4  prefixlen 64  scopeid 0x20<link>
        ether 42:01:0a:8a:00:04  txqueuelen 1000  (Ethernet)
        RX packets 5896679  bytes 504372582 (504.3 MB)
        RX errors 0  dropped 0  overruns 0  frame 0
        TX packets 9962136  bytes 1850543741 (1.8 GB)
        TX errors 0  dropped 0 overruns 0  carrier 0  collisions 0

lo: flags=73<UP,LOOPBACK,RUNNING>  mtu 65536
        inet 127.0.0.1  netmask 255.0.0.0
        inet6 ::1  prefixlen 128  scopeid 0x10<host>
        loop  txqueuelen 1000  (Local Loopback)
        RX packets 352  bytes 33742 (33.7 KB)
        RX errors 0  dropped 0  overruns 0  frame 0
        TX packets 352  bytes 33742 (33.7 KB)
        TX errors 0  dropped 0 overruns 0  carrier 0  collisions 0
```

Container runtimes create a virtual network interface for each pod on a host, so the list would be much longer on a typical Kubernetes node. We'll cover container networking in more detail in Chapter 3.

The Bridge Interface

The bridge interface (shown in Figure 2-1) allows system administrators to create multiple layer 2 networks on a single host. In other words, the bridge functions like a network switch between network interfaces on a host, seamlessly connecting them. Bridges allow pods, with their individual network interfaces, to interact with the broader network via the node's network interface.

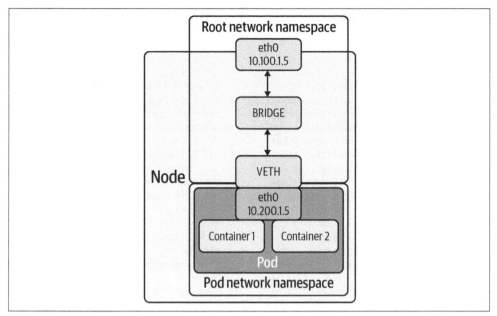

Figure 2-1. Bridge interface

You can read more about Linux bridging in the documentation
(*https://oreil.ly/4BRsA*).

In Example 2-3, we demonstrate how to create a bridge device named br0 and attach
a virtual Ethernet (veth) device, veth, and a physical device, eth0, using ip.

Example 2-3. Creating bridge interface and connecting veth pair

```
# # Add a new bridge interface named br0.
# ip link add br0 type bridge
# # Attach eth0 to our bridge.
# ip link set eth0 master br0
# # Attach veth to our bridge.
# ip link set veth master br0
```

Bridges can also be managed and created using the brctl command. Example 2-4
shows some options available with brctl.

Example 2-4. brctl options

```
$ brctl
$ commands:
        addbr           <bridge>                        add bridge
        delbr           <bridge>                        delete bridge
        addif           <bridge> <device>               add interface to bridge
        delif           <bridge> <device>               delete interface from bridge
        setageing       <bridge> <time>                 set ageing time
        setbridgeprio   <bridge> <prio>                 set bridge priority
        setfd           <bridge> <time>                 set bridge forward delay
        sethello        <bridge> <time>                 set hello time
        setmaxage       <bridge> <time>                 set max message age
        setpathcost     <bridge> <port> <cost>          set path cost
        setportprio     <bridge> <port> <prio>          set port priority
        show                                            show a list of bridges
        showmacs        <bridge>                        show a list of mac addrs
        showstp         <bridge>                        show bridge stp info
        stp             <bridge> <state>                turn stp on/off
```

The veth device is a local Ethernet tunnel. Veth devices are created in pairs, as shown in Figure 2-1, where the pod sees an eth0 interface from the veth. Packets transmitted on one device in the pair are immediately received on the other device. When either device is down, the link state of the pair is down. Adding a bridge to Linux can be done with using the brctl commands or ip. Use a veth configuration when namespaces need to communicate to the main host namespace or between each other.

Example 2-5 shows how to set up a veth configuration.

Example 2-5. Veth creation

```
# ip netns add net1
# ip netns add net2
# ip link add veth1 netns net1 type veth peer name veth2 netns net2
```

In Example 2-5, we show the steps to create two network namespaces (not to be confused with Kubernetes namespaces), net1 and net2, and a pair of veth devices, with veth1 assigned to namespace net1 and veth2 assigned to namespace net2. These two namespaces are connected with this veth pair. Assign a pair of IP addresses, and you can ping and communicate between the two namespaces.

Kubernetes uses this in concert with the CNI project to manage container network namespaces, interfaces, and IP addresses. We will cover more of this in Chapter 3.

Packet Handling in the Kernel

The Linux kernel is responsible for translating between packets, and a coherent stream of data for programs. In particular, we will look at how the kernel handles connections because routing and firewalling, key things in Kubernetes, rely heavily on Linux's underlying packet management.

Netfilter

Netfilter, included in Linux since 2.3, is a critical component of packet handling. Netfilter is a framework of kernel hooks, which allow userspace programs to handle packets on behalf of the kernel. In short, a program registers to a specific Netfilter hook, and the kernel calls that program on applicable packets. That program could tell the kernel to do something with the packet (like drop it), or it could send back a modified packet to the kernel. With this, developers can build normal programs that run in userspace and handle packets. Netfilter was created jointly with `iptables`, to separate kernel and userspace code.

 netfilter.org contains some excellent documentation on the design and use of both Netfilter and `iptables`.

Netfilter has five hooks, shown in Table 2-1.

Netfilter triggers each hook under specific stages in a packet's journey through the kernel. Understanding Netfilter's hooks is key to understanding `iptables` later in this chapter, as `iptables` directly maps its concept of *chains* to Netfilter hooks.

Table 2-1. Netfilter hooks

Netfilter hook	Iptables chain name	Description
NF_IP_PRE_ROUTING	PREROUTING	Triggers when a packet arrives from an external system.
NF_IP_LOCAL_IN	INPUT	Triggers when a packet's destination IP address matches this machine.
NF_IP_FORWARD	NAT	Triggers for packets where neither source nor destination matches the machine's IP addresses (in other words, packets that this machine is routing on behalf of other machines).
NF_IP_LOCAL_OUT	OUTPUT	Triggers when a packet, originating from the machine, is leaving the machine.
NF_IP_POST_ROUTING	POSTROUTING	Triggers when any packet (regardless of origin) is leaving the machine.

Netfilter triggers each hook during a specific phase of packet handling, and under specific conditions, we can visualize Netfilter hooks with a flow diagram, as shown in Figure 2-2.

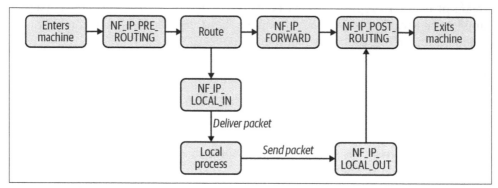

Figure 2-2. The possible flows of a packet through Netfilter hooks

We can infer from our flow diagram that only certain permutations of Netfilter hook calls are possible for any given packet. For example, a packet originating from a local process will always trigger NF_IP_LOCAL_OUT hooks and then NF_IP_POST_ROUTING hooks. In particular, the flow of Netfilter hooks for a packet depends on two things: if the packet source is the host and if the packet destination is the host. Note that if a process sends a packet destined for the same host, it triggers the NF_IP_LOCAL_OUT and then the NF_IP_POST_ROUTING hooks before "reentering" the system and triggering the NF_IP_PRE_ROUTING and NF_IP_LOCAL_IN hooks.

In some systems, it is possible to spoof such a packet by writing a fake source address (i.e., spoofing that a packet has a source and destination address of 127.0.0.1). Linux will normally filter such a packet when it arrives at an external interface. More broadly, Linux filters packets when a packet arrives at an interface and the packet's source address does not exist on that network. A packet with an "impossible" source IP address is called a *Martian packet*. It is possible to disable filtering of Martian packets in Linux. However, doing so poses substantial risk if any services on the host assume that traffic from localhost is "more trustworthy" than external traffic. This can be a common assumption, such as when exposing an API or database to the host without strong authentication.

Kubernetes has had at least one CVE, CVE-2020-8558, in which packets from another host, with the source IP address falsely set to 127.0.0.1, could access ports that should be accessible only locally. Among other things, this means that if a node in the Kubernetes control plane ran kube-proxy, other machines on the node's network could use "trust authentication" to connect to the API server, effectively owning the cluster.

This was not technically a case of Martian packets not being filtered, as offending packets would come from the loopback device, which *is* on the same network as 127.0.0.1. You can read the reported issue on GitHub (*https://oreil.ly/A5HtN*).

Table 2-2 shows the Netfilter hook order for various packet sources and destinations.

Table 2-2. Key netfilter packet flows

Packet source	Packet destination	Hooks (in order)
Local machine	Local machine	NF_IP_LOCAL_OUT, NF_IP_LOCAL_IN
Local machine	External machine	NF_IP_LOCAL_OUT, NF_IP_POST_ROUTING
External machine	Local machine	NF_IP_PRE_ROUTING, NF_IP_LOCAL_IN
External machine	External machine	NF_IP_PRE_ROUTING, NF_IP_FORWARD, NF_IP_POST_ROUTING

Note that packets from the machine to itself will trigger NF_IP_LOCAL_OUT and NF_IP_POST_ROUTING and then "leave" the network interface. They will "reenter" and be treated like packets from any other source.

Network address translation (NAT) only impacts local routing decisions in the NF_IP_PRE_ROUTING and NF_IP_LOCAL_OUT hooks (e.g., the kernel makes no routing decisions after a packet reaches the NF_IP_LOCAL_IN hook). We see this reflected in the design of iptables, where source and destination NAT can be performed only in specific hooks/chains.

Programs can register a hook by calling NF_REGISTER_NET_HOOK (NF_REGISTER_HOOK prior to Linux 4.13) with a handling function. The hook will be called every time a packet matches. This is how programs like iptables integrate with Netfilter, though you will likely never need to do this yourself.

There are several actions that a Netfilter hook can trigger, based on the return value:

Accept
Continue packet handling.

Drop
Drop the packet, without further processing.

Queue
Pass the packet to a userspace program.

Stolen
Doesn't execute further hooks, and allows the userspace program to take owner-ship of the packet.

Repeat
Make the packet "reenter" the hook and be reprocessed.

Hooks can also return mutated packets. This allows programs to do things such as reroute or masquerade packets, adjust packet TTLs, etc.

Conntrack

Conntrack is a component of Netfilter used to track the state of connections to (and from) the machine. Connection tracking directly associates packets with a particular connection. Without connection tracking, the flow of packets is much more opaque. Conntrack can be a liability or a valuable tool, or both, depending on how it is used. In general, Conntrack is important on systems that handle firewalling or NAT.

Connection tracking allows firewalls to distinguish between responses and arbitrary packets. A firewall can be configured to allow inbound packets that are part of an existing connection but disallow inbound packets that are not part of a connection. To give an example, a program could be allowed to make an outbound connection and perform an HTTP request, without the remote server being otherwise able to send data or initiate connections inbound.

NAT relies on Conntrack to function. iptables exposes NAT as two types: SNAT (source NAT, where iptables rewrites the source address) and DNAT (destination NAT, where iptables rewrites the destination address). NAT is extremely common; the odds are overwhelming that your home router uses SNAT and DNAT to fan traffic between your public IPv4 address and the local address of each device on the network. With connection tracking, packets are automatically associated with their connection and easily modified with the same SNAT/DNAT change. This enables consistent routing decisions, such as "pinning" a connection in a load balancer to a specific backend or machine. The latter example is highly relevant in Kubernetes, due to kube-proxy's implementation of service load balancing via iptables. Without connection tracking, every packet would need to be *deterministically* remapped to the same destination, which isn't doable (suppose the list of possible destinations could change…).

Conntrack identifies connections by a tuple, composed of source address, source port, destination address, destination port, and L4 protocol. These five pieces of information are the minimal identifiers needed to identify any given L4 connection. All L4 connections have an address and port on each side of the connection; after all, the internet uses addresses for routing, and computers use port numbers for application mapping. The final piece, the L4 protocol, is present because a program will bind to a port in TCP *or* UDP mode (and binding to one does not preclude binding to the other). Conntrack refers to these connections as *flows*. A flow contains metadata about the connection and its state.

Conntrack stores flows in a hash table, shown in Figure 2-3, using the connection tuple as a key. The size of the keyspace is configurable. A larger keyspace requires more memory to hold the underlying array but will result in fewer flows hashing to the same key and being chained in a linked list, leading to faster flow lookup times. The maximum number of flows is also configurable. A severe issue that can happen is when Conntrack runs out of space for connection tracking, and new connections cannot be made. There are other configuration options too, such as the timeout for a connection. On a typical system, default settings will suffice. However, a system that experiences a huge number of connections will run out of space. If your host runs directly exposed to the internet, overwhelming Conntrack with short-lived or incomplete connections is an easy way to cause a denial of service (DOS).

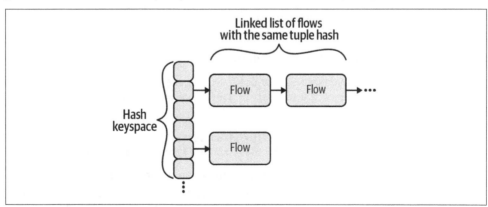

Figure 2-3. The structure of Conntrack flows

Conntrack's max size is normally set in /proc/sys/net/nf_conntrack_max, and the hash table size is normally set in /sys/module/nf_conntrack/parameters/hashsize.

Conntrack entries contain a connection state, which is one of four states. It is important to note that, as a layer 3 (Network layer) tool, Conntrack states are distinct from layer 4 (Protocol layer) states. Table 2-3 details the four states.

Table 2-3. Conntrack states

State	Description	Example
NEW	A valid packet is sent or received, with no response seen.	TCP SYN received.
ESTABLISHED	Packets observed in both directions.	TCP SYN received, and TCP SYN/ACK sent.
RELATED	An additional connection is opened, where metadata indicates that it is "related" to an original connection. Related connection handling is complex.	An FTP program, with an ESTABLISHED connection, opens additional data connections.
INVALID	The packet itself is invalid, or does not properly match another Conntrack connection state.	TCP RST received, with no prior connection.

Although Conntrack is built into the kernel, it may not be active on your system. Certain kernel modules must be loaded, and you must have relevant iptables rules (essentially, Conntrack is normally not active if nothing needs it to be). Conntrack requires the kernel module nf_conntrack_ipv4 to be active. lsmod | grep nf_conn track will show if the module is loaded, and sudo modprobe nf_conntrack will load it. You may also need to install the conntrack command-line interface (CLI) in order to view Conntrack's state.

When Conntrack is active, conntrack -L shows all current flows. Additional Conntrack flags will filter which flows are shown.

Let's look at the anatomy of a Conntrack flow, as displayed here:

```
tcp      6 431999 ESTABLISHED src=10.0.0.2 dst=10.0.0.1
sport=22 dport=49431 src=10.0.0.1 dst=10.0.0.2 sport=49431 dport=22 [ASSURED]
mark=0 use=1

<protocol> <protocol number> <flow TTL> [flow state>]
<source ip> <dest ip> <source port> <dest port> [] <expected return packet>
```

The expected return packet is of the form <source ip> <dest ip> <source port> <dest port>. This is the identifier that we expect to see when the remote system sends a packet. Note that in our example, the source and destination values are in reverse for address and ports. This is often, but not always, the case. For example, if a machine is behind a router, packets destined to that machine will be addressed to the router, whereas packets from the machine will have the machine address, not the router address, as the source.

In the previous example from machine `10.0.0.2`, `10.0.0.1` has established a TCP connection from port 49431 to port 22 on `10.0.0.2`. You may recognize this as being an SSH connection, although Conntrack is unable to show application-level behavior.

Tools like `grep` can be useful for examining Conntrack state and ad hoc statistics:

```
grep ESTABLISHED /proc/net/ip_conntrack | wc -l
```

Routing

When handling any packet, the kernel must decide where to send that packet. In most cases, the destination machine will not be within the same network. For example, suppose you are attempting to connect to `1.2.3.4` from your personal computer. `1.2.3.4` is not on your network; the best your computer can do is pass it to another host that is closer to being able to reach `1.2.3.4`. The route table serves this purpose by mapping known subnets to a gateway IP address and interface. You can list known routes with `route` (or `route -n` to show raw IP addresses instead of hostnames). A typical machine will have a route for the local network and a route for `0.0.0.0/0`. Recall that subnets can be expressed as a CIDR (e.g., `10.0.0.0/24`) or an IP address and a mask (e.g., `10.0.0.0` and `255.255.255.0`).

This is a typical routing table for a machine on a local network with access to the internet:

```
# route
Kernel IP routing table
Destination     Gateway         Genmask          Flags Metric Ref    Use Iface
0.0.0.0         10.0.0.1        0.0.0.0          UG    303    0        0 eth0
10.0.0.0        0.0.0.0         255.255.255.0    U     303    0        0 eth0
```

In the previous example, a request to `1.2.3.4` would be sent to `10.0.0.1`, on the `eth0` interface, because `1.2.3.4` is in the subnet described by the first rule (`0.0.0.0/0`) and not in the subnet described by the second rule (`10.0.0.0/24`). Subnets are specified by the destination and `genmask` values.

Linux prefers to route packets by *specificity* (how "small" a matching subnet is) and then by weight ("metric" in `route` output). Given our example, a packet addressed to `10.0.0.1` will always be sent to gateway `0.0.0.0` because that route matches a smaller set of addresses. If we had two routes with the same specificity, then the route with a lower metric wiould be preferred.

Some CNI plugins make heavy use of the route table.

Now that we've covered some key concepts in how the Linux kernel handles packets, we can look at how higher-level packet and connection routing works.

High-Level Routing

Linux has complex packet management abilities. Such tools allow Linux users to create firewalls, log traffic, route packets, and even implement load balancing. Kubernetes makes use of some of these tools to handle node and pod connectivity, as well as manage Kubernetes services. In this book, we will cover the three tools that are most commonly seen in Kubernetes. All Kubernetes setups will make some use of `iptables`, but there are many ways that services can be managed. We will also cover IPVS (which has built-in support in `kube-proxy`), and eBPF, which is used by Cilium (a `kube-proxy` alternative).

We will reference this section in Chapter 4, when we cover services and `kube-proxy`.

iptables

`iptables` is staple of Linux sysadmins and has been for many years. `iptables` can be used to create firewalls and audit logs, mutate and reroute packets, and even implement crude connection fan-out. `iptables` uses Netfilter, which allows `iptables` to intercept and mutate packets.

`iptables` rules can become extremely complex. There are many tools that provide a simpler interface for managing `iptables` rules; for example, firewalls like `ufw` and `firewalld`. Kubernetes components (specifically, `kubelet` and `kube-proxy`) generate `iptables` rules in this fashion. Understanding `iptables` is important to understand access and routing for pods and nodes in most clusters.

> Most Linux distributions are replacing `iptables` with `nftables`, a similar but more performant tool built atop Netfilter. Some distros already ship with a version of `iptables` that is powered by `nftables`.
>
> Kubernetes has many known issues with the `iptables`/`nftables` transition. We highly recommend not using a `nftables`-backed version of `iptables` for the foreseeable future.

There are three key concepts in `iptables`: tables, chains, and rules. They are considered hierarchical in nature: a table contains chains, and a chain contains rules.

Tables organize rules according to the type of effect they have. `iptables` has a broad range of functionality, which tables group together. The three most commonly applicable tables are: Filter (for firewall-related rules), NAT (for NAT-related rules), and Mangle (for non-NAT packet-mutating rules). `iptables` executes tables in a specific order, which we'll cover later.

Chains contain a list of rules. When a packet executes a chain, the rules in the chain are evaluated in order. Chains exist within a table and organize rules according to Netfilter hooks. There are five built-in, top-level chains, each of which corresponds to a Netfilter hook (recall that Netfilter was designed jointly with iptables). Therefore, the choice of which chain to insert a rule dictates if/when the rule will be evaluated for a given packet.

Rules are a combination condition and action (referred to as a *target*). For example, "if a packet is addressed to port 22, drop it." iptables evaluates individual packets, although chains and tables dictate which packets a rule will be evaluated against.

The specifics of table → chain → target execution are complex, and there is no end of fiendish diagrams available to describe the full state machine. Next, we'll examine each portion in more detail.

 It may help to refer to earlier material as you progress through this section. The designs of tables, chains, and rules are tightly intertwined, and it is hard to properly understand one without understanding the others.

iptables tables

A table in iptables maps to a particular *capability set*, where each table is "responsible" for a specific type of action. In more concrete terms, a table can contain only specific target types, and many target types can be used only in specific tables. iptables has five tables, which are listed in Table 2-4.

Table 2-4. iptables tables

Table	Purpose
Filter	The Filter table handles acceptance and rejection of packets.
NAT	The NAT table is used to modify the source or destination IP addresses.
Mangle	The Mangle table can perform general-purpose editing of packet headers, but it is not intended for NAT. It can also "mark" the packet with iptables-only metadata.
Raw	The Raw table allows for packet mutation before connection tracking and other tables are handled. Its most common use is to disable connection tracking for some packets.
Security	SELinux uses the Security table for packet handling. It is not applicable on a machine that is not using SELinux.

We will not discuss the Security table in more detail in this book; however, if you use SELinux, you should be aware of its use.

iptables executes tables in a particular order: Raw, Mangle, NAT, Filter. However, this order of execution is broken up by chains. Linux users generally accept the mantra of "tables contains chains," but this may feel misleading. The order of execution is chains, *then* tables. So, for example, a packet will trigger Raw PREROUTING, Mangle PREROUTING, NAT PREROUTING, and then trigger the Mangle table in either the INPUT or FORWARD chain (depending on the packet). We'll cover this in more detail in the next section on chains, as we put more pieces together.

iptables chains

iptables chains are a list of rules. When a packet triggers or passes through a chain, each rule is sequentially evaluated, until the packet matches a "terminating target" (such as DROP), or the packet reaches the end of the chain.

The built-in, "top-level" chains are PREROUTING, INPUT, NAT, OUTPUT, and POSTROUT ING. These are powered by Netfilter hooks. Each chain corresponds to a hook. Table 2-5 shows the chain and hook pairs. There are also user-defined subchains that exist to help organize rules.

Table 2-5. iptables chains and corresponding Netfilter hooks

iptables chain	Netfilter hook
PREROUTIN	NF_IP_PRE_ROUTING
INPUT	NF_IP_LOCAL_IN
NAT	NF_IP_FORWARD
OUTPUT	NF_IP_LOCAL_OUT
POSTROUTING	NF_IP_POST_ROUTING

Returning to our diagram of Netfilter hook ordering, we can infer the equivalent diagram of iptables chain execution and ordering for a given packet (see Figure 2-4).

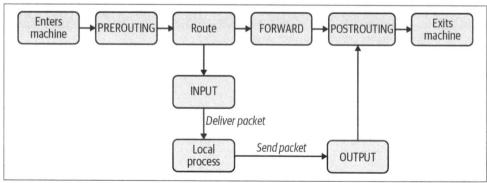

Figure 2-4. The possible flows of a packet through iptables chains

Again, like Netfilter, there are only a handful of ways that a packet can traverse these chains (assuming the packet is not rejected or dropped along the way). Let's use an example with three machines, with IP addresses `10.0.0.1`, `10.0.0.2`, and `10.0.0.3`, respectively. We will show some routing scenarios from the perspective of machine 1 (with IP address `10.0.0.1`). We examine them in Table 2-6.

Table 2-6. `iptables` *chains executed in various scenarios*

Packet description	Packet source	Packet destination	Tables processed
An inbound packet, from another machine.	`10.0.0.2`	`10.0.0.1`	PREROUTING, INPUT
An inbound packet, not destined for this machine.	`10.0.0.2`	`10.0.0.3`	PREROUTING, NAT, POSTROUTING
An outbound packet, originating locally, destined for another machine.	`10.0.0.1`	`10.0.0.2`	OUTPUT, POSTROUTING
A packet from a local program, destined for the same machine.	`127.0.0.1`	`127.0.0.1`	OUTPUT, POSTROUTING (then PREROUTING, INPUT as the packet re-enters via the loopback interface)

> You can experiment with chain execution behavior on your own using LOG rules. For example:
>
> ```
> iptables -A OUTPUT -p tcp --dport 22 -j LOG
> --log-level info --log-prefix "ssh-output"
> ```
>
> will log TCP packets to port 22 when they are processed by the OUTPUT chain, with the log prefix `"ssh-output"`. Be aware that log size can quickly become unwieldy. Log on important hosts with care.

Recall that when a packet triggers a chain, `iptables` executes tables within that chain (specifically, the rules within each table) in the following order:

1. Raw
2. Mangle
3. NAT
4. Filter

Most chains do not contain all tables; however, the relative execution order remains the same. This is a design decision to reduce redundancy. For example, the Raw table exists to manipulate packets "entering" `iptables`, and therefore has only PREROUTING and OUTPUT chains, in accordance with Netfilter's packet flow. The tables that contain each chain are laid out in Table 2-7.

Table 2-7. Which `iptables` tables (rows) contain which chains (columns)

	Raw	Mangle	NAT	Filter
PREROUTING	✓	✓	✓	
INPUT		✓	✓	✓
FORWARD		✓		✓
OUTPUT	✓	✓	✓	✓
POSTROUTING		✓	✓	

You can list the chains that correspond to a table yourself, with `iptables -L -t <table>`:

```
$ iptables -L -t filter
Chain INPUT (policy ACCEPT)
target     prot opt source               destination

Chain FORWARD (policy ACCEPT)
target     prot opt source               destination

Chain OUTPUT (policy ACCEPT)
target     prot opt source               destination
```

There is a small caveat for the NAT table: DNAT can be performed in `PREROUTING` or `OUTPUT`, and SNAT can be performed in only `INPUT` or `POSTROUTING`.

To give an example, suppose we have an inbound packet destined for our host. The order of execution would be:

1. PREROUTING
   a. Raw
   b. Mangle
   c. NAT
2. INPUT
   a. Mangle
   b. NAT
   c. Filter

Now that we've learned about Netfilter hooks, tables, and chains, let's take one last look at the flow of a packet through `iptables`, shown in Figure 2-5.

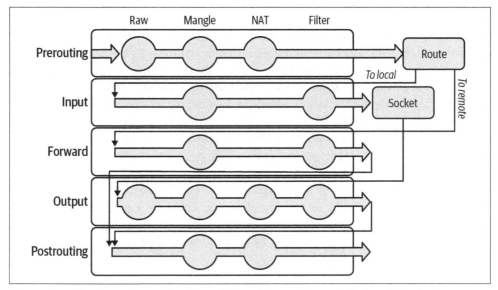

Figure 2-5. The flow of a packet through `iptables` *tables and chains. A circle denotes a table/hook combination that exists in* `iptables`.

All `iptables` rules belong to a table and chain, the possible combinations of which are represented as dots in our flow chart. `iptables` evaluates chains (and the rules in them, in order) based on the order of Netfilter hooks that a packet triggers. For the given chain, `iptables` evaluates that chain in each table that it is present in (note that some chain/table combinations do not exist, such as Filter/POSTROUTING). If we trace the flow of a packet originating from the local host, we see the following table/chains pairs evaluated, in order:

1. Raw/OUTPUT
2. Mangle/OUTPUT
3. NAT/OUTPUT
4. Filter/OUTPUT
5. Mangle/POSTROUTING
6. NAT/POSTROUTING

Subchains

The aforementioned chains are the top-level, or entry-point, chains. However, users can define their own subchains and execute them with the JUMP target. `iptables` executes such a chain in the same manner, target by target, until a terminating target matches. This can be useful for logical separation or reusing a series of targets that can be executed in more than one context (i.e., a similar motivation to why we might organize code into a function). Such organization of rules across chains can have a substantial impact on performance. `iptables` is, effectively, running tens or hundreds or thousands of `if` statements against every single packet that goes in or out of your system. That has measurable impact on packet latency, CPU use, and network throughput. A well-organized set of chains reduces this overhead by eliminating effectively redundant checks or actions. However, `iptables`'s performance given a service with many pods is still a problem in Kubernetes, which makes other solutions with less or no `iptables` use, such as IPVS or eBPF, more appealing.

Let's look at creating new chains in Example 2-6.

Example 2-6. Sample `iptables` chain for SSH firewalling

```
# Create incoming-ssh chain.
$ iptables -N incoming-ssh

# Allow packets from specific IPs.
$ iptables -A incoming-ssh -s 10.0.0.1 -j ACCEPT
$ iptables -A incoming-ssh -s 10.0.0.2 -j ACCEPT

# Log the packet.
$ iptables -A incoming-ssh -j LOG --log-level info --log-prefix "ssh-failure"

# Drop packets from all other IPs.
$ iptables -A incoming-ssh -j DROP

# Evaluate the incoming-ssh chain,
# if the packet is an inbound TCP packet addressed to port 22.
$ iptables -A INPUT -p tcp --dport 22 -j incoming-ssh
```

This example creates a new chain, `incoming-ssh`, which is evaluated for any TCP packets inbound on port 22. The chain allows packets from two specific IP addresses, and packets from other addresses are logged and dropped.

Filter chains end in a default action, such as dropping the packet if no prior target matched. Chains will default to `ACCEPT` if no default is specified. `iptables -P <chain> <target>` sets the default.

iptables rules

Rules have two parts: a match condition and an action (called a *target*). The match condition describes a packet attribute. If the packet matches, the action will be executed. If the packet does not match, `iptables` will move to check the next rule.

Match conditions check if a given packet meets some criteria, for example, if the packet has a specific source address. The order of operations from tables/chains is important to remember, as prior operations can impact the packet by mutating it, dropping it, or rejecting it. Table 2-8 shows some common match types.

Table 2-8. Some common `iptables` match types

Match type	Flag(s)	Description
Source	`-s, --src, --source`	Matches packets with the specified source address.
Destination	`-d, --dest, --destination`	Matches packets with the destination source address.
Protocol	`-p, --protocol`	Matches packets with the specified protocol.
In interface	`-i, --in-interface`	Matches packets that entered via the specified interface.
Out interface	`-o, --out-interface`	Matches packets that are leaving the specified interface.
State	`-m state --state <states>`	Matches packets from connections that are in one of the comma-separated states. This uses the Conntrack states (NEW, ESTABLISHED, RELATED, INVALID).

> Using `-m` or `--match`, `iptables` can use extensions for match criteria. Extensions range from nice-to-haves, such as specifying multiple ports in a single rule (multiport), to more complex features such as eBPF interactions. `man iptables-extensions` contains more information.

There are two kinds of target actions: terminating and nonterminating. A terminating target will stop `iptables` from checking subsequent targets in the chain, essentially acting as a final decision. A nonterminating target will allow `iptables` to continue checking subsequent targets in the chain. ACCEPT, DROP, REJECT, and RETURN are all terminating targets. Note that ACCEPT and RETURN are terminating only *within their chain*. That is to say, if a packet hits an ACCEPT target in a subchain, the parent chain will resume processing and could potentially drop or reject the target. Example 2-7 shows a set of rules that would reject packets to port 80, despite matching an ACCEPT at one point. Some command output has been removed for simplicity.

Example 2-7. Rule sequence which would reject some previously accepted packets

```
` ` `
$ iptables -L --line-numbers
Chain INPUT (policy ACCEPT)
num  target     prot opt source              destination
1    accept-all all  --  anywhere             anywhere
2    REJECT     tcp  --  anywhere            anywhere
     tcp dpt:80 reject-with icmp-port-unreachable

Chain accept-all (1 references)
num  target     prot opt source              destination
1               all  --  anywhere            anywhere
` ` `
```

Table 2-9 summarizes common target types and their behavior.

Table 2-9. Common `iptables` target types and behavior

Target type	Applicable tables	Description
AUDIT	All	Records data about accepted, dropped, or rejected packets.
ACCEPT	Filter	Allows the packet to continue unimpeded and without further modification.
DNAT	NAT	Modifies the destination address.
DROPs	Filter	Discards the packet. To an external observer, it will appear as though the packet was never received.
JUMP	All	Executes another chain. Once that chain finishes executing, execution of the parent chain will continue.
LOG	All	Logs the packet contents, via the kernel log.
MARK	All	Sets a special integer for the packet, used as an identifier by Netfilter. The integer can be used in other `iptables` decisions and is not written to the packet itself.
MASQUER ADE	NAT	Modifies the source address of the packet, replacing it with the address of a specified network interface. This is similar to SNAT, but does not require the machine's IP address to be known in advance.
REJECT	Filter	Discards the packet and sends a rejection reason.
RETURN	All	Stops processing the current chain (or subchain). Note that this is *not* a terminating target, and if there is a parent chain, that chain will continue to be processed.
SNAT	NAT	Modifies the source address of the packet, replacing it with a fixed address. See also: MAS QUERADE.

Each target type may have specific options, such as ports or log strings, that apply to the rule. Table 2-10 shows some example commands and explanations.

Table 2-10. `iptables` target command examples

Command	Explanation
iptables -A INPUT -s 10.0.0.1	Accepts an inbound packet if the source address is 10.0.0.1.
iptables -A INPUT -p ICMP	Accepts all inbound ICMP packets.
iptables -A INPUT -p tcp --dport 443	Accepts all inbound TCP packets to port 443.
iptables -A INPUT -p tcp --dport 22 -j DROP	Drops all inbound TCP ports to port 22.

A target belongs to both a table and a chain, which control when (if at all) `iptables` executes the aforementioned target for a given packet. Next, we'll put together what we've learned and look at `iptables` commands in practice.

Practical iptables

You can show `iptables` chains with `iptables -L`:

```
$ iptables -L
Chain INPUT (policy ACCEPT)
target     prot opt source              destination

Chain FORWARD (policy ACCEPT)
target     prot opt source              destination

Chain OUTPUT (policy ACCEPT)
target     prot opt source              destination
```

There is a distinct but nearly identical program, `ip6tables`, for managing IPv6 rules. `iptables` and `ip6tables` rules are completely separate. For example, dropping all packets to TCP `0.0.0.0:22` with `iptables` will not prevent connections to TCP `[::]:22`, and vice versa for `ip6tables`.

For simplicity, we will refer only to `iptables` and IPv4 addresses in this section.

`--line-numbers` shows numbers for each rule in a chain. This can be helpful when inserting or deleting rules. `-I <chain> <line>` inserts a rule at the specified line number, before the previous rule at that line.

The typical format of a command to interact with `iptables` rules is:

```
iptables [-t table] {-A|-C|-D} chain rule-specification
```

where `-A` is for *append*, `-C` is for *check*, and `-D` is for *delete*.

 `iptables` rules aren't persisted across restarts. `iptables` provides `iptables-save` and `iptables-restore` tools, which can be used manually or with simple automation to capture or reload rules. This is something that most firewall tools paper over by automatically creating their own `iptables` rules every time the system starts.

`iptables` can masquerade connections, making it appear as if the packets came from their own IP address. This is useful to provide a simplified exterior to the outside world. A common use case is to provide a known host for traffic, as a security bastion, or to provide a predictable set of IP addresses to third parties. In Kubernetes, masquerading can make pods use their node's IP address, despite the fact that pods have unique IP addresses. This is necessary to communicate outside the cluster in many setups, where pods have internal IP addresses that cannot communicate directly with the internet. The `MASQUERADE` target is similar to SNAT; however, it does not require a `--source-address` to be known and specified in advance. Instead, it uses the address of a specified interface. This is slightly less performant than SNAT in cases where the new source address is static, as `iptables` must continuously fetch the address:

```
$iptables -t nat -A POSTROUTING -o eth0 -j MASQUERADE
```

`iptables` can perform connection-level load balancing or more accurately, connection fan-out. This technique relies on DNAT rules and random selection (to prevent every connection from being routed to the first DNAT target):

```
$ iptables -t nat -A OUTPUT -p tcp --dport 80 -d $FRONT_IP -m statistic \
--mode random --probability 0.5 -j DNAT --to-destination $BACKEND1_IP:80
$ iptables -t nat -A OUTPUT -p tcp --dport 80 -d $FRONT_IP \
-j DNAT --to-destination $BACKEND2_IP:80
```

In the previous example, there is a 50% chance of routing to the first backend. Otherwise, the packet proceeds to the next rule, which is guaranteed to route the connection to the second backend. The math gets a little tedious for adding more backends. To have an equal chance of routing to any backend, the nth backend must have a 1/n chance of being routed to. If there were three backends, the probabilities would need to be 0.3 (repeating), 0.5, and 1:

```
Chain KUBE-SVC-I7EAKVFJLYM7WH25 (1 references)
target        prot opt source                destination
KUBE-SEP-LXP5RGXOX6SCIC6C  all  --  anywhere           anywhere
     statistic mode random probability 0.25000000000
KUBE-SEP-XRJTEP3YTXUYFBMK  all  --  anywhere           anywhere
     statistic mode random probability 0.33332999982
KUBE-SEP-OMZR4HWUSCJLN33U  all  --  anywhere           anywhere
     statistic mode random probability 0.50000000000
KUBE-SEP-EELL7LVIDZU4CPY6  all  --  anywhere           anywhere
```

When Kubernetes uses `iptables` load balancing for a service, it creates a chain as shown previously. If you look closely, you can see rounding errors in one of the probability numbers.

Using DNAT fan-out for load balancing has several caveats. It has no feedback for the load of a given backend and will always map application-level queries on the same connection to the same backend. Because the DNAT result lasts the lifetime of the connection, if long-lived connections are common, many downstream clients may stick to the same upstream backend if that backend is longer lived than others. To give a Kubernetes example, suppose a gRPC service has only two replicas and then additional replicas scale up. gRPC reuses the same HTTP/2 connection, so existing downstream clients (using the Kubernetes service and not gRPC load balancing) will stay connected to the initial two replicas, skewing the load profile among gRPC backends. Because of this, many developers use a smarter client (such as making use of gRPC's client-side load balancing), force periodic reconnects at the server and/or client, or use service meshes to externalize the problem. We'll discuss load balancing in more detail in Chapters 4 and 5.

Although `iptables` is widely used in Linux, it can become slow in the presence of a huge number of rules and offers limited load balancing functionality. Next we'll look at IPVS, an alternative that is more purpose-built for load balancing.

IPVS

IP Virtual Server (IPVS) is a Linux connection (L4) load balancer. Figure 2-6 shows a simple diagram of IPVS's role in routing packets.

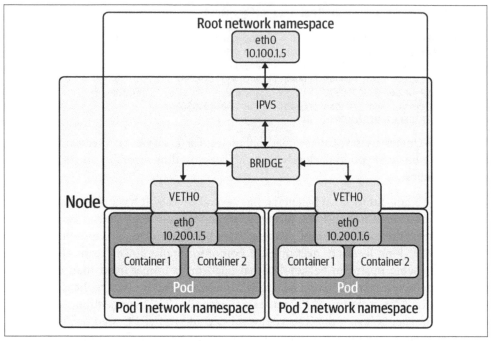

Figure 2-6. IPVS

`iptables` can do simple L4 load balancing by randomly routing connections, with the randomness shaped by the weights on individual DNAT rules. IPVS supports multiple load balancing modes (in contrast with the `iptables` one), which are outlined in Table 2-11. This allows IPVS to spread load more effectively than `iptables`, depending on IPVS configuration and traffic patterns.

Table 2-11. IPVS modes supported in Kubernetes

Name	Shortcode	Description
Round-robin	`rr`	Sends subsequent connections to the "next" host in a cycle. This increases the time between subsequent connections sent to a given host, compared to random routing like `iptables` enables.
Least connection	`lc`	Sends connections to the host that currently has the least open connections.
Destination hashing	`dh`	Sends connections deterministically to a specific host, based on the connections' destination addresses.
Source hashing	`sh`	Sends connections deterministically to a specific host, based on the connections' source addresses.
Shortest expected delay	`sed`	Sends connections to the host with the lowest connections to weight ratio.
Never queue	`nq`	Sends connections to any host with no existing connections, otherwise uses "shortest expected delay" strategy.

IPVS supports packet forwarding modes:

- NAT rewrites source and destination addresses.
- DR encapsulates IP datagrams within IP datagrams.
- IP tunneling directly routes packets to the backend server by rewriting the MAC address of the data frame with the MAC address of the selected backend server.

There are three aspects to look at when it comes to issues with `iptables` as a load balancer:

Number of nodes in the cluster
Even though Kubernetes already supports 5,000 nodes in release v1.6, `kube-proxy` with `iptables` is a bottleneck to scale the cluster to 5,000 nodes. One example is that with a NodePort service in a 5,000-node cluster, if we have 2,000 services and each service has 10 pods, this will cause at least 20,000 `iptables` records on each worker node, which can make the kernel pretty busy.

Time
The time spent to add one rule when there are 5,000 services (40,000 rules) is 11 minutes. For 20,000 services (160,000 rules), it's 5 hours.

Latency
There is latency to access a service (routing latency); each packet must traverse the `iptables` list until a match is made. There is latency to add/remove rules, inserting and removing from an extensive list is an intensive operation at scale.

IPVS also supports session affinity, which is exposed as an option in services (`Service.spec.sessionAffinity` and `Service.spec.sessionAffinityConfig`). Repeated connections, within the session affinity time window, will route to the same host. This can be useful for scenarios such as minimizing cache misses. It can also make routing in any mode effectively stateful (by indefinitely routing connections from the same address to the same host), but the routing stickiness is less absolute in Kubernetes, where individual pods come and go.

To create a basic load balancer with two equally weighted destinations, run `ipvsadm -A -t <address> -s <mode>`. `-A`, `-E`, and `-D` are used to add, edit, and delete virtual services, respectively. The lowercase counterparts, `-a`, `-e`, and `-d`, are used to add, edit, and delete host backends, respectively:

```
# ipvsadm -A -t 1.1.1.1:80 -s lc
# ipvsadm -a -t 1.1.1.1:80 -r 2.2.2.2 -m -w 100
# ipvsadm -a -t 1.1.1.1:80 -r 3.3.3.3 -m -w 100
```

You can list the IPVS hosts with `-L`. Each virtual server (a unique IP address and port combination) is shown, with its backends:

```
# ipvsadm -L
IP Virtual Server version 1.2.1 (size=4096)
Prot LocalAddress:Port Scheduler Flags
  -> RemoteAddress:Port           Forward Weight ActiveConn InActConn
TCP  1.1.1.1.80:http lc
  -> 2.2.2.2:http                 Masq    100   0          0
  -> 3.3.3.3:http                 Masq    100   0          0
```

-L supports multiple options, such as --stats, to show additional connection statistics.

eBPF

eBPF is a programming system that allows special sandboxed programs to run in the kernel without passing back and forth between kernel and user space, like we saw with Netfilter and iptables.

Before eBPF, there was the Berkeley Packet Filter (BPF). BPF is a technology used in the kernel, among other things, to analyze network traffic. BPF supports filtering packets, which allows a userspace process to supply a filter that specifies which packets it wants to inspect. One of BPF's use cases is tcpdump, shown in Figure 2-7. When you specify a filter on tcpdump, it compiles it as a BPF program and passes it to BPF. The techniques in BPF have been extended to other processes and kernel operations.

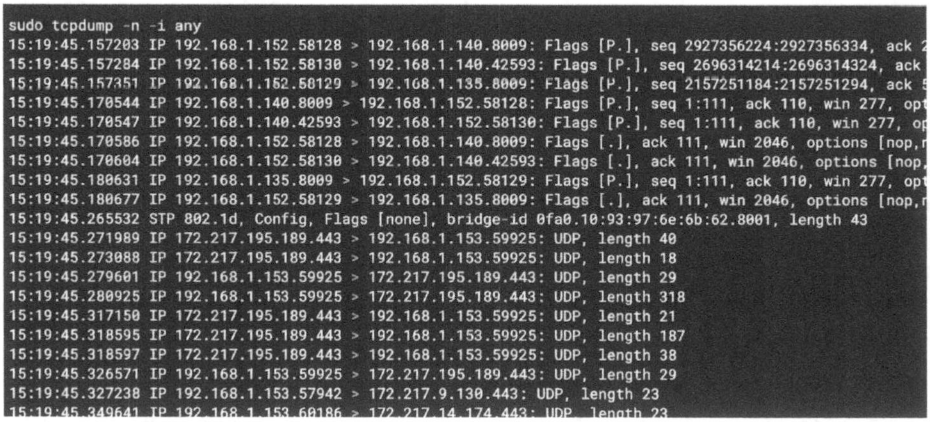

```
sudo tcpdump -n -i any
15:19:45.157203 IP 192.168.1.152.58128 > 192.168.1.140.8009: Flags [P.], seq 2927356224:2927356334, ack 2
15:19:45.157284 IP 192.168.1.152.58130 > 192.168.1.140.42593: Flags [P.], seq 2696314214:2696314324, ack
15:19:45.157351 IP 192.168.1.152.58129 > 192.168.1.135.8009: Flags [P.], seq 2157251184:2157251294, ack 5
15:19:45.170544 IP 192.168.1.140.8009 > 192.168.1.152.58128: Flags [P.], seq 1:111, ack 110, win 277, opt
15:19:45.170547 IP 192.168.1.140.42593 > 192.168.1.152.58130: Flags [P.], seq 1:111, ack 110, win 277, op
15:19:45.170586 IP 192.168.1.152.58128 > 192.168.1.140.8009: Flags [.], ack 111, win 2046, options [nop,r
15:19:45.170604 IP 192.168.1.152.58130 > 192.168.1.140.42593: Flags [.], ack 111, win 2046, options [nop,
15:19:45.180631 IP 192.168.1.135.8009 > 192.168.1.152.58129: Flags [P.], seq 1:111, ack 110, win 277, opt
15:19:45.180677 IP 192.168.1.152.58129 > 192.168.1.135.8009: Flags [.], ack 111, win 2046, options [nop,r
15:19:45.265532 STP 802.1d, Config, Flags [none], bridge-id 0fa0.10:93:97:6e:6b:62.8001, length 43
15:19:45.271989 IP 172.217.195.189.443 > 192.168.1.153.59925: UDP, length 40
15:19:45.273088 IP 172.217.195.189.443 > 192.168.1.153.59925: UDP, length 18
15:19:45.279601 IP 192.168.1.153.59925 > 172.217.195.189.443: UDP, length 29
15:19:45.280925 IP 192.168.1.153.59925 > 172.217.195.189.443: UDP, length 318
15:19:45.317150 IP 172.217.195.189.443 > 192.168.1.153.59925: UDP, length 21
15:19:45.318595 IP 172.217.195.189.443 > 192.168.1.153.59925: UDP, length 187
15:19:45.318597 IP 172.217.195.189.443 > 192.168.1.153.59925: UDP, length 38
15:19:45.326571 IP 192.168.1.153.59925 > 172.217.195.189.443: UDP, length 29
15:19:45.327238 IP 192.168.1.153.57942 > 172.217.9.130.443: UDP, length 23
15:19:45.349641 IP 192.168.1.153.60186 > 172.217.14.174.443: UDP, length 23
```

Figure 2-7. tcpdump

An eBPF program has direct access to syscalls. eBPF programs can directly watch and block syscalls, without the usual approach of adding kernel hooks to a userspace program. Because of its performance characteristics, it is well suited for writing networking software.

You can learn more about eBPF on its website (*http://ebpf.io*).

In addition to socket filtering, other supported attach points in the kernel are as follows:

Kprobes
Dynamic kernel tracing of internal kernel components.

Uprobes
User-space tracing.

Tracepoints
Kernel static tracing. These are programed into the kernel by developers and are more stable as compared to kprobes, which may change between kernel versions.

perf_events
Timed sampling of data and events.

XDP
Specialized eBPF programs that can go lower than kernel space to access driver space to act directly on packets.

Let's return to `tcpdump` as an example. Figure 2-8 shows a simplified rendition of `tcpdump`'s interactions with eBPF.

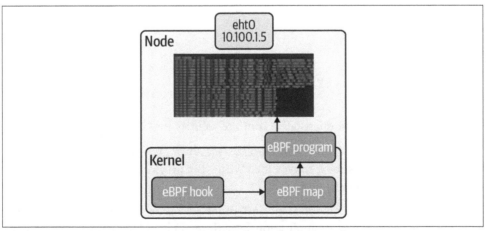

Figure 2-8. eBPF example

Suppose we run `tcpdump -i any`.

The string is compiled by `pcap_compile` into a BPF program. The kernel will then use this BPF program to filter all packets that go through all the network devices we specified, any with the `-I` in our case.

It will make this data available to `tcpdump` via a map. Maps are a data structure consisting of key-value pairs used by the BPF programs to exchange data.

There are many reasons to use eBPF with Kubernetes:

Performance (hashing table versus `iptables` list)
> For every service added to Kubernetes, the list of `iptables` rules that have to be traversed grows exponentially. Because of the lack of incremental updates, the entire list of rules has to be replaced each time a new rule is added. This leads to a total duration of 5 hours to install the 160,000 `iptables` rules representing 20,000 Kubernetes services.

Tracing
> Using BPF, we can gather pod and container-level network statistics. The BPF socket filter is nothing new, but the BPF socket filter per cgroup is. Introduced in Linux 4.10, `cgroup-bpf` allows attaching eBPF programs to cgroups. Once attached, the program is executed for all packets entering or exiting any process in the cgroup.

Auditing `kubectl exec` with eBPF
> With eBPF, you can attach a program that will record any commands executed in the `kubectl exec` session and pass those commands to a userspace program that logs those events.

Security

> *Seccomp*
>> Secured computing that restricts what syscalls are allowed. Seccomp filters can be written in eBPF.

> *Falco*
>> Open source container-native runtime security that uses eBPF.

The most common use of eBPF in Kubernetes is Cilium, CNI and service implementation. Cilium replaces `kube-proxy`, which writes `iptables` rules to map a service's IP address to its corresponding pods.

Through eBPF, Cilium can intercept and route all packets directly in the kernel, which is faster and allows for application-level (layer 7) load balancing. We will cover `kube-proxy` in Chapter 4.

Network Troubleshooting Tools

Troubleshooting network-related issues with Linux is a complex topic and could easily fill its own book. In this section, we will introduce some key troubleshooting tools and the basics of their use (Table 2-12 is provided as a simple cheat sheet of tools and applicable use cases). Think of this section as a jumping-off point for common Kubernetes-related tool uses. Man pages, `--help`, and the internet can guide you further. There is substantial overlap in the tools that we describe, so you may find learning about some tools (or tool features) redundant. Some are better suited to a given task than others (for example, multiple tools will catch TLS errors, but OpenSSL provides the richest debugging information). Exact tool use may come down to preference, familiarity, and availability.

Table 2-12. Cheat sheet of common debugging cases and tools

Case	Tools
Checking connectivity	`traceroute`, `ping`, `telnet`, `netcat`
Port scanning	`nmap`
Checking DNS records	`dig`, commands mentioned in "Checking Connectivity"
Checking HTTP/1	cURL, `telnet`, `netcat`
Checking HTTPS	OpenSSL, cURL
Checking listening programs	`netstat`

Some networking tools that we describe likely won't be preinstalled in your distro of choice, but all should be available through your distro's package manager. We will sometimes use `# Truncated` in command output where we have omitted text to avoid examples becoming repetitive or overly long.

Security Warning

Before we get into tooling details, we need to talk about security. An attacker can utilize any tool listed here in order to explore and access additional systems. There are many strong opinions on this topic, but we consider it best practice to leave the fewest possible networking tools installed on a given machine.

An attacker may still be able to download tools themselves (e.g., by downloading a binary from the internet) or use the standard package manager (if they have sufficient permission). In most cases, you are simply introducing some additional friction prior to exploring and exploiting. However, in some cases you can reduce an attacker's capabilities by not preinstalling networking tools.

Linux file permissions include something called the *setuid bit* that is sometimes used by networking tools. If a file has the setuid bit set, executing said file causes the file to be executed *as the user who owns the file*, rather than the current user. You can observe this by looking for an s rather than an x in the permission readout of a file:

```
$ ls -la /etc/passwd
-rwsr-xr-x 1 root root 68208 May 28  2020 /usr/bin/passwd
```

This allows programs to expose limited, privileged capabilities (for example, passwd uses this ability to allow a user to update their password, without allowing arbitrary writes to the password file). A number of networking tools (ping, nmap, etc.) may use the setuid bit on some systems to send raw packets, sniff packets, etc. If an attacker downloads their own copy of a tool and cannot gain root privileges, they will be able to do less with said tool than if it was installed by the system with the setuid bit set.

ping

ping is a simple program that sends ICMP ECHO_REQUEST packets to networked devices. It is a common, simple way to test network connectivity from one host to another.

ICMP is a layer 4 protocol, like TCP and UDP. Kubernetes services support TCP and UDP, but not ICMP. This means that pings to a Kubernetes service will always fail. Instead, you will need to use telnet or a higher-level tool such as cURL to check connectivity to a service. Individual pods may still be reachable by ping, depending on your network configuration.

 Firewalls and routing software are aware of ICMP packets and can be configured to filter or route specific ICMP packets. It is common, but not guaranteed (or necessarily advisable), to have permissive rules for ICMP packets. Some network administrators, network software, or cloud providers will allow ICMP packets by default.

The basic use of ping is simply ping <address>. The address can be an IP address or a domain. ping will send a packet, wait, and report the status of that request when a response or timeout happens.

By default, ping will send packets forever, and must be manually stopped (e.g., with Ctrl-C). -c <count> will make ping perform a fixed number before shutting down. On shutdown, ping also prints a summary:

```
$ ping -c 2 k8s.io
PING k8s.io (34.107.204.206): 56 data bytes
64 bytes from 34.107.204.206: icmp_seq=0 ttl=117 time=12.665 ms
64 bytes from 34.107.204.206: icmp_seq=1 ttl=117 time=12.403 ms

--- k8s.io ping statistics ---
```

```
2 packets transmitted, 2 packets received, 0.0% packet loss
round-trip min/avg/max/stddev = 12.403/12.534/12.665/0.131 ms
```

Table 2-13 shows common ping options.

Table 2-13. Useful ping options

Option	Description
-c <count>	Sends the specified number of packets. Exits after the final packet is received or times out.
-i <seconds>	Sets the wait interval between sending packets. Defaults to 1 second. Extremely low values are not recommended, as ping can flood the network.
-o	Exit after receiving 1 packet. Equivalent to -c 1.
-S <source address>	Uses the specified source address for the packet.
-W <milliseconds>	Sets the wait interval to receive a packet. If ping receives the packet later than the wait time, it will still count toward the final summary.

traceroute

traceroute shows the network route taken from one host to another. This allows users to easily validate and debug the route taken (or where routing fails) from one machine to another.

traceroute sends packets with specific IP time-to-live values. Recall from Chapter 1 that each host that handles a packet decrements the time-to-live (TTL) value on packets by 1, therefore limiting the number of hosts that a request can be handled by. When a host receives a packet and decrements the TTL to 0, it sends a TIME_EXCEE DED packet and discards the original packet. The TIME_EXCEEDED response packet contains the source address of the machine where the packet timed out. By starting with a TTL of 1 and raising the TTL by 1 for each packet, traceroute is able to get a response from each host along the route to the destination address.

traceroute displays hosts line by line, starting with the first external machine. Each line contains the hostname (if available), IP address, and response time:

```
$traceroute k8s.io
traceroute to k8s.io (34.107.204.206), 64 hops max, 52 byte packets
 1  router (10.0.0.1)  8.061 ms  2.273 ms  1.576 ms
 2  192.168.1.254 (192.168.1.254)  2.037 ms  1.856 ms  1.835 ms
 3  adsl-71-145-208-1.dsl.austtx.sbcglobal.net (71.145.208.1)
4.675 ms  7.179 ms  9.930 ms
 4  * * *
 5  12.122.149.186 (12.122.149.186)  20.272 ms  8.142 ms  8.046 ms
 6  sffca22crs.ip.att.net (12.122.3.70)  14.715 ms  8.257 ms  12.038 ms
 7  12.122.163.61 (12.122.163.61)  5.057 ms  4.963 ms  5.004 ms
 8  12.255.10.236 (12.255.10.236)  5.560 ms
    12.255.10.238 (12.255.10.238)  6.396 ms
    12.255.10.236 (12.255.10.236)  5.729 ms
 9  * * *
```

```
10  206.204.107.34.bc.googleusercontent.com (34.107.204.206)
64.473 ms  10.008 ms  9.321 ms
```

If `traceroute` receives no response from a given hop before timing out, it prints a *.
Some hosts may refuse to send a `TIME_EXCEEDED` packet, or a firewall along the way
may prevent successful delivery.

Table 2-14 shows common `traceroute` options.

Table 2-14. Useful `traceroute` options

Option	Syntax	Description
First TTL	`-f <TTL>`, `-M <TTL>`	Set the starting IP TTL (default value: 1). Setting the TTL to n will cause `traceroute` to not report the first n-1 hosts en route to the destination.
Max TTL	`-m <TTL>`	Set the maximum TTL, i.e., the maximum number of hosts that `traceroute` will attempt to route through.
Protocol	`-P <protocol>`	Send packets of the specified protocol (TCP, UDP, ICMP, and sometimes other options). UDP is default.
Source address	`-s <address>`	Specify the source IP address of outgoing packets.
Wait	`-w <seconds>`	Set the time to wait for a probe response.

dig

`dig` is a DNS lookup tool. You can use it to make DNS queries from the command
line and display the results.

The general form of a `dig` command is `dig [options] <domain>`. By default, `dig` will
display the CNAME, A, and AAAA records:

```
$ dig kubernetes.io

; <<>> DiG 9.10.6 <<>> kubernetes.io
;; global options: +cmd
;; Got answer:
;; ->>HEADER<<- opcode: QUERY, status: NOERROR, id: 51818
;; flags: qr rd ra; QUERY: 1, ANSWER: 1, AUTHORITY: 0, ADDITIONAL: 1

;; OPT PSEUDOSECTION:
; EDNS: version: 0, flags:; udp: 1452
;; QUESTION SECTION:
;kubernetes.io.                 IN      A

;; ANSWER SECTION:
kubernetes.io.          960     IN      A       147.75.40.148

;; Query time: 12 msec
;; SERVER: 2600:1700:2800:7d4f:6238:e0ff:fe08:6a7b#53
(2600:1700:2800:7d4f:6238:e0ff:fe08:6a7b)
```

```
;; WHEN: Mon Jul 06 00:10:35 PDT 2020
;; MSG SIZE  rcvd: 71
```

To display a particular type of DNS record, run dig <domain> <type> (or dig -t
<type> <domain>). This is overwhelmingly the main use case for dig:

```
$ dig kubernetes.io TXT

; <<>> DiG 9.10.6 <<>> -t TXT kubernetes.io
;; global options: +cmd
;; Got answer:
;; ->>HEADER<<- opcode: QUERY, status: NOERROR, id: 16443
;; flags: qr rd ra; QUERY: 1, ANSWER: 2, AUTHORITY: 0, ADDITIONAL: 1

;; OPT PSEUDOSECTION:
; EDNS: version: 0, flags:; udp: 512
;; QUESTION SECTION:
;kubernetes.io.                 IN      TXT

;; ANSWER SECTION:
kubernetes.io.          3599    IN      TXT
"v=spf1 include:_spf.google.com ~all"
kubernetes.io.          3599    IN      TXT
"google-site-verification=oPORCoq9XU6CmaR7G_bV00CLmEz-wLGOL7SXpeEuTt8"

;; Query time: 49 msec
;; SERVER: 2600:1700:2800:7d4f:6238:e0ff:fe08:6a7b#53
(2600:1700:2800:7d4f:6238:e0ff:fe08:6a7b)
;; WHEN: Sat Aug 08 18:11:48 PDT 2020
;; MSG SIZE  rcvd: 171
```

Table 2-15 shows common dig options.

Table 2-15. Useful dig options

Option	Syntax	Description
IPv4	-4	Use IPv4 only.
IPv6	-6	Use IPv6 only.
Address	-b <address>[#<port>]	Specify the address to make a DNS query to. Port can optionally be included, preceded by #.
Port	-p <port>	Specify the port to query, in case DNS is exposed on a nonstandard port. The default is 53, the DNS standard.
Domain	-q <domain>	The domain name to query. The domain name is usually specified as a positional argument.
Record Type	-t <type>	The DNS record type to query. The record type can alternatively be specified as a positional argument.

telnet

telnet is both a network protocol and a tool for using said protocol. telnet was once used for remote login, in a manner similar to SSH. SSH has become dominant due to having better security, but telnet is still extremely useful for debugging servers that use a text-based protocol. For example, with telnet, you can connect to an HTTP/1 server and manually make requests against it.

The basic syntax of telnet is telnet <address> <port>. This establishes a connection and provides an interactive command-line interface. Pressing Enter twice will send a command, which easily allows multiline commands to be written. Press Ctrl-J to exit the session:

```
$ telnet kubernetes.io
Trying 147.75.40.148...
Connected to kubernetes.io.
Escape character is '^]'.
> HEAD / HTTP/1.1
> Host: kubernetes.io
>
HTTP/1.1 301 Moved Permanently
Cache-Control: public, max-age=0, must-revalidate
Content-Length: 0
Content-Type: text/plain
Date: Thu, 30 Jul 2020 01:23:53 GMT
Location: https://kubernetes.io/
Age: 2
Connection: keep-alive
Server: Netlify
X-NF-Request-ID: a48579f7-a045-4f13-af1a-eeaa69a81b2f-23395499
```

To make full use of telnet, you will need to understand how the application protocol that you are using works. telnet is a classic tool to debug servers running HTTP, HTTPS, POP3, IMAP, and so on.

nmap

nmap is a port scanner, which allows you to explore and examine services on your network.

The general syntax of nmap is nmap [options] <target>, where target is a domain, IP address, or IP CIDR. nmap's default options will give a fast and brief summary of open ports on a host:

```
$ nmap 1.2.3.4
Starting Nmap 7.80 ( https://nmap.org ) at 2020-07-29 20:14 PDT
Nmap scan report for my-host (1.2.3.4)
Host is up (0.011s latency).
Not shown: 997 closed ports
PORT     STATE SERVICE
```

```
22/tcp   open  ssh
3000/tcp open  ppp
5432/tcp open  postgresql

Nmap done: 1 IP address (1 host up) scanned in 0.45 seconds
```

In the previous example, nmap detects three open ports and guesses which service is running on each port.

 Because nmap can quickly show you which services are accessible from a remote machine, it can be a quick and easy way to spot services that should *not* be exposed. nmap is a favorite tool for attackers for this reason.

nmap has a dizzying number of options, which change the scan behavior and level of detail provided. As with other commands, we will summarize some key options, but we *highly* recommend reading nmap's help/man pages.

Table 2-16 shows common nmap options.

Table 2-16. Useful nmap options

Option	Syntax	Description
Additional detection	-A	Enable OS detection, version detection, and more.
Decrease verbosity	-d	Decrease the command verbosity. Using multiple d's (e.g., -dd) increases the effect.
Increase verbosity	-v	Increase the command verbosity. Using multiple v's (e.g., -vv) increases the effect.

netstat

netstat can display a wide range of information about a machine's network stack and connections:

```
$ netstat
Active internet connections (w/o servers)
Proto Recv-Q Send-Q Local Address          Foreign Address        State
tcp       0    164 my-host:ssh             laptop:50113           ESTABLISHED
tcp       0      0 my-host:50051           example-host:48760     ESTABLISHED
tcp6      0      0 2600:1700:2800:7d:54310 2600:1901:0:bae2::https TIME_WAIT
udp6      0      0 localhost:38125         localhost:38125        ESTABLISHED
Active UNIX domain sockets (w/o servers)
Proto RefCnt Flags    Type     State   I-Node Path
unix  13     [ ]      DGRAM            8451   /run/systemd/journal/dev-log
unix  2      [ ]      DGRAM            8463   /run/systemd/journal/syslog
[Cut for brevity]
```

Invoking netstat with no additional arguments will display all *connected* sockets on the machine. In our example, we see three TCP sockets, one UDP socket, and a multitude of UNIX sockets. The output includes the address (IP address and port) on both sides of a connection.

We can use the `-a` flag to show all connections or `-l` to show only listening connections:

```
$ netstat -a
Active internet connections (servers and established)
Proto Recv-Q Send-Q Local Address         Foreign Address      State
tcp        0      0 0.0.0.0:ssh           0.0.0.0:*            LISTEN
tcp        0      0 0.0.0.0:postgresql    0.0.0.0:*            LISTEN
tcp        0    172 my-host:ssh           laptop:50113        ESTABLISHED
[Content cut]
```

A common use of `netstat` is to check which process is listening on a specific port. To do that, we run `sudo netstat -lp` - `l` for "listening" and `p` for "program." `sudo` may be necessary for `netstat` to view all program information. The output for `-l` shows which address a service is listening on (e.g., `0.0.0.0` or `127.0.0.1`).

We can use simple tools like `grep` to get a clear output from `netstat` when we are looking for a specific result:

```
$ sudo netstat -lp | grep 3000
tcp6       0      0 [::]:3000       [::]:*       LISTEN      613/grafana-server
```

Table 2-17 shows common `netstat` options.

Table 2-17. Useful `netstat` commands

Option	Syntax	Description
Show all sockets	`netstat -a`	Shows all sockets, not only open connections.
Show statistics	`netstat -s`	Shows networking statistics. By default, `netstat` shows stats from all protocols.
Show listening sockets	`netstat -l`	Shows sockets that are listening. This is an easy way to find running services.
TCP	`netstat -t`	The `-t` flag shows only TCP data. It can be used with other flags, e.g., `-lt` (show sockets listening with TCP).
UDP	`netstat -u`	The `-u` flag shows only UDP data. It can be used with other flags, e.g., `-lu` (show sockets listening with UDP).

netcat

`netcat` is a multipurpose tool for making connections, sending data, or listening on a socket. It can be helpful as a way to "manually" run a server or client to inspect what happens in greater detail. `netcat` is arguably similar to `telnet` in this regard, though `netcat` is capable of many more things.

nc is an alias for `netcat` on most systems.

netcat can connect to a server when invoked as `netcat <address> <port>`. `netcat` has an interactive `stdin`, which allows you to manually type data or pipe data to `net cat`. It's very `telnet`-esque so far:

```
$ echo -e "GET / HTTP/1.1\nHost: localhost\n" > cmd
$ nc localhost 80 < cmd
HTTP/1.1 302 Found
Cache-Control: no-cache
Content-Type: text/html; charset=utf-8
[Content cut]
```

Openssl

The OpenSSL technology powers a substantial chunk of the world's HTTPS connections. Most heavy lifting with OpenSSL is done with language bindings, but it also has a CLI for operational tasks and debugging. `openssl` can do things such as creating keys and certificates, signing certificates, and, most relevant to us, testing TLS/SSL connections. Many other tools, including ones outlined in this chapter, can test TLS/SSL connections. However, `openssl` stands out for its feature-richness and level of detail.

Commands usually take the form `openssl [sub-command] [arguments] [options]`. `openssl` has a vast number of subcommands (for example, `openssl rand` allows you to generate pseudo random data). The `list` subcommand allows you to list capabilities, with some search options (e.g., `openssl list --commands` for commands). To learn more about individual sub commands, you can check `openssl <subcommand> --help` or its man page (`man openssl-<subcommand>` or just `man <subcommand>`).

`openssl s_client -connect` will connect to a server and display detailed information about the server's certificate. Here is the default invocation:

```
openssl s_client -connect k8s.io:443
CONNECTED(00000003)
depth=2 O = Digital Signature Trust Co., CN = DST Root CA X3
verify return:1
depth=1 C = US, O = Let's Encrypt, CN = Let's Encrypt Authority X3
verify return:1
depth=0 CN = k8s.io
verify return:1
---
Certificate chain
0 s:CN = k8s.io
```

```
i:C = US, O = Let's Encrypt, CN = Let's Encrypt Authority X3
1 s:C = US, O = Let's Encrypt, CN = Let's Encrypt Authority X3
i:O = Digital Signature Trust Co., CN = DST Root CA X3
---
Server certificate
-----BEGIN CERTIFICATE-----
[Content cut]
-----END CERTIFICATE-----
subject=CN = k8s.io

issuer=C = US, O = Let's Encrypt, CN = Let's Encrypt Authority X3

---
No client certificate CA names sent
Peer signing digest: SHA256
Peer signature type: RSA-PSS
Server Temp Key: X25519, 253 bits
---
SSL handshake has read 3915 bytes and written 378 bytes
Verification: OK
---
New, TLSv1.3, Cipher is TLS_AES_256_GCM_SHA384
Server public key is 2048 bit
Secure Renegotiation IS NOT supported
Compression: NONE
Expansion: NONE
No ALPN negotiated
Early data was not sent
Verify return code: 0 (ok)
---
```

If you are using a self-signed CA, you can use -CAfile <path> to use that CA. This will allow you to establish and verify connections against a self-signed certificate.

cURL

cURL is a data transfer tool that supports multiple protocols, notably HTTP and HTTPS.

wget is a similar tool to the command curl. Some distros or administrators may install it instead of curl.

cURL commands are of the form curl [options] <URL>. cURL prints the URL's contents and sometimes cURL-specific messages to stdout. The default behavior is to make an HTTP GET request:

```
$ curl example.org
<!doctype html>
<html>
<head>
    <title>Example Domain</title>
# Truncated
```

By default, cURL does not follow redirects, such as HTTP 301s or protocol upgrades. The -L flag (or --location) will enable redirect following:

```
$ curl kubernetes.io
Redirecting to https://kubernetes.io

$ curl -L kubernetes.io
<!doctype html><html lang=en class=no-js><head>
# Truncated
```

Use the -X option to perform a specific HTTP verb; e.g., use curl -X DELETE foo/bar to make a DELETE request.

You can supply data (for a POST, PUT, etc.) in a few ways:

- URL encoded: -d "key1=value1&key2=value2"
- JSON: -d '{"key1":"value1", "key2":"value2"}'
- As a file in either format: -d @data.txt

The -H option adds an explicit header, although basic headers such as Content-Type are added automatically:

-H "Content-Type: application/x-www-form-urlencoded"

Here are some examples:

```
$ curl -d "key1=value1" -X PUT localhost:8080

$ curl -H "X-App-Auth: xyz" -d "key1=value1&key2=value2"
-X POST https://localhost:8080/demo
```

 cURL can be of some help when debugging TLS issues, but more specialized tools such as openssl may be more helpful.

cURL can help diagnose TLS issues. Just like a reputable browser, cURL validates the certificate chain returned by HTTP sites and checks against the host's CA certs:

```
$ curl https://expired-tls-site
curl: (60) SSL certificate problem: certificate has expired
More details here: https://curl.haxx.se/docs/sslcerts.html
```

```
curl failed to verify the legitimacy of the server and therefore could not
establish a secure connection to it. To learn more about this situation and
how to fix it, please visit the web page mentioned above.
```

Like many programs, cURL has a verbose flag, -v, which will print more information about the request and response. This is extremely valuable when debugging a layer 7 protocol such as HTTP:

```
$ curl https://expired-tls-site -v
*   Trying 1.2.3.4...
* TCP_NODELAY set
* Connected to expired-tls-site (1.2.3.4) port 443 (#0)
* ALPN, offering h2
* ALPN, offering http/1.1
* successfully set certificate verify locations:
*   CAfile: /etc/ssl/cert.pem
  CApath: none
* TLSv1.2 (OUT), TLS handshake, Client hello (1):
* TLSv1.2 (IN), TLS handshake, Server hello (2):
* TLSv1.2 (IN), TLS handshake, Certificate (11):
* TLSv1.2 (OUT), TLS alert, certificate expired (557):
* SSL certificate problem: certificate has expired
* Closing connection 0
curl: (60) SSL certificate problem: certificate has expired
More details here: https://curl.haxx.se/docs/sslcerts.html

# Truncated
```

cURL has many additional features that we have not covered, such as the ability to use timeouts, custom CA certs, custom DNS, and so on.

Conclusion

This chapter has provided you with a whirlwind tour of networking in Linux. We focused primarily on concepts that are required to understand Kubernetes' implementation, cluster setup constraints, and debugging Kubernetes-related networking problems (in workloads on Kubernetes, or Kubernetes itself). This chapter was by no means exhaustive, and you may find it valuable to learn more.

Next, we will start to look at containers in Linux and how containers interact with the network.

Container Networking Basics

Now that we've discussed networking basics and Linux networking, we'll discuss how networking is implemented in containers. Like networking, containers have a long history. This chapter will review the history, discuss various options for running containers, and explore the networking setup available. The industry, for now, has settled on Docker as the container runtime standard. Thus, we'll dive into the Docker networking model, explain how the CNI differs from the Docker network model, and end the chapter with examples of networking modes with Docker containers.

Introduction to Containers

In this section, we will discuss the evolution of running applications that has led us to containers. Some, rightfully, will talk about containers as not being real. They are yet another abstraction of the underlying technology in the OS kernel. Being technically right misses the point of the technology and leads us nowhere down the road of solving the hard problem that is application management and deployment.

Applications

Running applications has always had its challenges. There are many ways to serve applications nowadays: in the cloud, on-prem, and, of course, with containers. Application developers and system administrators face many issues, such as dealing with different versions of libraries, knowing how to complete deployments, and having old versions of the application itself. For the longest time, developers of applications had to deal with these issues. Bash scripts and deployment tools all have their drawbacks and issues. Every new company has its way of deploying applications, so every new developer has to learn these techniques. Separation of duties, permissions controls, and maintaining system stability require system administrators to limit access to developers for deployments. Sysadmins also manage multiple applications on the same host machine to drive up that machine's efficiency, thus creating contention between developers wanting to deploy new features and system administrators wanting to maintain the whole ecosystem's stability.

A general-purpose OS supports as many types of applications as possible, so its kernel includes all kinds of drivers, protocol libraries, and schedulers. Figure 3-1 shows one machine, with one operating system, but there are many ways to deploy an application to that host. Application deployment is a problem all organizations must solve.

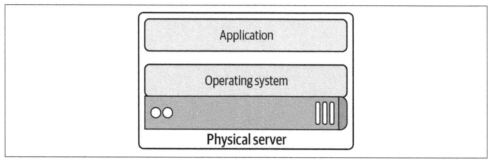

Figure 3-1. Application server

From a networking perspective, with one operating system, there is one TCP/IP stack. That single stack creates issues with port conflicts on the host machine. System administrators host multiple applications on the same machine to increase the machine's utilization, and each application will have to run on its port. So now, the system administrators, the application developers, and the network engineers have to coordinate all of this together. More tasks to add to the deployment checklist are creating troubleshooting guides and dealing with all the IT requests. Hypervisors are a way to increase one host machine's efficiency and remove the one operating system/networking stack issues.

Hypervisor

A hypervisor emulates hardware resources, CPU, and memory from a host machine to create guest operating systems or virtual machines. In 2001, VMware released its x86 hypervisor; earlier versions included IBM's z/Architecture and FreeBSD jails. The year 2003 saw the release of Xen, the first open source hypervisor, and in 2006 Kernel-based Virtual Machine (KVM) was released. A hypervisor allows system administrators to share the underlying hardware with multiple guest operating systems; Figure 3-2 demonstrates this. This resource sharing increases the host machine's efficiency, alleviating one of the sysadmins issues.

Hypervisors also gave each application development team a separate networking stack, removing the port conflict issues on shared systems. For example, team A's Tomcat application can run on port 8080, while team B's can also run on port 8080 since each application can now have its guest operating system with a separate network stack. Library versions, deployment, and other issues remain for the application developer. How can they package and deploy everything their application needs while maintaining the efficiency introduced by the hypervisor and virtual machines? This concern led to the development of containers.

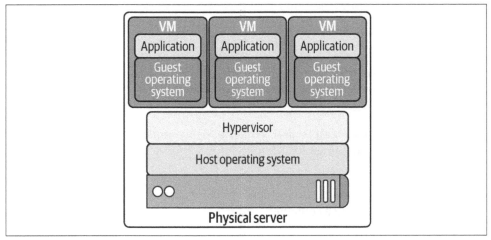

Figure 3-2. Hypervisor

Containers

In Figure 3-3, we see the benefits of the containerization of applications; each container is independent. Application developers can use whatever they need to run their application without relying on underlying libraries or host operating systems. Each container also has its own network stack. The container allows developers to package and deploy applications while maintaining efficiencies for the host machine.

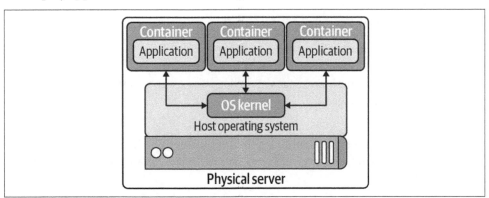

Figure 3-3. Containers running on host OS

With any technology comes a history of changes, competitors, and innovations, and containers are no different. The following is a list of terms that can be confusing when learning about containers. First, we list the distinction between container runtimes, discuss each runtime's functionality, and show how they relate to Kubernetes. The functionality of container runtimes breaks down to "high level" and "low level":

Container
> A running container image.

Image
> A container image is the file that is pulled down from a registry server and used locally as a mount point when starting a container.

Container engine
> A container engine accepts user requests via command-line options to pull images and run a container.

Container runtime
> The container runtime is the low-level piece of software in a container engine that deals with running a container.

Base image
> A starting point for container images; to reduce build image sizes and complexity, users can start with a base image and make incremental changes on top of it.

Image layer
> Repositories are often referred to as images or container images, but actually they are made up of one or more layers. Image layers in a repository are connected in a parent-child relationship. Each image layer represents changes between itself and the parent layer.

Image format
> Container engines have their own container image format, such as LXD, RKT, and Docker.

Registry
> A registry stores container images and allows for users to upload, download, and update container images.

Repository
> Repositories can be equivalent to a container image. The important distinction is that repositories are made up of layers and metadata about the image; this is the manifest.

Tag
> A tag is a user-defined name for different versions of a container image.

Container host

The container host is the system that runs the container with a container engine.

Container orchestration

This is what Kubernetes does! It dynamically schedules container workloads for a cluster of container hosts.

 Cgroups and namespaces are Linux primitives to create containers; they are discussed in the next section.

An example of "low-level" functionality is creating cgroups and namespaces for containers, the bare minimum to run one. Developers require more than that when working with containers. They need to build and test containers and deploy them; these are considered a "high-level" functionality. Each container runtime offers various levels of functionality. The following is a list of high and low functionality:

Low-level container runtime functionality

- Creating containers

- Running containers

High-level container runtime functionality

- Formatting container images

- Building container images

- Managing container images

- Managing instances of containers

- Sharing container images

Over the next few pages, we will discuss runtimes that implement the previous functionality. Each of the following projects has its strengths and weaknesses to provide high- and low-level functionality. Some are good to know about for historical reasons but no longer exist or have merged with other projects:

Low-level container runtimes

LXC

C API for creating Linux containers

runC

CLI for OCI-compliant containers

High-level container runtimes

> *containerd*
>> Container runtime split off from Docker, a graduated CNCF project

> *CRI-O*
>> Container runtime interface using the Open Container Initiative (OCI) specification, an incubating CNCF project

> *Docker*
>> Open source container platform

> *lmctfy*
>> Google containerization platform

> *rkt*
>> CoreOS container specification

OCI

OCI promotes common, minimal, open standards, and specifications for container technology.

The idea for creating a formal specification for container image formats and runtimes allows a container to be portable across all major operating systems and platforms to ensure no undue technical barriers. The three values guiding the OCI project are as follows:

Composable
> Tools for managing containers should have clean interfaces. They should also not be bound to specific projects, clients, or frameworks and should work across all platforms.

Decentralized
> The format and runtime should be well specified and developed by the community, not one organization. Another goal of the OCI project is independent implementations of tools to run the same container.

Minimalist
> The OCI spec strives to do several things well, be minimal and stable, and enable innovation and experimentation.

Docker donated a draft for the base format and runtime. It also donated code for a reference implementation to the OCI. Docker took the contents of the libcontainer project, made it run independently of Docker, and donated it to the OCI project. That codebase is runC, which can be found on GitHub (*https://oreil.ly/A49v0*).

Let's discuss several early container initiatives and their capabilities. This section will end with where Kubernetes is with container runtimes and how they work together.

LXC

Linux Containers, LXC, was created in 2008. LXC combines cgroups and namespaces to provide an isolated environment for running applications. LXC's goal is to create an environment as close as possible to a standard Linux without the need for a separate kernel. LXC has separate components: the liblxc library, several programming language bindings, Python versions 2 and 3, Lua, Go, Ruby, Haskell, a set of standard tools, and container templates.

runC

runC is the most widely used container runtime developed initially as part of Docker and was later extracted as a separate tool and library. runC is a command-line tool for running applications packaged according to the OCI format and is a compliant implementation of the OCI spec. runC uses libcontainer, which is the same container library powering a Docker engine installation. Before version 1.11, the Docker engine was used to manage volumes, networks, containers, images, etc. Now, the Docker architecture has several components, and the runC features include the following:

- Full support for Linux namespaces, including user namespaces
- Native support for all security features available in Linux
  - SELinux, AppArmor, seccomp, control groups, capability drop, pivot_root, UID/GID dropping, etc.
- Native support of Windows 10 containers
- Planned native support for the entire hardware manufacturer's ecosystem
- A formally specified configuration format, governed by the OCI under the Linux Foundation

containerd

containerd is a high-level runtime that was split off from Docker. containerd is a background service that acts as an API facade for various container runtimes and OSs. containerd has various components that provide it with high-level functionality. containerd is a service for Linux and Windows that manages its host system's complete container life cycle, image transfer, storage, container execution, and network attachment. containerd's client CLI tool is ctr, and it is for development and debugging purposes for direct communication with containerd. containerd-shim is the component that allows for daemonless containers. It resides as the parent of the container's process to facilitate a few things. containerd allows the runtimes, i.e., runC, to exit after it starts the container. This way, we do not need the long-running runtime processes for containers. It also keeps the standard I/O and other file descriptors open for the container if containerd and Docker die. If the shim does not run, then the pipe's parent side would be closed, and the container would exit. containerd-shim also allows the container's exit status to be reported back to a higher-level tool like Docker without having the container process's actual parent do it.

lmctfy

Google started lmctfy as its open source Linux container technology in 2013. lmctfy is a high-level container runtime that provides the ability to create and delete containers but is no longer actively maintained and was porting over to libcontainer, which is now containerd. lmctfy provided an API-driven configuration without developers worrying about the details of cgroups and namespace internals.

rkt

rkt started at CoreOS as an alternative to Docker in 2014. It is written in Go, uses pods as its basic compute unit, and allows for a self-contained environment for applications. rkt's native image format was the App Container Image (ACI), defined in the App Container spec; this was deprecated in favor of the OCI format and specification support. It supports the CNI specification and can run Docker images and OCI images. The rkt project was archived in February 2020 by the maintainers.

Docker

Docker, released in 2013, solved many of the problems that developers had running containers end to end. It has all this functionality for developers to create, maintain, and deploy containers:

- Formatting container images
- Building container images
- Managing container images
- Managing instances of containers
- Sharing container images
- Running containers

Figure 3-4 shows us the architecture of the Docker engine and its various components. Docker began as a monolith application, building all the previous functionality into a single binary known as the *Docker engine*. The engine contained the Docker client or CLI that allows developers to build, run, and push containers and images. The Docker server runs as a daemon to manage the data volumes and networks for running containers. The client communicates to the server through the Docker API.

It uses containerd to manage the container life cycle, and it uses runC to spawn the container process.

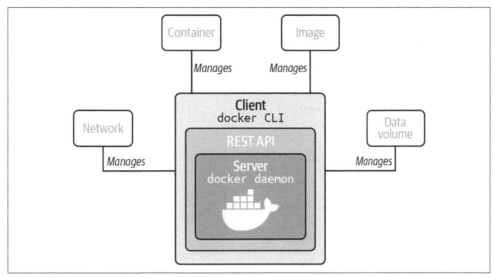

Figure 3-4. Docker engine

In the past few years, Docker has broken apart this monolith into separate components. To run a container, the Docker engine creates the image and passes it to containerd. containerd calls containerd-shim, which uses runC to run the container. Then, containerd-shim allows the runtime (runC in this case) to exit after it starts the container. This way, we can run daemonless containers because we do not need the long-running runtime processes for containers.

Docker provides a separation of concerns for application developers and system administrators. It allows the developers to focus on building their apps, and system admins focus on deployment. Docker provides a fast development cycle; to test new versions of Golang for our web app, we can update the base image and run tests against it. Docker provides application portability between running on-premise, in the cloud, or in any other data center. Its motto is to build, ship, and run anywhere. A new container can quickly be provisioned for scalability and run more apps on one host machine, increasing that machine's efficiency.

CRI-O

CRI-O is an OCI-based implementation of the Kubernetes CRI, while the OCI is a set of specifications that container runtime engines must implement. Red Hat started the CRI project in 2016 and in 2019 contributed it to the CNCF. CRI is a plugin interface that enables Kubernetes, via Kubelet, to communicate with any container runtime that satisfies the CRI interface. CRI-O development began in 2016 after the

Kubernetes project introduced CRI, and CRI-O 1.0 was released in 2017. The CRI-O is a lightweight CRI runtime made as a Kubernetes-specific high-level runtime built on gRPC and Protobuf over a UNIX socket. Figure 3-5 points out where the CRI fits into the whole picture with the Kubernetes architecture. CRI-O provides stability in the Kubernetes project, with a commitment to passing Kubernetes tests.

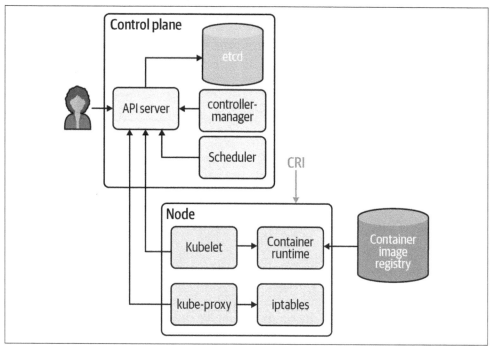

Figure 3-5. CRI about Kubernetes

There have been many companies, technologies, and innovations in the container space. This section has been a brief history of that. The industry has landed on making sure the container landscape remains an open OCI project for all to use across various ways to run containers. Kubernetes has helped shaped this effort as well with the adaption of the CRI-O interface. Understanding the components of the container is vital to all administrators of container deployments and developers using containers. A recent example of this importance is in Kubernetes 1.20, where dockershim support will be deprecated. The Docker runtime utilizing the dockershim for administrators is deprecated, but developers can still use Docker to build OCI-compliant containers to run.

The first CRI implementation was the dockershim, which provided a layer of abstraction in front of the Docker engine.

Now we will dive deeper into the container technology that powers them.

Container Primitives

No matter if you are using Docker or containerd, runC starts and manages the actual containers for them. In this section, we will review what runC takes care of for developers from a container perspective. Each of our containers has Linux primitives known as *control groups* and *namespaces*. Figure 3-6 shows an example of what this looks like; cgroups control access to resources in the kernel for our containers, and namespaces are individual slices of resources to manage separately from the root namespaces, i.e., the host.

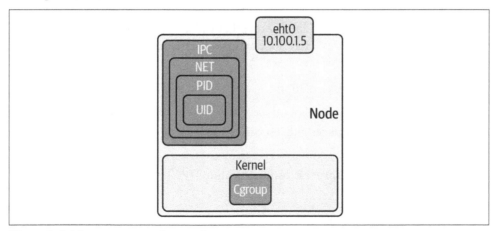

Figure 3-6. Namespaces and control groups

To help solidify these concepts, let's dig into control groups and namespaces a bit further.

Control Groups

In short, a cgroup is a Linux kernel feature that limits, accounts for, and isolates resource usage. Initially released in Linux 2.6.24, cgroups allow administrators to control different CPU systems and memory for particulate processes. Cgroups are provided through pseudofilesystems and are maintained by the core kernel code in cgroups. These separate subsystems maintain various cgroups in the kernel:

CPU
    The process can be guaranteed a minimum number of CPU shares.

Memory
    These set up memory limits for a process.

Disk I/O
    This and other devices are controlled via the device's cgroup subsystem.

Network
    This is maintained by the `net_cls` and marks packets leaving the cgroup.

`lscgroup` is a command-line tool that lists all the cgroups currently in the system.

runC will create the cgroups for the container at creation time. A cgroup controls how much of a resource a container can use, while namespaces control what processes inside the container can see.

Namespaces

Namespaces are features of the Linux kernel that isolate and virtualize system resources of a collection of processes. Here are examples of virtualized resources:

PID namespace
    Processes ID, for process isolation

Network namespace
    Manages network interfaces and a separate networking stack

IPC namespace
    Manages access to interprocess communication (IPC) resources

Mount namespace
    Manages filesystem mount points

UTS namespace
    UNIX time-sharing; allows single hosts to have different host and domain names for different processes

UID namespaces
    User ID; isolates process ownership with separate user and group assignments

A process's user and group IDs can be different inside and outside a user's namespace. A process can have an unprivileged user ID outside a user namespace while at the same time having a user ID of 0 inside the container user namespace. The process has root privileges for execution inside the user namespace but is unprivileged for operations outside the namespace.

Example 3-1 is an example of how to inspect the namespaces for a process. All information for a process is on the /proc filesystem in Linux. PID 1's PID namespace is 4026531836, and listing all the namespaces shows that the PID namespace IDs match.

Example 3-1. Namespaces of a single process

```
vagrant@ubuntu-xenial:~$ sudo ps -p 1 -o pid,pidns
  PID      PIDNS
    1 4026531836

vagrant@ubuntu-xenial:~$ sudo ls -l /proc/1/ns
total 0
lrwxrwxrwx 1 root root 0 Dec 12 20:41 cgroup -> cgroup:[4026531835]
lrwxrwxrwx 1 root root 0 Dec 12 20:41 ipc -> ipc:[4026531839]
lrwxrwxrwx 1 root root 0 Dec 12 20:41 mnt -> mnt:[4026531840]
lrwxrwxrwx 1 root root 0 Dec 12 20:41 net -> net:[4026531957]
lrwxrwxrwx 1 root root 0 Dec 12 20:41 pid -> pid:[4026531836]
lrwxrwxrwx 1 root root 0 Dec 12 20:41 user -> user:[4026531837]
lrwxrwxrwx 1 root root 0 Dec 12 20:41 uts -> uts:[4026531838]
```

Figure 3-7 shows that effectively these two Linux primitives allow application developers to control and manage their applications separate from the hosts and other applications either in containers or by running natively on the host.

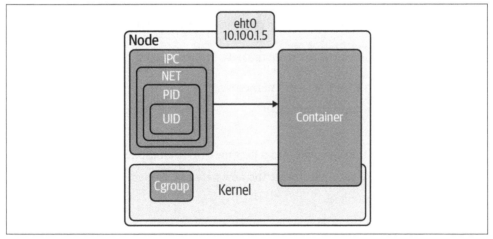

Figure 3-7. Cgroups and namespaces powers combined

The following examples use Ubuntu 16.04 LTS Xenial Xerus. If you want to follow along on your system, more information can be found in this book's code repo. The repo contains the tools and configurations for building the Ubuntu VM and Docker containers. Let's get started with setting up and testing our namespaces.

Setting Up Namespaces

Figure 3-8 outlines a basic container network setup. In the following pages, we will walk through all the Linux commands that the low-level runtimes complete for container network creation.

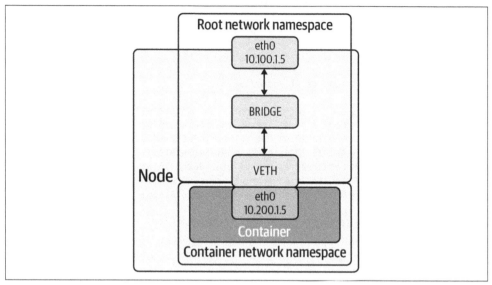

Figure 3-8. Root network namespace and container network namespace

The following steps show how to create the networking setup shown in Figure 3-8:

1. Create a host with a root network namespace.
2. Create a new network namespace.
3. Create a veth pair.
4. Move one side of the veth pair into a new network namespace.
5. Address side of the veth pair inside the new network namespace.
6. Create a bridge interface.
7. Address the bridge interface.
8. Attach the bridge to the host interface.
9. Attach one side of the veth pair to the bridge interface.
10. Profit.

The following are all the Linux commands needed to create the network namespace, bridge, and veth pairs and wire them together:

```
$ echo 1 > /proc/sys/net/ipv4/ip_forward
$ sudo ip netns add net1
$ sudo ip link add veth0 type veth peer name veth1
$ sudo ip link set veth1 netns net1
$ sudo ip link add veth0 type veth peer name veth1
$ sudo ip netns exec net1 ip addr add 192.168.1.101/24 dev veth1
$ sudo ip netns exec net1 ip link set dev veth1 up
$ sudo ip link add br0 type bridge
$ sudo ip link set dev br0 up
$ sudo ip link set enp0s3 master br0
$ sudo ip link set veth0 master br0
$ sudo ip netns exec net1  ip route add default via 192.168.1.100
```

Let's dive into an example and outline each command.

The ip Linux command sets up and controls the network namespaces.

 You can find more information about ip on its man page (*https://oreil.ly/jBKL7*).

In Example 3-2, we have used Vagrant and VirtualBox to create a fresh installation of Ubuntu for our testing purposes.

Example 3-2. Ubuntu testing virtual machine

```
$ vagrant up
Bringing machine 'default' up with 'virtualbox' provider...
==> default: Importing base box 'ubuntu/xenial64'...
==> default: Matching MAC address for NAT networking...
==> default: Checking if box 'ubuntu/xenial64' version '20200904.0.0' is up to date...
==> default: Setting the name of the VM:
advanced_networking_code_examples_default_1600085275588_55198
==> default: Clearing any previously set network interfaces...
==> default: Available bridged network interfaces:
1) en12: USB 10/100 /1000LAN
2) en5: USB Ethernet(?)
3) en0: Wi-Fi (Wireless)
4) llw0
5) en11: USB 10/100/1000 LAN 2
6) en4: Thunderbolt 4
7) en1: Thunderbolt 1
8) en2: Thunderbolt 2
9) en3: Thunderbolt 3
==> default: When choosing an interface, it is usually the one that is
==> default: being used to connect to the internet.
==> default:
    default: Which interface should the network bridge to? 1
==> default: Preparing network interfaces based on configuration...
```

```
      default: Adapter 1: nat
      default: Adapter 2: bridged
==> default: Forwarding ports...
      default: 22 (guest) => 2222 (host) (adapter 1)
==> default: Running 'pre-boot' VM customizations...
==> default: Booting VM...
==> default: Waiting for machine to boot. This may take a few minutes...
      default: SSH address: 127.0.0.1:2222
      default: SSH username: vagrant
      default: SSH auth method: private key
      default: Warning: Connection reset. Retrying...
      default:
      default: Vagrant insecure key detected. Vagrant will automatically replace
      default: this with a newly generated keypair for better security.
      default:
      default: Inserting generated public key within guest...
      default: Removing insecure key from the guest if it's present...
      default: Key inserted! Disconnecting and reconnecting using new SSH key...
==> default: Machine booted and ready!
==> default: Checking for guest additions in VM...
==> default: Configuring and enabling network interfaces...
==> default: Mounting shared folders...
      default: /vagrant =>
      /Users/strongjz/Documents/code/advanced_networking_code_examples
```

Refer to the book repo for the Vagrantfile to reproduce this.

 Vagrant (*https://oreil.ly/o8Qo0*) is a local virtual machine manager created by HashiCorp.

After Vagrant boots our virtual machine, we can use Vagrant to ssh into this VM:

```
$± |master U:2 ?:2 X| → vagrant ssh
Welcome to Ubuntu 16.04.7 LTS (GNU/Linux 4.4.0-189-generic x86_64)

vagrant@ubuntu-xenial:~$
```

IP forwarding is an operating system's ability to accept incoming network packets on one interface, recognize them for another, and pass them on to that network accordingly. When enabled, IP forwarding allows a Linux machine to receive incoming packets and forward them. A Linux machine acting as an ordinary host would not need to have IP forwarding enabled because it generates and receives IP traffic for its purposes. By default, it is turned off; let's enable it on our Ubuntu instance:

```
vagrant@ubuntu-xenial:~$ sysctl net.ipv4.ip_forward
net.ipv4.ip_forward = 0
vagrant@ubuntu-xenial:~$ sudo echo 1 > /proc/sys/net/ipv4/ip_forward
```

```
vagrant@ubuntu-xenial:~$ sysctl net.ipv4.ip_forward
net.ipv4.ip_forward = 1
```

With our install of the Ubuntu instance, we can see that we do not have any additional network namespaces, so let's create one:

```
vagrant@ubuntu-xenial:~$ sudo ip netns list
```

ip netns allows us to control the namespaces on the server. Creating one is as easy as typing ip netns add net1:

```
vagrant@ubuntu-xenial:~$ sudo ip netns add net1
```

As we work through this example, we can see the network namespace we just created:

```
vagrant@ubuntu-xenial:~$ sudo ip netns list
net1
```

Now that we have a new network namespace for our container, we will need a veth pair for communication between the root network namespace and the container network namespace net1.

ip again allows administrators to create the veth pairs with a straightforward command. Remember from Chapter 2 that veth comes in pairs and acts as a conduit between network namespaces, so packets from one end are automatically forwarded to the other.

```
vagrant@ubuntu-xenial:~$ sudo ip link add veth0 type veth peer name veth1
```

Interfaces 4 and 5 are the veth pairs in the command output. We can also see which are paired with each other, veth1@veth0 and veth0@veth1.

The ip link list command verifies the veth pair creation:

```
vagrant@ubuntu-xenial:~$ ip link list
1: lo: <LOOPBACK,UP,LOWER_UP> mtu 65536 qdisc noqueue state
UNKNOWN mode DEFAULT group default qlen 1
    link/loopback 00:00:00:00:00:00 brd 00:00:00:00:00:00
2: enp0s3: <BROADCAST,MULTICAST,UP,LOWER_UP> mtu 1500 qdisc
pfifo_fast state UP mode DEFAULT group default qlen 1000
    link/ether 02:8f:67:5f:07:a5 brd ff:ff:ff:ff:ff:ff
3: enp0s8: <BROADCAST,MULTICAST,UP,LOWER_UP> mtu 1500 qdisc
pfifo_fast state UP mode DEFAULT group default qlen 1000
    link/ether 08:00:27:0f:4e:0d brd ff:ff:ff:ff:ff:ff
4: veth1@veth0: <BROADCAST,MULTICAST,M-DOWN> mtu 1500 qdisc
noop state DOWN mode DEFAULT group default qlen 1000
    link/ether 72:e4:03:03:c1:96 brd ff:ff:ff:ff:ff:ff
5: veth0@veth1: <BROADCAST,MULTICAST,M-DOWN> mtu 1500 qdisc
noop state DOWN mode DEFAULT group default qlen 1000
```

```
    link/ether 26:1a:7f:2c:d4:48 brd ff:ff:ff:ff:ff:ff
vagrant@ubuntu-xenial:~$
```

Now let's move `veth1` into the new network namespace created previously:

```
vagrant@ubuntu-xenial:~$ sudo ip link set veth1 netns net1
```

`ip netns exec` allows us to verify the network namespace's configuration. The output verifies that `veth1` is now in the network namespace `net`:

```
vagrant@ubuntu-xenial:~$ sudo ip netns exec net1 ip link list
4: veth1@if5: <BROADCAST,MULTICAST> mtu 1500 qdisc noop state
DOWN mode DEFAULT group default qlen 1000
    link/ether 72:e4:03:03:c1:96 brd ff:ff:ff:ff:ff:ff link-netnsid 0
```

Network namespaces are entirely separate TCP/IP stacks in the Linux kernel. Being a new interface and in a new network namespace, the veth interface will need IP addressing in order to carry packets from the `net1` namespace to the root namespace and beyond the host:

```
vagrant@ubuntu-xenial:~$ sudo ip netns exec
net1 ip addr add 192.168.1.100/24 dev veth1
```

As with host networking interfaces, they will need to be "turned on":

```
vagrant@ubuntu-xenial:~$ sudo ip netns exec net1 ip link set dev veth1 up
```

The state has now transitioned to `LOWERLAYERDOWN`. The status `NO-CARRIER` points in the right direction. Ethernet needs a cable to be connected; our upstream veth pair is not on yet either. The `veth1` interface is up and addressed but effectively still "unplugged":

```
vagrant@ubuntu-xenial:~$ sudo ip netns exec net1 ip link list veth1
4: veth1@if5: <NO-CARRIER,BROADCAST,MULTICAST,UP> mtu 1500
qdisc noqueue state LOWERLAYERDOWN mode DEFAULT
group default qlen 1000 link/ether 72:e4:03:03:c1:96
brd ff:ff:ff:ff:ff:ff link-netnsid 0
```

Let's turn up the `veth0` side of the pair now:

```
vagrant@ubuntu-xenial:~$ sudo ip link set dev veth0 up
vagrant@ubuntu-xenial:~$ sudo ip link list
5: veth0@if4: <BROADCAST,MULTICAST,UP,LOWER_UP> mtu 1500
qdisc noqueue state UP mode DEFAULT group default qlen 1000
link/ether 26:1a:7f:2c:d4:48 brd ff:ff:ff:ff:ff:ff link-netnsid 0
```

Now the veth pair inside the `net1` namespace is UP:

```
vagrant@ubuntu-xenial:~$ sudo ip netns exec net1 ip link list
4: veth1@if5: <BROADCAST,MULTICAST,UP,LOWER_UP> mtu 1500
qdisc noqueue state UP mode DEFAULT group default qlen 1000
link/ether 72:e4:03:03:c1:96 brd ff:ff:ff:ff:ff:ff link-netnsid 0
```

Both sides of the veth pair report up; we need to connect the root namespace veth side to the bridge interface. Make sure to select the interface you're working with, in this case enp0s8; it may be different for others:

```
vagrant@ubuntu-xenial:~$ sudo ip link add br0 type bridge
vagrant@ubuntu-xenial:~$ sudo ip link set dev br0 up
vagrant@ubuntu-xenial:~$ sudo ip link set enp0s8 master br0
vagrant@ubuntu-xenial:~$ sudo ip link set veth0 master br0
```

We can see that the enp0s8 and veth0 report are part of the bridge br0 interface, master br0 state up.

Next, let's test connectivity to our network namespace:

```
vagrant@ubuntu-xenial:~$ ping 192.168.1.100 -c 4
PING 192.168.1.100 (192.168.1.100) 56(84) bytes of data.
From 192.168.1.10 icmp_seq=1 Destination Host Unreachable
From 192.168.1.10 icmp_seq=2 Destination Host Unreachable
From 192.168.1.10 icmp_seq=3 Destination Host Unreachable
From 192.168.1.10 icmp_seq=4 Destination Host Unreachable

--- 192.168.1.100 ping statistics ---
4 packets transmitted, 0 received, +4 errors, 100% packet loss, time 6043ms
```

Our new network namespace does not have a default route, so it does not know where to route our packets for the ping requests:

```
$ sudo ip netns exec net1
ip route add default via 192.168.1.100
$ sudo ip netns exec net1 ip r
default via 192.168.1.100 dev veth1
192.168.1.0/24 dev veth1  proto kernel  scope link  src 192.168.1.100
```

Let's try that again:

```
$ ping 192.168.2.100 -c 4
PING 192.168.2.100 (192.168.2.100) 56(84) bytes of data.
64 bytes from 192.168.2.100: icmp_seq=1 ttl=64 time=0.018 ms
64 bytes from 192.168.2.100: icmp_seq=2 ttl=64 time=0.028 ms
64 bytes from 192.168.2.100: icmp_seq=3 ttl=64 time=0.036 ms
64 bytes from 192.168.2.100: icmp_seq=4 ttl=64 time=0.043 ms

--- 192.168.2.100 ping statistics ---
4 packets transmitted, 4 received, 0% packet loss, time 2997ms

$ ping 192.168.2.101 -c 4
PING 192.168.2.101 (192.168.2.101) 56(84) bytes of data.
64 bytes from 192.168.2.101: icmp_seq=1 ttl=64 time=0.016 ms
64 bytes from 192.168.2.101: icmp_seq=2 ttl=64 time=0.017 ms
64 bytes from 192.168.2.101: icmp_seq=3 ttl=64 time=0.016 ms
64 bytes from 192.168.2.101: icmp_seq=4 ttl=64 time=0.021 ms

--- 192.168.2.101 ping statistics ---
```

```
4 packets transmitted, 4 received, 0% packet loss, time 2997ms
rtt min/avg/max/mdev = 0.016/0.017/0.021/0.004 ms
```

Success! We have created the bridge interface and veth pairs, migrated one to the new
network namespace, and tested connectivity. Example 3-3 is a recap of all the commands we ran to accomplish that.

Example 3-3. Recap network namespace creation

```
$ echo 1 > /proc/sys/net/ipv4/ip_forward
$ sudo ip netns add net1
$ sudo ip link add veth0 type veth peer name veth1
$ sudo ip link set veth1 netns net1
$ sudo ip link add veth0 type veth peer name veth1
$ sudo ip netns exec net1 ip addr add 192.168.1.101/24 dev veth1
$ sudo ip netns exec net1 ip link set dev veth1 up
$ sudo ip link add br0 type bridge
$ sudo ip link set dev br0 up
$ sudo ip link set enp0s3 master br0
$ sudo ip link set veth0 master br0
$ sudo ip netns exec net1  ip route add default via 192.168.1.100
```

For a developer not familiar with all these commands, that is a lot to remember and
very easy to bork up! If the bridge information is incorrect, it could take down an
entire part of the network with network loops. These issues are ones that system
administrators would like to avoid, so they prevent developers from making those
types of networking changes on the system. Fortunately, containers help remove the
developers' strain to remember all these commands and alleviate system admins' fear
of giving devs access to run those commands.

These commands are all needed just for the network namespace for *every* container creation and deletion. The namespace creation in Example 3-3 is the container runtime's job. Docker manages this for us, in its way. The CNI project
standardizes the network creation for all systems. The CNI, much like the OCI, is a
way for developers to standardize and prioritize specific tasks for managing parts of
the container's life cycle. In later sections, we will discuss CNI.

Container Network Basics

The previous section showed us all the commands needed to create namespaces for
our networking. Let's investigate how Docker does this for us. We also only used the
bridge mode; there several other modes for container networking. This section will
deploy several Docker containers and examine their networking and explain how
containers communicate externally to the host and with each other.

Let's start by discussing the several network "modes" used when working with
containers:

None

No networking disables networking for the container. Use this mode when the container does not need network access.

Bridge

In bridge networking, the container runs in a private network internal to the host. Communication with other containers in the network is open. Communication with services outside the host goes through Network Address Translation (NAT) before exiting the host. Bridge mode is the default mode of networking when the `--net` option is not specified.

Host

In host networking, the container shares the same IP address and the network namespace as that of the host. Processes running inside this container have the same network capabilities as services running directly on the host. This mode is useful if the container needs access to network resources on the hosts. The container loses the benefit of network segmentation with this mode of networking. Whoever is deploying the containers will have to manage and contend with the ports of services running this node.

> The host networking driver works only on Linux hosts. Docker Desktop for Mac and Windows, or Docker EE for Windows Server, does not support host networking mode.

Macvlan

Macvlan uses a parent interface. That interface can be a host interface such as eth0, a subinterface, or even a bonded host adapter that bundles Ethernet interfaces into a single logical interface. Like all Docker networks, Macvlan networks are segmented from each other, providing access within a network, but not between networks. Macvlan allows a physical interface to have multiple MAC and IP addresses using Macvlan subinterfaces. Macvlan has four types: Private, VEPA, Bridge (which Docker default uses), and Passthrough. With a bridge, use NAT for external connectivity. With Macvlan, since hosts are directly mapped to the physical network, external connectivity can be done using the same DHCP server and switch that the host uses.

> Most cloud providers block Macvlan networking. Administrative access to networking equipment is needed.

IPvlan

> IPvlan is similar to Macvlan, with a significant difference: IPvlan does not assign MAC addresses to created subinterfaces. All subinterfaces share the parent's interface MAC address but use different IP addresses. IPvlan has two modes, L2 or L3. In IPvlan, L2, or layer 2, mode is analog to the Macvlan bridge mode. IPvlan L3, or layer 3, mode masquerades as a layer 3 device between the subinterfaces and parent interface.

Overlay

> Overlay allows for the extension of the same network across hosts in a container cluster. The overlay network virtually sits on top of the underlay/physical networks. Several open source projects create these overlay networks, which we will discuss later in the chapter.

Custom

> Custom bridge networking is the same as bridge networking but uses a bridge explicitly created for that container. An example of using this would be a container that runs on a database bridge network. A separate container can have an interface on the default and database bridge, enabling it to communicate with both networks as needed.

Container-defined networking allows a container to share the address and network configuration of another container. This sharing enables process isolation between containers, where each container runs one service but where services can still communicate with one another on `127.0.0.1`.

To test all these modes, we need to continue to use a Vagrant Ubuntu host but now with Docker installed. Docker for Mac and Windows does not support host networking mode, so we must use Linux for this example. You can do this with the provisioned machine in Example 1-1 or use the Docker Vagrant version in the book's code repo. The Ubuntu Docker install directions are as follows if you want to do it manually:

```
$ vagrant up
Bringing machine 'default' up with 'virtualbox' provider...
==> default: Importing base box 'ubuntu/xenial64'...
==> default: Matching MAC address for NAT networking...
==> default: Checking if box
'ubuntu/xenial64' version '20200904.0.0' is up to date...
==> default: Setting the name of the VM:
advanced_networking_code_examples_default_1600085275588_55198
==> default: Clearing any previously set network interfaces...
==> default: Available bridged network interfaces:
1) en12: USB 10/100 /1000LAN
2) en5: USB Ethernet(?)
3) en0: Wi-Fi (Wireless)
4) llw0
5) en11: USB 10/100/1000 LAN 2
```

```
6) en4: Thunderbolt 4
7) en1: Thunderbolt 1
8) en2: Thunderbolt 2
9) en3: Thunderbolt 3
==> default: When choosing an interface, it is usually the one that is
==> default: being used to connect to the internet.
==> default:
    default: Which interface should the network bridge to? 1
==> default: Preparing network interfaces based on configuration...
    default: Adapter 1: nat
    default: Adapter 2: bridged
==> default: Forwarding ports...
    default: 22 (guest) => 2222 (host) (adapter 1)
==> default: Running 'pre-boot' VM customizations...
==> default: Booting VM...
==> default: Waiting for machine to boot. This may take a few minutes...
    default: SSH address: 127.0.0.1:2222
    default: SSH username: vagrant
    default: SSH auth method: private key
    default: Warning: Connection reset. Retrying...
    default:
    default: Vagrant insecure key detected. Vagrant will automatically replace
    default: this with a newly generated keypair for better security.
    default:
    default: Inserting generated public key within guest...
    default: Removing insecure key from the guest if it's present...
    default: Key inserted! Disconnecting and reconnecting using new SSH key...
==> default: Machine booted and ready!
==> default: Checking for guest additions in VM...
==> default: Configuring and enabling network interfaces...
==> default: Mounting shared folders...
    default: /vagrant =>
    /Users/strongjz/Documents/code/advanced_networking_code_examples
    default: + sudo docker run hello-world
    default: Unable to find image 'hello-world:latest' locally
    default: latest: Pulling from library/hello-world
    default: 0e03bdcc26d7:
    default: Pulling fs layer
    default: 0e03bdcc26d7:
    default: Verifying Checksum
    default: 0e03bdcc26d7:
    default: Download complete
    default: 0e03bdcc26d7:
    default: Pull complete
    default: Digest:
    sha256:4cf9c47f86df71d48364001ede3a4fcd85ae80ce02ebad74156906caff5378bc
    default: Status: Downloaded newer image for hello-world:latest
    default:
    default: Hello from Docker!
    default: This message shows that your
    default: installation appears to be working correctly.
    default:
```

```
default: To generate this message, Docker took the following steps:
default:  1. The Docker client contacted the Docker daemon.
default:  2. The Docker daemon pulled the "hello-world" image
default: from the Docker Hub.
default:     (amd64)
default:  3. The Docker daemon created a new container from that image
default: which runs the executable that produces the output you are
default: currently reading.
default:  4. The Docker daemon streamed that output to the Docker
default: client, which sent it to your terminal.
default:
default: To try something more ambitious, you can run an Ubuntu
default: container with:
default:  $ docker run -it ubuntu bash
default:
default: Share images, automate workflows, and more with a free Docker ID:
default:  https://hub.docker.com
default:
default: For more examples and ideas, visit:
default:  https://docs.docker.com/get-started
```

Now that we have the host up, let's begin investigating the different networking setups
we have to work with in Docker. Example 3-4 shows that Docker creates three network types during the install: bridge, host, and none.

Example 3-4. Docker networks

```
vagrant@ubuntu-xenial:~$ sudo docker network ls
NETWORK ID          NAME         DRIVER       SCOPE
1fd1db59c592        bridge       bridge       local
eb34a2105b0f        host         host         local
941ce103b382        none         null         local
vagrant@ubuntu-xenial:~$
```

The default is a Docker bridge, and a container gets attached to it and provisioned
with an IP address in the 172.17.0.0/16 default subnet. Example 3-5 is a view of
Ubuntu's default interfaces and the Docker install that creates the docker0 bridge
interface for the host.

Example 3-5. Docker bridge interface

```
vagrant@ubuntu-xenial:~$ ip a
1: lo: <LOOPBACK,UP,LOWER_UP> mtu 65536 qdisc
noqueue state UNKNOWN group default qlen 1 ❶
    link/loopback 00:00:00:00:00:00 brd 00:00:00:00:00:00
    inet 127.0.0.1/8 scope host lo
    valid_lft forever preferred_lft forever
    inet6 ::1/128 scope host
    valid_lft forever preferred_lft forever
2: enp0s3:
```

```
<BROADCAST,MULTICAST,UP,LOWER_UP> mtu 1500 qdisc pfifo_fast state UP group
default qlen 1000 ❷
    link/ether 02:8f:67:5f:07:a5 brd ff:ff:ff:ff:ff:ff
    inet 10.0.2.15/24 brd 10.0.2.255 scope global enp0s3
    valid_lft forever preferred_lft forever
    inet6 fe80::8f:67ff:fe5f:7a5/64 scope link
    valid_lft forever preferred_lft forever
3: enp0s8:
<BROADCAST,MULTICAST,UP,LOWER_UP> mtu 1500 qdisc pfifo_fast state UP group
default qlen 1000 ❸
    link/ether 08:00:27:22:0e:46 brd ff:ff:ff:ff:ff:ff
    inet 192.168.1.19/24 brd 192.168.1.255 scope global enp0s8
    valid_lft forever preferred_lft forever
    inet 192.168.1.20/24 brd 192.168.1.255 scope global secondary enp0s8
    valid_lft forever preferred_lft forever
    inet6 2605:a000:160d:517:a00:27ff:fe22:e46/64 scope global mngtmpaddr dynamic
    valid_lft 604600sec preferred_lft 604600sec
    inet6 fe80::a00:27ff:fe22:e46/64 scope link
    valid_lft forever preferred_lft forever
4: docker0:
<NO-CARRIER,BROADCAST,MULTICAST,UP> mtu 1500 qdisc noqueue state DOWN group
default ❹
    link/ether 02:42:7d:50:c7:01 brd ff:ff:ff:ff:ff:ff
    inet 172.17.0.1/16 brd 172.17.255.255 scope global docker0
    valid_lft forever preferred_lft forever
    inet6 fe80::42:7dff:fe50:c701/64 scope link
    valid_lft forever preferred_lft forever
```

❶ This is the loopback interface.

❷ enp0s3 is our NAT'ed virtual box interface.

❸ enp0s8 is the host interface; this is on the same network as our host and uses
    DHCP to get the 192.168.1.19 address of default Docker bridge.

❹ The default Docker container interface uses bridge mode.

Example 3-6 started a busybox container with the docker run command and requested that the Docker returns the container's IP address. Docker default NATed address
is 172.17.0.0/16, with our busybox container getting 172.17.0.2.

Example 3-6. Docker bridge

```
vagrant@ubuntu-xenial:~$ sudo docker run -it busybox ip a
Unable to find image 'busybox:latest' locally
latest: Pulling from library/busybox
df8698476c65: Pull complete
Digest: sha256:d366a4665ab44f0648d7a00ae3fae139d55e32f9712c67accd604bb55df9d05a
Status: Downloaded newer image for busybox:latest
```

```
1: lo: <LOOPBACK,UP,LOWER_UP> mtu 65536 qdisc noqueue qlen 1
    link/loopback 00:00:00:00:00:00 brd 00:00:00:00:00:00
    inet 127.0.0.1/8 scope host lo
    valid_lft forever preferred_lft forever
7: eth0@if8: <BROADCAST,MULTICAST,UP,LOWER_UP,M-DOWN> mtu 1500 qdisc noqueue
    link/ether 02:42:ac:11:00:02 brd ff:ff:ff:ff:ff:ff
    inet 172.17.0.2/16 brd 172.17.255.255 scope global eth0
    valid_lft forever preferred_lft forever
```

The host networking in Example 3-7 shows that the container shares the same network namespace as the host. We can see that the interfaces are the same as that of the host; enp0s3, enp0s8, and docker0 are present in the container `ip a` command output.

Example 3-7. Docker host networking

```
vagrant@ubuntu-xenial:~$ sudo docker run -it --net=host busybox ip a
1: lo: <LOOPBACK,UP,LOWER_UP> mtu 65536 qdisc noqueue qlen 1
    link/loopback 00:00:00:00:00:00 brd 00:00:00:00:00:00
    inet 127.0.0.1/8 scope host lo
    valid_lft forever preferred_lft forever
    inet6 ::1/128 scope host
    valid_lft forever preferred_lft forever`
2: enp0s3: <BROADCAST,MULTICAST,UP,LOWER_UP> mtu 1500 qdisc pfifo_fast qlen 1000
    link/ether 02:8f:67:5f:07:a5 brd ff:ff:ff:ff:ff:ff
    inet 10.0.2.15/24 brd 10.0.2.255 scope global enp0s3
    valid_lft forever preferred_lft forever
    inet6 fe80::8f:67ff:fe5f:7a5/64 scope link
    valid_lft forever preferred_lft forever
3: enp0s8: <BROADCAST,MULTICAST,UP,LOWER_UP> mtu 1500 qdisc pfifo_fast qlen 1000
    link/ether 08:00:27:22:0e:46 brd ff:ff:ff:ff:ff:ff
    inet 192.168.1.19/24 brd 192.168.1.255 scope global enp0s8
    valid_lft forever preferred_lft forever
    inet 192.168.1.20/24 brd 192.168.1.255 scope global secondary enp0s8
    valid_lft forever preferred_lft forever
    inet6 2605:a000:160d:517:a00:27ff:fe22:e46/64 scope global dynamic
    valid_lft 604603sec preferred_lft 604603sec
    inet6 fe80::a00:27ff:fe22:e46/64 scope link
    valid_lft forever preferred_lft forever
4: docker0: <NO-CARRIER,BROADCAST,MULTICAST,UP> mtu 1500 qdisc noqueue
    link/ether 02:42:7d:50:c7:01 brd ff:ff:ff:ff:ff:ff
    inet 172.17.0.1/16 brd 172.17.255.255 scope global docker0
    valid_lft forever preferred_lft forever
    inet6 fe80::42:7dff:fe50:c701/64 scope link
    valid_lft forever preferred_lft forever
```

From the veth bridge example previously set up, let's see how much simpler it is when Docker manages that for us. To view this, we need a process to keep the container running. The following command starts up a busybox container and drops into an `sh` command line:

```
vagrant@ubuntu-xenial:~$ sudo docker run -it --rm busybox /bin/sh
/#
```

We have a loopback interface, lo, and an Ethernet interface eth0 connected to veth12, with a Docker default IP address of 172.17.0.2. Since our previous command only outputted an ip a result and the container exited afterward, Docker reused the IP address 172.17.0.2 for the running busybox container:

```
/# ip a
1: lo: <LOOPBACK,UP,LOWER_UP> mtu 65536 qdisc noqueue qlen 1
    link/loopback 00:00:00:00:00:00 brd 00:00:00:00:00:00
    inet 127.0.0.1/8 scope host lo
    valid_lft forever preferred_lft forever
11: eth0@if12: <BROADCAST,MULTICAST,UP,LOWER_UP,M-DOWN> mtu 1500 qdisc noqueue
    link/ether 02:42:ac:11:00:02 brd ff:ff:ff:ff:ff:ff
    inet 172.17.0.2/16 brd 172.17.255.255 scope global eth0
    valid_lft forever preferred_lft forever
```

Running the ip r inside the container's network namespace, we can see that the container's route table is automatically set up as well:

```
/ # ip r
default via 172.17.0.1 dev eth0
172.17.0.0/16 dev eth0 scope link  src 172.17.0.2
```

If we open a new terminal and vagrant ssh into our Vagrant Ubuntu instance and run the docker ps command, it shows all the information in the running busybox container:

```
vagrant@ubuntu-xenial:~$ sudo docker ps
CONTAINER ID       IMAGE         COMMAND
3b5a7c3a74d5       busybox       "/bin/sh"

CREATED            STATUS         PORTS      NAMES
47 seconds ago  Up 46 seconds               competent_mendel
```

We can see the veth interface Docker set up for the container veth68b6f80@if11 on the same host's networking namespace. It is a member of the bridge for docker0 and is turned on master docker0 state UP:

```
vagrant@ubuntu-xenial:~$ ip a
1: lo: <LOOPBACK,UP,LOWER_UP> mtu 65536 qdisc noqueue state UNKNOWN group
default qlen 1
    link/loopback 00:00:00:00:00:00 brd 00:00:00:00:00:00
    inet 127.0.0.1/8 scope host lo
    valid_lft forever preferred_lft forever
    inet6 ::1/128 scope host
    valid_lft forever preferred_lft forever
2: enp0s3: <BROADCAST,MULTICAST,UP,LOWER_UP> mtu 1500 qdisc pfifo_fast state UP
group default qlen 1000
    link/ether 02:8f:67:5f:07:a5 brd ff:ff:ff:ff:ff:ff
    inet 10.0.2.15/24 brd 10.0.2.255 scope global enp0s3
```

```
        valid_lft forever preferred_lft forever
    inet6 fe80::8f:67ff:fe5f:7a5/64 scope link
        valid_lft forever preferred_lft forever
3: enp0s8: <BROADCAST,MULTICAST,UP,LOWER_UP> mtu 1500 qdisc pfifo_fast state UP
group default qlen 1000
    link/ether 08:00:27:22:0e:46 brd ff:ff:ff:ff:ff:ff
    inet 192.168.1.19/24 brd 192.168.1.255 scope global enp0s8
        valid_lft forever preferred_lft forever
    inet 192.168.1.20/24 brd 192.168.1.255 scope global secondary enp0s8
        valid_lft forever preferred_lft forever
    inet6 2605:a000:160d:517:a00:27ff:fe22:e46/64 scope global mngtmpaddr dynamic
        valid_lft 604745sec preferred_lft 604745sec
    inet6 fe80::a00:27ff:fe22:e46/64 scope link
        valid_lft forever preferred_lft forever
4: docker0: <BROADCAST,MULTICAST,UP,LOWER_UP> mtu 1500 qdisc noqueue state UP
group default
    link/ether 02:42:7d:50:c7:01 brd ff:ff:ff:ff:ff:ff
    inet 172.17.0.1/16 brd 172.17.255.255 scope global docker0
        valid_lft forever preferred_lft forever
    inet6 fe80::42:7dff:fe50:c701/64 scope link
        valid_lft forever preferred_lft forever
12: veth68b6f80@if11: <BROADCAST,MULTICAST,UP,LOWER_UP> mtu 1500 qdisc noqueue
master docker0 state UP group default
    link/ether 3a:64:80:02:87:76 brd ff:ff:ff:ff:ff:ff link-netnsid 0
    inet6 fe80::3864:80ff:fe02:8776/64 scope link
        valid_lft forever preferred_lft forever
```

The Ubuntu host's route table shows Docker's routes for reaching containers running on the host:

```
vagrant@ubuntu-xenial:~$ ip r
default via 192.168.1.1 dev enp0s8
10.0.2.0/24 dev enp0s3  proto kernel  scope link  src 10.0.2.15
172.17.0.0/16 dev docker0  proto kernel  scope link  src 172.17.0.1
192.168.1.0/24 dev enp0s8  proto kernel  scope link  src 192.168.1.19
```

By default, Docker does not add the network namespaces it creates to /var/run where ip netns list expects newly created network namespaces. Let's work through how we can see those namespaces now. Three steps are required to list the Docker network namespaces from the ip command:

1. Get the running container's PID.

2. Soft link the network namespace from /proc/PID/net/ to /var/run/netns.

3. List the network namespace.

`docker ps` outputs the container ID needed to inspect the running PID on the host PID namespace:

```
vagrant@ubuntu-xenial:~$ sudo docker ps
CONTAINER ID        IMAGE               COMMAND
1f3f62ad5e02        busybox             "/bin/sh"

CREATED             STATUS              PORTS NAMES
11 minutes ago      Up 11 minutes       determined_shamir
```

`docker inspect` allows us to parse the output and get the host's process's PID. If we run `ps -p` on the host PID namespace, we can see it is running `sh`, which tracks our `docker run` command:

```
vagrant@ubuntu-xenial:~$ sudo docker inspect -f '{{.State.Pid}}' 1f3f62ad5e02
25719
vagrant@ubuntu-xenial:~$ ps -p 25719
  PID TTY          TIME CMD
25719 pts/0    00:00:00 sh
```

`1f3f62ad5e02` is the container ID, and `25719` is the PID of the busybox container running `sh`, so now we can create a symbolic link for the container's network namespace created by Docker to where `ip` expects with the following command:

```
$ sudo ln -sfT /proc/25719/ns/net /var/run/netns/1f3f62ad5e02
```

 When using the container ID and process ID from the examples, keep in mind they will be different on your systems.

Now the `ip netns exec` commands return the same IP address, `172.17.0.2`, that the `docker exec` command does:

```
vagrant@ubuntu-xenial:~$ sudo ip netns exec 1f3f62ad5e02 ip a
1: lo:
<LOOPBACK,UP,LOWER_UP> mtu 65536 qdisc noqueue state UNKNOWN group default qlen 1
    link/loopback 00:00:00:00:00:00 brd 00:00:00:00:00:00
    inet 127.0.0.1/8 scope host lo
       valid_lft forever preferred_lft forever
13: eth0@if14:
<BROADCAST,MULTICAST,UP,LOWER_UP> mtu 1500 qdisc noqueue state UP group default
    link/ether 02:42:ac:11:00:02 brd ff:ff:ff:ff:ff:ff link-netnsid 0
    inet 172.17.0.2/16 brd 172.17.255.255 scope global eth0
       valid_lft forever preferred_lft forever
```

We can verify with `docker exec` and run `ip an` inside the busybox container. The IP address, MAC address, and network interfaces all match the output:

```
vagrant@ubuntu-xenial:~$ sudo docker exec 1f3f62ad5e02 ip a
1: lo: <LOOPBACK,UP,LOWER_UP> mtu 65536 qdisc noqueue qlen 1
    link/loopback 00:00:00:00:00:00 brd 00:00:00:00:00:00
    inet 127.0.0.1/8 scope host lo
       valid_lft forever preferred_lft forever
13: eth0@if14: <BROADCAST,MULTICAST,UP,LOWER_UP,M-DOWN> mtu 1500 qdisc noqueue
    link/ether 02:42:ac:11:00:02 brd ff:ff:ff:ff:ff:ff
    inet 172.17.0.2/16 brd 172.17.255.255 scope global eth0
       valid_lft forever preferred_lft forever
```

Docker starts our container; creates the network namespace, the veth pair, and the docker0 bridge (if it does not already exist); and then attaches them all for every container creation and deletion, in a single command! That is powerful from an application developer's perspective. There's no need to remember all those Linux commands and possibly break the networking on a host. This discussion has mostly been about a single host. How Docker coordinates container communication between hosts in a cluster is discussed in the next section.

Docker Networking Model

Libnetwork is Docker's take on container networking, and its design philosophy is in the container networking model (CNM). Libnetwork implements the CNM and works in three components: the sandbox, endpoint, and network. The sandbox implements the management of the Linux network namespaces for all containers running on the host. The network component is a collection of endpoints on the same network. Endpoints are hosts on the network. The network controller manages all of this via APIs in the Docker engine.

On the endpoint, Docker uses `iptables` for network isolation. The container publishes a port to be accessed externally. Containers do not receive a public IPv4 address; they receive a private RFC 1918 address. Services running on a container must be exposed port by port, and container ports have to be mapped to the host port so conflicts are avoided. When Docker starts, it creates a virtual bridge interface, docker0, on the host machine and assigns it a random IP address from the private 1918 range. This bridge passes packets between two connected devices, just like a physical bridge does. Each new container gets one interface automatically attached to the docker0 bridge; Figure 3-9 represents this and is similar to the approach we demonstrated in the previous sections.

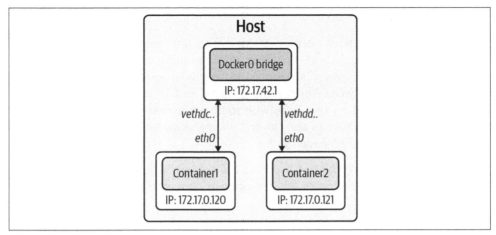

Figure 3-9. Docker bridge

The CNM maps the network modes to drives we have already discussed. Here is a list of the networking mode and the Docker engine equivalent:

Bridge
Default Docker bridge (see Figure 3-9, and our previous examples show this)

Custom or Remote
User-defined bridge, or allows users to create or use their plugin

Overlay
Overlay

Null
No networking options

Bridge networks are for containers running on the same host. Communicating with containers running on different hosts can use an overlay network. Docker uses the concept of local and global drivers. Local drivers, a bridge, for example, are host-centric and do not do cross-node coordination. That is the job of global drivers such as Overlay. Global drivers rely on libkv, a key-value store abstraction, to coordinate across machines. The CNM does not provide the key-value store, so external ones like Consul, etcd, and Zookeeper are needed.

The next section will discuss in depth the technologies enabling overlay networks.

Overlay Networking

Thus far, our examples have been on a single host, but production applications at scale do not run on a single host. For applications running in containers on separate nodes to communicate, several issues need to be solved, such as how to coordinate routing information between hosts, port conflicts, and IP address management, to name a few. One technology that helps with routing between hosts for containers is a VXLAN. In Figure 3-10, we can see a layer 2 overlay network created with a VXLAN running over the physical L3 network.

We briefly discussed VXLANs in Chapter 1, but a more in-depth explanation of how the data transfer works to enable the container-to-container communication is warranted here.

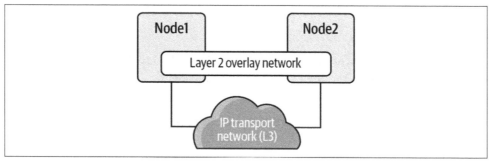

Figure 3-10. VXLAN tunnel

A VXLAN is an extension of the VLAN protocol creating 16 million unique identifiers. Under IEEE 802.1Q, the maximum number of VLANs on a given Ethernet network is 4,094. The transport protocol over a physical data center network is IP plus UDP. VXLAN defines a MAC-in-UDP encapsulation scheme where the original layer 2 frame has a VXLAN header added wrapped in a UDP IP packet. Figure 3-11 shows the IP packet encapsulated in the UDP packet and its headers.

A VXLAN packet is a MAC-in-UDP encapsulated packet. The layer 2 frame has a VXLAN header added to it and is placed in a UDP-IP packet. The VXLAN identifier is 24 bits. That is how a VXLAN can support 16 million segments.

Figure 3-11 is a more detailed version of Chapter 1. We have the VXLAN tunnel endpoints, VTEPs, on both hosts, and they are attached to the host's bridge interfaces with the containers attached to the bridge. The VTEP performs data frame encapsulation and decapsulation. The VTEP peer interaction ensures that the data gets forwarded to the relevant destination container addresses. The data leaving the containers is encapsulated with VXLAN information and transferred over the VXLAN tunnels to be de-encapsulated by the peer VTEP.

Overlay networking enables cross-host communication on the network for containers. The CNM still has other issues that make it incompatible with Kubernetes. The Kubernetes maintainers decided to use the CNI project started at CoreOS. It is simpler than CNM, does not require daemons, and is designed to be cross-platform.

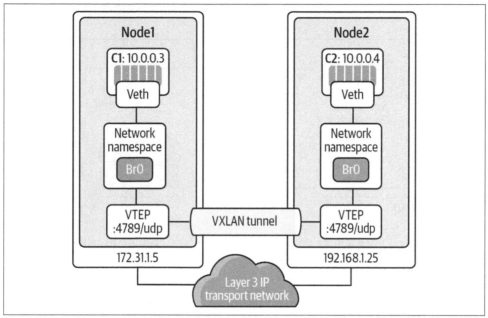

Figure 3-11. VXLAN tunnel detailed

Container Network Interface

CNI is the software interface between the container runtime and the network implementation. There are many options to choose from when implementing a CNI; we will discuss a few notable ones. CNI started at CoreOS as part of the rkt project; it is now a CNCF project. The CNI project consists of a specification and libraries for developing plugins to configure network interfaces in Linux containers. CNI is concerned with a container's network connectivity by allocating resources when the container gets created and removing them when deleted. A CNI plugin is responsible for associating a network interface to the container network namespace and making any necessary changes to the host. It then assigns the IP to the interface and sets up the routes for it. Figure 3-12 outlines the CNI architecture. The container runtime uses a configuration file for the host's network information; in Kubernetes, the Kubelet also uses this configuration file. The CNI and container runtime communicate with each other and apply commands to the configured CNI plugin.

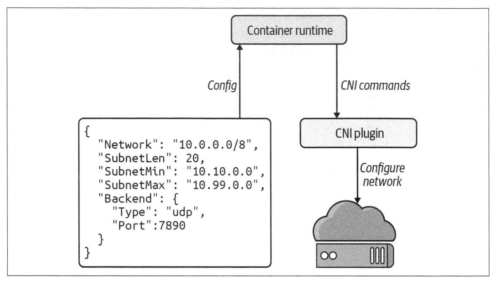

```
{
  "Network": "10.0.0.0/8",
  "SubnetLen": 20,
  "SubnetMin": "10.10.0.0",
  "SubnetMax": "10.99.0.0",
  "Backend": {
    "Type": "udp",
    "Port":7890
  }
}
```

Figure 3-12. CNI architecture

There are several open source projects that implement CNI plugins with various features and functionality. Here is an outline of several:

Cilium

Cilium is open source software for securing network connectivity between application containers. Cilium is an L7/HTTP-aware CNI and can enforce network policies on L3–L7 using an identity-based security model decoupled from network addressing. A Linux technology eBPF powers it.

Flannel

Flannel is a simple way to configure a layer 3 network fabric designed for Kubernetes. Flannel focuses on networking. Flannel uses the Kubernetes cluster's existing `etcd` datastore to store its state information to avoid providing a dedicated one.

Calico

According to Calico, it "combines flexible networking capabilities with run-anywhere security enforcement to provide a solution with native Linux kernel performance and true cloud-native scalability." It has full network policy support and works well in conjunction with other CNIs. Calico does not use an overlay network. Instead, Calico configures a layer 3 network that uses the BGP routing protocol to route packets between hosts. Calico can also integrate with Istio, a service mesh, to interpret and enforce policy for workloads within the cluster, both at the service mesh and the network infrastructure layers.

AWS

AWS has its open source implementation of a CNI, the AWS VPC CNI. It provides high throughput and availability by being directly on the AWS network. There is low latency using this CNI by providing little overhead because of no additional overlay network and minimal network jitter running on the AWS network. Cluster and network administrators can apply existing AWS VPC networking and security best practices for building Kubernetes networks on AWS. They can accomplish those best practices because the AWS CNI includes the capability to use native AWS services like VPC flow logs for analyzing network events and patterns, VPC routing policies for traffic management, and security groups and network access control lists for network traffic isolation. We will discuss more about the AWS VPC CNI in Chapter 6.

 The Kubernetes.io website offers a list of the CNI options available (*https://oreil.ly/imDMP*).

There are many more options for a CNI, and it is up to the cluster administrator, network admins, and application developers to best decide which CNI solves their business use cases. In later chapters, we will walk through use cases and deploy several to help admins make a decision.

In our next section, we will walk through container connectivity examples using the Golang web server and Docker.

Container Connectivity

Like we experimented with in the previous chapter, we will use the Go minimal web server to walk through the concept of container connectivity. We will explain what is happening at the container level when we deploy the web server as a container on our Ubuntu host.

The following are the two networking scenarios we will walk through:

- Container to container on the Docker host
- Container to container on separate hosts

The Golang web server is hardcoded to run on port 8080, http.ListenAnd Serve("0.0.0.0:8080", nil), as we can see in Example 3-8.

Example 3-8. Minimal web server in Go

```go
package main

import (
        "fmt"
        "net/http"
)

func hello(w http.ResponseWriter, _ *http.Request) {
        fmt.Fprintf(w, "Hello")
}

func main() {
        http.HandleFunc("/", hello)
        http.ListenAndServe("0.0.0.0:8080", nil)
}
```

To provision our minimal Golang web server, we need to create it from a Dockerfile. Example 3-9 displays our Golang web server's Dockerfile. The Dockerfile contains instructions to specify what to do when building the image. It begins with the FROM instruction and specifies what the base image should be. The RUN instruction specifies a command to execute. Comments start with #. Remember, each line in a Dockerfile creates a new layer if it changes the image's state. Developers need to find the right balance between having lots of layers created for the image and the readability of the Dockerfile.

Example 3-9. Dockerfile for Golang minimal web server

```dockerfile
FROM golang:1.15 AS builder ❶
WORKDIR /opt ❷
COPY web-server.go . ❸
RUN CGO_ENABLED=0 GOOS=linux go build -o web-server . ❹

FROM golang:1.15 ❺
WORKDIR /opt ❻
COPY --from=0 /opt/web-server . ❼
CMD ["/opt/web-server"] ❽
```

❶ Since our web server is written in Golang, we can compile our Go server in a container to reduce the image's size to only the compiled Go binary. We start by using the Golang base image with version 1.15 for our web server.

❷ WORKDIR sets the working directory for all the subsequent commands to run from.

❸ COPY copies the `web-server.go` file that defines our application as the working directory.

❹ RUN instructs Docker to compile our Golang application in the builder container.

❺ Now to run our application, we define `FROM` for the application base image, again as `golang:1.15`; we can further minimize the final size of the image by using other minimal images like alpine.

❻ Being a new container, we again set the working directory to `/opt`.

❼ COPY here will copy the compiled Go binary from the builder container into the application container.

❽ CMD instructs Docker that the command to run our application is to start our web server.

There are some Dockerfile best practices that developers and admins should adhere to when containerizing their applications:

- Use one `ENTRYPOINT` per Dockerfile. The `ENTRYPOINT` or `CMD` tells Docker what process starts inside the running container, so there should be only one running process; containers are all about process isolation.
- To cut down on the container layers, developers should combine similar commands into one using & & and \. Each new command in the Dockerfile adds a layer to the Docker container image, thus increasing its storage.
- Use the caching system to improve the containers' build times. If there is no change to a layer, it should be at the top of the Dockerfile. Caching is part of the reason that the order of statements is essential. Add files that are least likely to change first and the ones most likely to change last.
- Use multistage builds to reduce the size of the final image drastically.
- Do not install unnecessary tools or packages. Doing this will reduce the containers' attack surface and size, reducing network transfer times from the registry to the hosts running the containers.

Let's build our Golang web server and review the Docker commands to do so.

`docker build` instructs Docker to build our images from the Dockerfile instructions:

```
$ sudo docker build .
Sending build context to Docker daemon   4.27MB
Step 1/8 : FROM golang:1.15 AS builder
1.15: Pulling from library/golang
```

```
57df1a1f1ad8: Pull complete
71e126169501: Pull complete
1af28a55c3f3: Pull complete
03f1c9932170: Pull complete
f4773b341423: Pull complete
fb320882041b: Pull complete
24b0ad6f9416: Pull complete
Digest:
sha256:da7ff43658854148b401f24075c0aa390e3b52187ab67cab0043f2b15e754a68
Status: Downloaded newer image for golang:1.15
 ---> 05c8f6d2538a
Step 2/8 : WORKDIR /opt
 ---> Running in 20c103431e6d
Removing intermediate container 20c103431e6d
 ---> 74ba65cfdf74
Step 3/8 : COPY web-server.go .
 ---> 7a36ec66be52
Step 4/8 : RUN CGO_ENABLED=0 GOOS=linux go build -o web-server .
 ---> Running in 5ea1c0a85422
Removing intermediate container 5ea1c0a85422
 ---> b508120db6ba
Step 5/8 : FROM golang:1.15
 ---> 05c8f6d2538a
Step 6/8 : WORKDIR /opt
 ---> Using cache
 ---> 74ba65cfdf74
Step 7/8 : COPY --from=0 /opt/web-server .
 ---> dde6002760cd
Step 8/8 : CMD ["/opt/web-server"]
 ---> Running in 2bcb7c8f5681
Removing intermediate container 2bcb7c8f5681
 ---> 72fd05de6f73
Successfully built 72fd05de6f73
```

The Golang minimal web server for our testing has the container ID 72fd05de6f73, which is not friendly to read, so we can use the docker tag command to give it a friendly name:

```
$ sudo docker tag 72fd05de6f73 go-web:v0.0.1
```

docker images returns the list of locally available images to run. We have one from the test on the Docker installation and the busybox we have been using to test our networking setup. If a container is not available locally, it is downloaded from the registry; network load times impact this, so we need to have as small an image as possible:

```
$ sudo docker images
REPOSITORY      TAG        IMAGE ID        SIZE
<none>          <none>     b508120db6ba    857MB
go-web          v0.0.1     72fd05de6f73    845MB
golang          1.15       05c8f6d2538a    839MB
```

```
busybox        latest    6858809bf669    1.23MB
hello-world    latest    bf756fb1ae65    13.3kB
```

`docker ps` shows us the running containers on the host. From our network name-space example, we still have one running busybox container:

```
$ sudo docker ps
CONTAINER ID IMAGE     COMMAND      STATUS          PORTS NAMES
1f3f62ad5e02 busybox   "/bin/sh"    Up 11 minutes   determined_shamir
```

`docker logs` will print out any logs that the container is producing from standard out; currently, our busybox image is not printing anything out for us to see:

```
vagrant@ubuntu-xenial:~$ sudo docker logs 1f3f62ad5e02
vagrant@ubuntu-xenial:~$
```

`docker exec` allows devs and admins to execute commands inside the Docker container. We did this previously while investigating the Docker networking setups:

```
vagrant@ubuntu-xenial:~$ sudo docker exec 1f3f62ad5e02 ip a
1: lo: <LOOPBACK,UP,LOWER_UP> mtu 65536 qdisc noqueue qlen 1
link/loopback 00:00:00:00:00:00 brd 00:00:00:00:00:00
inet 127.0.0.1/8 scope host lo
valid_lft forever preferred_lft forever
7: eth0@if8: <BROADCAST,MULTICAST,UP,LOWER_UP,M-DOWN> mtu 1500 qdisc noqueue
link/ether 02:42:ac:11:00:02 brd ff:ff:ff:ff:ff:ff
inet 172.17.0.2/16 brd 172.17.255.255 scope global eth0
valid_lft forever preferred_lft forever
vagrant@ubuntu-xenial:~$
```

 You can find more commands for the Docker CLI in the documentation (*https://oreil.ly/xWkad*).

In the previous section, we built the Golang web server as a container. To test the connectivity, we will also employ the `dnsutils` image used by end-to-end testing for Kubernetes. That image is available from the Kubernetes project at `gcr.io/kubernetes-e2e-test-images/dnsutils:1.3`.

The image name will copy the Docker images from the Google container registry to our local Docker filesystem:

```
$ sudo docker pull gcr.io/kubernetes-e2e-test-images/dnsutils:1.3
1.3: Pulling from kubernetes-e2e-test-images/dnsutils
5a3ea8efae5d: Pull complete
7b7e943444f2: Pull complete
59c439aa0fa7: Pull complete
3702870470ee: Pull complete
Digest: sha256:b31bcf7ef4420ce7108e7fc10b6c00343b21257c945eec94c21598e72a8f2de0
```

```
Status: Downloaded newer image for gcr.io/kubernetes-e2e-test-images/dnsutils:1.3
gcr.io/kubernetes-e2e-test-images/dnsutils:1.3
```

Now that our Golang application can run as a container, we can explore the container networking scenarios.

Container to Container

Our first walk-through is the communication between two containers running on the same host. We begin by starting the dnsutils image and getting in a shell:

```
$ sudo docker run -it gcr.io/kubernetes-e2e-test-images/dnsutils:1.3 /bin/sh
/ #
```

The default Docker network setup gives the dnsutils image connectivity to the internet:

```
/ # ping google.com -c 4
PING google.com (172.217.9.78): 56 data bytes
64 bytes from 172.217.9.78: seq=0 ttl=114 time=39.677 ms
64 bytes from 172.217.9.78: seq=1 ttl=114 time=38.180 ms
64 bytes from 172.217.9.78: seq=2 ttl=114 time=43.150 ms
64 bytes from 172.217.9.78: seq=3 ttl=114 time=38.140 ms

--- google.com ping statistics ---
4 packets transmitted, 4 packets received, 0% packet loss
round-trip min/avg/max = 38.140/39.786/43.150 ms
/ #
```

The Golang web server starts with the default Docker bridge; in a separate SSH connection, then our Vagrant host, we start the Golang web server with the following command:

```
$ sudo docker run -it -d -p 80:8080 go-web:v0.0.1
a568732bc191bb1f5a281e30e34ffdeabc624c59d3684b93167456a9a0902369
```

The -it options are for interactive processes (such as a shell); we must use -it to allocate a TTY for the container process. -d runs the container in detached mode; this allows us to continue to use the terminal and outputs the full Docker container ID. The -p is probably the essential option in terms of the network; this one creates the port connections between the host and the containers. Our Golang web server runs on port 8080 and exposes that port on port 80 on the host.

docker ps verifies that we now have two containers running: the Go web server container with port 8080 exposed on the host port 80 and the shell running inside our dnsutils container:

```
vagrant@ubuntu-xenial:~$ sudo docker ps
CONTAINER ID   IMAGE          COMMAND             CREATED        STATUS
906fd860f84d   go-web:v0.0.1  "/opt/web-server"   4 minutes ago  Up 4 minutes
25ded12445df   dnsutils:1.3   "/bin/sh"           6 minutes ago  Up 6 minutes
```

```
PORTS                    NAMES
0.0.0.0:8080->8080/tcp   frosty_brown
                         brave_zhukovsky
```

Let's use the `docker inspect` command to get the Docker IP address of the Golang web server container:

```
$ sudo docker inspect
-f '{{range .NetworkSettings.Networks}}{{.IPAddress}}{{end}}'
906fd860f84d
172.17.0.2
```

On the `dnsutils` image, we can use the Docker network address of the Golang web server 172.17.0.2 and the container port 8080:

```
/ # wget 172.17.0.2:8080
Connecting to 172.17.0.2:8080 (172.17.0.2:8080)
index.html           100% |****************************************|
                     5   0:00:00 ETA
/ # cat index.html
Hello/ #
```

Each container can reach the other over the `docker0` bridge and the container ports because they are on the same Docker host and the same network. The Docker host has routes to the container's IP address to reach the container on its IP address and port:

```
vagrant@ubuntu-xenial:~$ curl 172.17.0.2:8080
Hello
```

But it does not for the Docker IP address and host port from the `docker run` command:

```
vagrant@ubuntu-xenial:~$ curl 172.17.0.2:80
curl: (7) Failed to connect to 172.17.0.2 port 80: Connection refused
vagrant@ubuntu-xenial:~$ curl 172.17.0.2:8080
Hello
```

Now for the reverse, using the loopback interface, we demonstrate that the host can reach the web server only on the host port exposed, 80, not the Docker port, 8080:

```
vagrant@ubuntu-xenial:~$ curl 127.0.0.1:8080
curl: (7) Failed to connect to 127.0.0.1 port 8080: Connection refused
vagrant@ubuntu-xenial:~$ curl 127.0.0.1:80
Hellovagrant@ubuntu-xenial:~$
```

Now back on the `dnsutils`, the same is true: the `dnsutils` image on the Docker network, using the Docker IP address of the Go web container, can use only the Docker port, 8080, not the exposed host port 80:

```
/ # wget 172.17.0.2:8080 -qO-
Hello/ #
```

```
/ # wget 172.17.0.2:80 -qO-
wget: can't connect to remote host (172.17.0.2): Connection refused
```

Now to show it is an entirely separate stack, let's try the `dnsutils` loopback address and both the Docker port and the exposed host port:

```
/ # wget localhost:80 -qO-
wget: can't connect to remote host (127.0.0.1): Connection refused
/ # wget localhost:8080 -qO-
wget: can't connect to remote host (127.0.0.1): Connection refused
```

Neither works as expected; the `dnsutils` image has a separate network stack and does not share the Go web server's network namespace. Knowing why it does not work is vital in Kubernetes to understand since pods are a collection of containers that share the same network namespace. Now we will examine how two containers communicate on two separate hosts.

Container to Container Separate Hosts

Our previous example showed us how a container network runs on a local system, but how can two containers across the network on separate hosts communicate? In this example, we will deploy containers on separate hosts and investigate that and how it differs from being on the same host.

Let's start a second Vagrant Ubuntu host, `host-2`, and SSH into it as we did with our Docker host. We can see that our IP address is different from the Docker host running our Golang web server:

```
vagrant@host-2:~$ ifconfig enp0s8
enp0s8    Link encap:Ethernet  HWaddr 08:00:27:f9:77:12
          inet addr:192.168.1.23  Bcast:192.168.1.255  Mask:255.255.255.0
          inet6 addr: fe80::a00:27ff:fef9:7712/64 Scope:Link
          UP BROADCAST RUNNING MULTICAST  MTU:1500  Metric:1
          RX packets:65630 errors:0 dropped:0 overruns:0 frame:0
          TX packets:2967 errors:0 dropped:0 overruns:0 carrier:0
          collisions:0 txqueuelen:1000
          RX bytes:96493210 (96.4 MB)  TX bytes:228989 (228.9 KB)
```

We can access our web server from the Docker host's IP address, `192.168.1.20`, on port 80 exposed in the docker `run` command options. Port 80 is exposed on the Docker host but not reachable on container port 8080 with the host IP address:

```
vagrant@ubuntu-xenial:~$ curl 192.168.1.20:80
Hellovagrant@ubuntu-xenial:~$
vagrant@host-2:~$ curl 192.168.1.20:8080
curl: (7) Failed to connect to 192.168.1.20 port 8080: Connection refused
vagrant@ubuntu-xenial:~$
```

The same is true if host-2 tries to reach the container on the containers' IP address, using either the Docker port or the host port. Remember, Docker uses the private address range, 172.17.0.0/16:

```
vagrant@host-2:~$ curl 172.17.0.2:8080 -t 5
curl: (7) Failed to connect to 172.17.0.2 port 8080: No route to host
vagrant@host-2:~$ curl 172.17.0.2:80 -t 5
curl: (7) Failed to connect to 172.17.0.2 port 80: No route to host
vagrant@host-2:~$
```

For the host to route to the Docker IP address, it uses an overlay network or some external routing outside Docker. Routing is also external to Kubernetes; many CNIs help with this issue, and this is explored when looking at deploy clusters in Chapter 6.

The previous examples used the Docker default network bridge with exposed ports to the hosts. That is how host-2 was able to communicate to the Docker container running on the Docker host. This chapter only scratches the surface of container networks. There are many more abstractions to explore, like ingress and egress traffic to the entire cluster, service discovery, and routing internal and external to the cluster. Later chapters will continue to build on these container networking basics.

Conclusion

In this introduction to container networking, we worked through how containers have evolved to help with application deployment and advance host efficiency by allowing and segmenting multiple applications on a host. We have walked through the myriad history of containers with the various projects that have come and gone. Containers are powered and managed with namespaces and cgroups, features inside the Linux kernel. We walked through the abstractions that container runtimes maintain for application developers and learned how to deploy them ourselves. Understanding those Linux kernel abstractions is essential to deciding which CNI to deploy and its trade-offs and benefits. Administrators now have a base understanding of how container runtimes manage the Linux networking abstractions.

We have completed the basics of container networking! Our knowledge has expanded from using a simple network stack to running different unrelated stacks inside our containers. Knowing about namespaces, how ports are exposed, and communication flow empowers administrators to troubleshoot networking issues quickly and prevent downtime of their applications running in a Kubernetes cluster. Troubleshooting port issues or testing if a port is open on the host, on the container, or across the network is a must-have skill for any network engineer and indispensable for developers to troubleshoot their container issues. Kubernetes is built on these basics and abstracts them for developers. The next chapter will review how Kubernetes creates those abstractions and integrates them into the Kubernetes networking model.

CHAPTER 4

Kubernetes Networking Introduction

Now that we have covered Linux and container networking's critical components, we are ready to discuss Kubernetes networking in greater detail. In this chapter, we will discuss how pods connect internally and externally to the cluster. We will also cover how the internal components of Kubernetes connect. Higher-level network abstractions around discovery and load balancing, such as services and ingresses, will be covered in the next chapter.

Kubernetes networking looks to solve these four networking issues:

- Highly coupled container-to-container communications
- Pod-to-pod communications
- Pod-to-service communications
- External-to-service communications

The Docker networking model uses a virtual bridge network by default, which is defined per host and is a private network where containers attach. The container's IP address is allocated a private IP address, which implies containers running on different machines cannot communicate with each other. Developers will have to map host ports to container ports and then proxy the traffic to reach across nodes with Docker. In this scenario, it is up to the Docker administrators to avoid port clashes between containers; usually, this is the system administrators. The Kubernetes networking handles this differently.

The Kubernetes Networking Model

The Kubernetes networking model natively supports multihost cluster networking. Pods can communicate with each other by default, regardless of which host they are deployed on. Kubernetes relies on the CNI project to comply with the following requirements:

- All containers must communicate with each other without NAT.

- Nodes can communicate with containers without NAT.

- A container's IP address is the same as those outside the container that it sees itself as.

The unit of work in Kubernetes is called a *pod*. A pod contains one or more containers, which are always scheduled and run "together" on the same node. This connectivity allows individual instances of a service to be separated into distinct containers. For example, a developer may choose to run a service in one container and a log forwarder in another container. Running processes in distinct containers allows them to have separate resource quotas (e.g., "the log forwarder cannot use more than 512 MB of memory"). It also allows container build and deployment machinery to be separated by reducing the scope necessary to build a container.

The following is a minimal pod definition. We have omitted many options. Kubernetes manages various fields, such as the status of the pods, that are read-only:

```
apiVersion: v1
kind: Pod
metadata:
  name: go-web
  namespace: default
spec:
  containers:
  - name: go-web
    image: go-web:v0.0.1
    ports:
    - containerPort: 8080
      protocol: TCP
```

Kubernetes users typically do not create pods directly. Instead, users create a high-level workload, such as a deployment, which manages pods according to some intended spec. In the case of a deployment, as shown in Figure 4-1, users specify a *template* for pods, along with how many pods (often called *replicas*) that they want to exist. There are several other ways to manage workloads such as ReplicaSets and StatefulSets that we will review in the next chapter. Some provide abstractions over an intermediate type, while others manage pods directly. There are also third-party workload types, in the form of custom resource definitions (CRDs). Workloads in

Kubernetes are a complex topic, and we will only attempt to cover the very basics and the parts applicable to the networking stack.

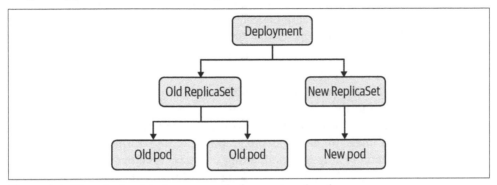

Figure 4-1. The relationship between a deployment and pods

Pods themselves are ephemeral, meaning they are deleted and replaced with new versions of themselves. The short life span of pods is one of the main surprises and challenges to developers and operators familiar with more semipermanent, traditional physical or virtual machines. Local disk state, node scheduling, and IP addresses will all be replaced regularly during a pod's life cycle.

A pod has a unique IP address, which is shared by all containers in the pod. The primary motivation behind giving every pod an IP address is to remove constraints around port numbers. In Linux, only one program can listen on a given address, port, and protocol. If pods did not have unique IP addresses, then two pods on a node could contend for the same port (such as two web servers, both trying to listen on port 80). If they were the same, it would require a runtime configuration to fix, such as a `--port` flag. Alternatively, it would take an ugly script to update a config file in the case of third-party software.

In some cases, third-party software could not run on custom ports at all, which would require more complex workarounds, such as `iptables` DNAT rules on the node. Web servers have the additional problem of expecting conventional port numbers in their software, such as 80 for HTTP and 443 for HTTPS. Breaking from these conventions requires reverse-proxying through a load balancer or making downstream consumers aware of the various ports (which is much easier for internal systems than external ones). Some systems, such as Google's Borg, use this model. Kubernetes chose the IP per pod model to be more comfortable for developers to adopt and make it easier to run third-party workloads. Unfortunately for us, allocating and routing an IP address for every pod adds *substantial* complexity to a Kubernetes cluster.

By default, Kubernetes will allow any traffic to or from any pod. This passive connectivity means, among other things, that any pod in a cluster can connect to any other pod in that same cluster. That can easily lead to abuse, especially if services do not use authentication or if an attacker obtains credentials.

See "Popular CNI Plugins" on page 156 for more.

Pods created and deleted with their own IP addresses can cause issues for beginners who do not understand this behavior. Suppose we have a small service running on Kubernetes, in the form of a deployment with three pod replicas. When someone updates a container image in the deployment, Kubernetes performs a *rolling upgrade*, deleting old pods and creating new pods using the new container image. These new pods will likely have new IP addresses, making the old IP addresses unreachable. It can be a common beginner's mistake to reference pod IPs in config or DNS records manually, only to have them fail to resolve. This error is what services and endpoints attempt to solve, and this is discussed in the next chapter.

When explicitly creating a pod, it is possible to specify the IP address. StatefulSets are a built-in workload type intended for workloads such as databases, which maintain a pod identity concept and give a new pod the same name and IP address as the pod it replaces. There are other examples in the form of third-party CRDs, and it is possible to write a CRD for specific networking purposes.

 Custom resources are extensions of the Kubernetes API defined by the writer. It allows software developers to customize the installation of their software in a Kubernetes environment. You can find more information on writing a CRD in the documentation (*https://oreil.ly/vVcrE*).

Every Kubernetes node runs a component called the *Kubelet*, which manages pods on the node. The networking functionality in the Kubelet comes from API interactions with a CNI plugin on the node. The CNI plugin is what manages pod IP addresses and individual container network provisioning. We mentioned the eponymous interface portion of the CNI in the previous chapter; the CNI defines a standard interface to manage a container's network. The reason for making the CNI an interface is to have an interoperable standard, where there are multiple CNI plugin implementations. The CNI plugin is responsible for assigning pod IP addresses and maintaining a route between all (applicable) pods. Kubernetes does not ship with a default CNI plugin, which means that in a standard installation of Kubernetes, pods cannot use the network.

Let's begin the discussion on how the pod network is enabled by the CNI and the different network layouts.

Node and Pod Network Layout

The cluster must have a group of IP addresses that it controls to assign an IP address to a pod, for example, `10.1.0.0/16`. Nodes and pods must have L3 connectivity in this IP address space. Recall from Chapter 1 that in L3, the Internet layer, connectivity means packets with an IP address can route to a host with that IP address. It is important to note that the ability to deliver *packets* is more fundamental than creating connections (an L4 concept). In L4, firewalls may choose to allow connections from host A to B but reject connections initiating from host B to A. L4 connections from A to B, connections at L3, A to B and B to A, must be allowed. Without L3 connectivity, TCP handshakes would not be possible, as the SYN-ACK could not be delivered.

Generally, pods do not have MAC addresses. Therefore, L2 connectivity to pods is not possible. The CNI will determine this for pods.

There are no requirements in Kubernetes about L3 connectivity to the outside world. Although the majority of clusters have internet connectivity, some are more isolated for security reasons.

We will broadly discuss both ingress (traffic leaving a host or cluster) and egress (traffic entering a host or cluster). Our use of "ingress" here shouldn't be confused with the Kubernetes ingress resource, which is a specific HTTP mechanism to route traffic to Kubernetes services.

There are broadly three approaches, with many variations, to structuring a cluster's network: isolated, flat, and island networks. We will discuss the general approaches here and then get more in-depth into specific implementation details when covering CNI plugins later this chapter.

Isolated Networks

In an isolated cluster network, nodes are routable on the broader network (i.e., hosts that are not part of the cluster can reach nodes in the cluster), but pods are not. Figure 4-2 shows such a cluster. Note that pods cannot reach other pods (or any other hosts) outside the cluster.

Because the cluster is not routable from the broader network, multiple clusters can even use the same IP address space. Note that the Kubernetes API server will need to be routable from the broader network, if external systems or users should be able to access the Kubernetes API. Many managed Kubernetes providers have a "secure cluster" option like this, where no direct traffic is possible between the cluster and the internet.

That isolation to the local cluster can be splendid for security if the cluster's workloads permit/require such a setup, such as clusters for batch processing. However, it is not reasonable for all clusters. The majority of clusters will need to reach and/or be reached by external systems, such as clusters that must support services that have dependencies on the broader internet. Load balancers and proxies can be used to breach this barrier and allow internet traffic into or out of an isolated cluster.

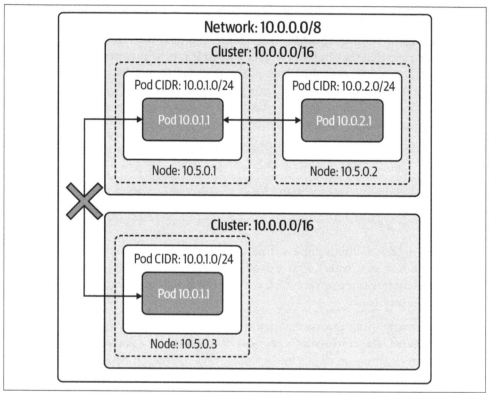

Figure 4-2. Two isolated clusters in the same network

Flat Networks

In a flat network, all pods have an IP address that is routable from the broader network. Barring firewall rules, any host on the network can route to any pod inside or outside the cluster. This configuration has numerous upsides around network simplicity and performance. Pods can connect directly to arbitrary hosts in the network.

Note in Figure 4-3 that no two nodes' pod CIDRs overlap between the two clusters, and therefore no two pods will be assigned the same IP address. Because the broader network can route every pod IP address to that pod's node, any host on the network is reachable to and from any pod.

This openness allows any host with sufficient service discovery data to decide which pod will receive those packets. A load balancer outside the cluster can load balance pods, such as a gRPC client in another cluster.

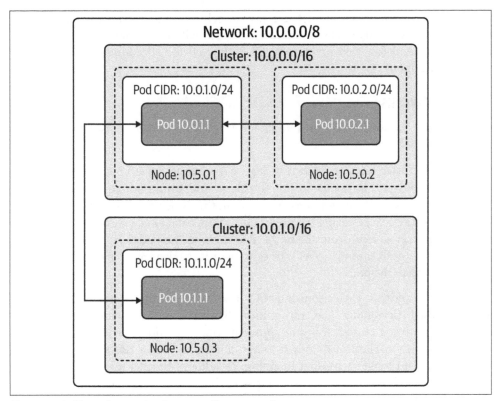

Figure 4-3. Two clusters in the same flat network

External pod traffic (and incoming pod traffic, when the connection's destination is a specific pod IP address) has low latency and low overhead. Any form of proxying or packet rewriting incurs a latency and processing cost, which is small but nontrivial (especially in an application architecture that involves many backend services, where each delay adds up).

Unfortunately, this model requires a large, contiguous IP address space for each cluster (i.e., a range of IP addresses where every IP address in the range is under your control). Kubernetes requires a single CIDR for pod IP addresses (for each IP family). This model is achievable with a private subnet (such as 10.0.0.0/8 or 172.16.0.0/12); however, it is much harder and more expensive to do with public IP addresses, especially IPv4 addresses. Administrators will need to use NAT to connect a cluster running in a private IP address space to the internet.

Aside from needing a large IP address space, administrators also need an easily programmable network. The CNI plugin must allocate pod IP addresses and ensure a route exists to a given pod's node.

Flat networks, on a private subnet, are easy to achieve in a cloud provider environment. The vast majority of cloud provider networks will provide large private subnets and have an API (or even preexisting CNI plugins) for IP address allocation and route management.

Island Networks

Island cluster networks are, at a high level, a combination of isolated and flat networks.

In an island cluster setup, as shown in Figure 4-4, nodes have L3 connectivity with the broader network, but pods do not. Traffic to and from pods must pass through some form of proxy, through nodes. Most often, this is achieved by `iptables` source NAT on a pod's packets leaving the node. This setup, called *masquerading*, uses SNAT to rewrite packet sources from the pod's IP address to the node's IP address (refer to Chapter 2 for a refresher on SNAT). In other words, packets appear to be "from" the node, rather than the pod.

Sharing an IP address while also using NAT hides the individual pod IP addresses. IP address–based firewalling and recognition becomes difficult across the cluster boundary. Within a cluster, it is still apparent which IP address is which pod (and, therefore, which application). Pods in other clusters, or other hosts on the broader network, will no longer have that mapping. IP address-based firewalling and allow lists are not sufficient security on their own but are a valuable and sometimes required layer.

Now let's see how we configure any of these network layouts with the kube-controller-manager. *Control plane* refers to all the functions and processes that determine which path to use to send the packet or frame. *Data plane* refers to all the functions and processes that forward packets/frames from one interface to another based on control plane logic.

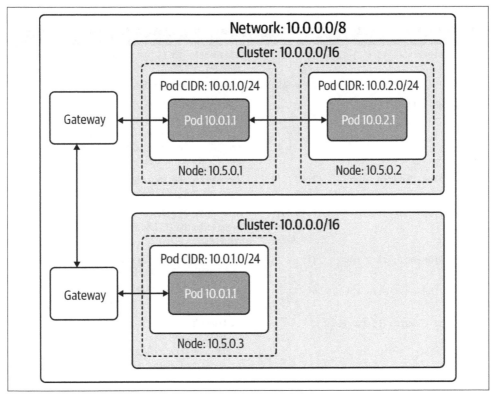

Figure 4-4. Two in the "island network" configuration

kube-controller-manager Configuration

The `kube-controller-manager` runs most individual Kubernetes controllers in one binary and one process, where most Kubernetes logic lives. At a high level, a controller in Kubernetes terms is software that watches resources and takes action to synchronize or enforce a specific state (either the desired state or reflecting the current state as a status). Kubernetes has many controllers, which generally "own" a specific object type or specific operation.

`kube-controller-manager` includes multiple controllers that manage the Kubernetes network stack. Notably, administrators set the cluster CIDR here.

`kube-controller-manager`, due to running a significant number of controllers, also has a substantial number of flags. Table 4-1 highlights some notable network configuration flags.

Table 4-1. Kube-controller-manager options

Flag	Default	Description
`--allocate-node-cidrs`	true	Sets whether CIDRs for pods should be allocated and set on the cloud provider.
`--CIDR-allocator-type string`	RangeAllocator	Type of CIDR allocator to use.
`--cluster-CIDR`		CIDR range from which to assign pod IP addresses. Requires `--allocate-node-cidrs` to be true. If `kube-controller-manager` has `IPv6DualStack` enabled, `--cluster-CIDR` accepts a comma-separated pair of IPv4 and IPv6 CIDRs.
`--configure-cloud-routes`	true	Sets whether CIDRs should be allocated by `allocate-node-cidrs` and configured on the cloud provider.
`--node-CIDR-mask-size`	24 for IPv4 clusters, 64 for IPv6 clusters	Mask size for the node CIDR in a cluster. Kubernetes will assign each node 2^(`node-CIDR-mask-size`) IP addresses.
`--node-CIDR-mask-size-ipv4`	24	Mask size for the node CIDR in a cluster. Use this flag in dual-stack clusters to allow both IPv4 and IPv6 settings.
`--node-CIDR-mask-size-ipv6`	64	Mask size for the node CIDR in a cluster. Use this flag in dual-stack clusters to allow both IPv4 and IPv6 settings.
`--service-cluster-ip-range`		CIDR range for services in the cluster to allocate service ClusterIPs. Requires `--allocate-node-cidrs` to be true. If `kube-controller-manager` has `IPv6DualStack` enabled, `--service-cluster-ip-range` accepts a comma-separated pair of IPv4 and IPv6 CIDRs.

 All Kubernetes binaries have documentation for their flags in the online docs. See all `kube-controller-manager` options in the documentation (*https://oreil.ly/xDGIE*).

Now that we have discussed high-level network architecture and network configuration in the Kubernetes control plane, let's look closer at how Kubernetes worker nodes handle networking.

The Kubelet

The Kubelet is a single binary that runs on every worker node in a cluster. At a high level, the Kubelet is responsible for managing any pods scheduled to the node and providing status updates for the node and pods on it. However, the Kubelet primarily acts as a coordinator for other software on the node. The Kubelet manages a container networking implementation (via the CNI) and a container runtime (via the CRI).

We define worker nodes as Kubernetes nodes that can run pods. Some clusters technically run the API server and etcd on restricted worker nodes. This setup can allow control plane components to be managed with the same automation as typical workloads but exposes additional failure modes and security vulnerabilities.

When a controller (or user) creates a pod in the Kubernetes API, it initially exists as only the pod API object. The Kubernetes scheduler watches for such a pod and attempts to select a valid node to schedule the pod to. There are several constraints to this scheduling. Our pod with its CPU/memory requests must not exceed the unrequested CPU/memory remaining on the node. Many selection options are available, such as affinity/anti-affinity to labeled nodes or other labeled pods or taints on nodes. Assuming the scheduler finds a node that satisfies all the pod's constraints, the scheduler writes that node's name to our pod's nodeName field. Let's say Kubernetes schedules the pod to node-1:

```
apiVersion: v1
kind: Pod
metadata:
  name: example
spec:
  nodeName: "node-1"
  containers:
    - name: example
      image: example:1.0
```

The Kubelet on node-1 watches for all of the pods scheduled to it. The equivalent kubectl command would be kubectl get pods -w --field-selector spec.nodeName=node-1. When the Kubelet observes that our pod exists but is not present on the node, it creates it. We will skip over the CRI details and the creation of the container itself. Once the container exists, the Kubelet makes an ADD call to the CNI, which tells the CNI plugin to create the pod network. We will cover the interface and plugins in our next section.

Pod Readiness and Probes

Pod readiness is an additional indication of whether the pod is ready to serve traffic. Pod readiness determines whether the pod address shows up in the Endpoints object from an external source. Other Kubernetes resources that manage pods, like deployments, take pod readiness into account for decision-making, such as advancing during a rolling update. During rolling deployment, a new pod becomes ready, but a service, network policy, or load balancer is not yet prepared for the new pod due to whatever reason. This may cause service disruption or loss of backend capacity. It should be noted that if a pod spec does contain probes of any type, Kubernetes defaults to success for all three types.

Users can specify pod readiness checks in the pod spec. From there, the Kubelet executes the specified check and updates the pod status based on successes or failures.

Probes effect the `.Status.Phase` field of a pod. The following is a list of the pod phases and their descriptions:

Pending
> The pod has been accepted by the cluster, but one or more of the containers has not been set up and made ready to run. This includes the time a pod spends waiting to be scheduled as well as the time spent downloading container images over the network.

Running
> The pod has been scheduled to a node, and all the containers have been created. At least one container is still running or is in the process of starting or restarting. Note that some containers may be in a failed state, such as in a CrashLoopBackoff.

Succeeded
> All containers in the pod have terminated in success and will not be restarted.

Failed
> All containers in the pod have terminated, and at least one container has terminated in failure. That is, the container either exited with nonzero status or was terminated by the system.

Unknown
> For some reason the state of the pod could not be determined. This phase typically occurs due to an error in communicating with the Kubelet where the pod should be running.

The Kubelet performs several types of health checks for individual containers in a pod: *liveness probes* (`livenessProbe`), *readiness probes* (`readinessProbe`), and *startup probes* (`startupProbe`). The Kubelet (and, by extension, the node itself) must be able to connect to all containers running on that node in order to perform any HTTP health checks.

Each probe has one of three results:

Success
> The container passed the diagnostic.

Failure
> The container failed the diagnostic.

Unknown
> The diagnostic failed, so no action should be taken.

The probes can be exec probes, which attempt to execute a binary within the container, TCP probes, or HTTP probes. If the probe fails more than the `failureThreshold` number of times, Kubernetes will consider the check to have failed. The effect of this depends on the type of probe.

When a container's readiness probe fails, the Kubelet does not terminate it. Instead, the Kubelet writes the failure to the pod's status.

If the liveness probes fail, the Kubelet will terminate the container. Liveness probes can easily cause unexpected failures if misused or misconfigured. The intended use case for liveness probes is to let the Kubelet know when to restart a container. However, as humans, we quickly learn that if "something is wrong, restart it" is a dangerous strategy. For example, suppose we create a liveness probe that loads the main page of our web app. Further, suppose that some change in the system, outside our container's code, causes the main page to return a 404 or 500 error. There are frequent causes of such a scenario, such as a backend database failure, a required service failure, or a feature flag change that exposes a bug. In any of these scenarios, the liveness probe would restart the container. At best, this would be unhelpful; restarting the container will not solve a problem elsewhere in the system and could quickly worsen the problem. Kubernetes has container restart backoffs (`CrashLoopBackoff`), which add increasing delay to restarting failed containers. With enough pods or rapid enough failures, the application may go from having an error on the home page to being hard-down. Depending on the application, pods may also lose cached data upon a restart; it may be strenuous to fetch or impossible to fetch during the hypothetical degradation. Because of this, use liveness probes with caution. When pods use them, they only depend on the container they are testing, with no other dependencies. Many engineers have specific health check endpoints, which provide minimal validation of criteria, such as "PHP is running and serving my API."

A startup probe can provide a grace period before a liveness probe can take effect. Liveness probes will not terminate a container before the startup probe has succeeded. An example use case is to allow a container to take many minutes to start, but to terminate a container quickly if it becomes unhealthy after starting.

In Example 4-1, our Golang web server has a liveness probe that performs an HTTP GET on port 8080 to the path `/healthz`, while the readiness probe uses / on the same port.

Example 4-1. Kubernetes podspec for Golang minimal webserver

```
apiVersion: v1
kind: Pod
metadata:
  labels:
    test: liveness
  name: go-web
spec:
  containers:
  - name: go-web
    image: go-web:v0.0.1
    ports:
    - containerPort: 8080
    livenessProbe:
      httpGet:
        path: /healthz
        port: 8080
      initialDelaySeconds: 5
      periodSeconds: 5
    readinessProbe:
      httpGet:
        path: /
        port: 8080
      initialDelaySeconds: 5
      periodSeconds: 5
```

This status does not affect the pod itself, but other Kubernetes mechanisms react to it. One key example is ReplicaSets (and, by extension, deployments). A failing readiness probe causes the ReplicaSet controller to count the pod as unready, giving rise to a halted deployment when too many new pods are unhealthy. The `Endpoints/End pointsSlice` controllers also react to failing readiness probes. If a pod's readiness probe fails, the pod's IP address will not be in the endpoint object, and the service will not route traffic to it. We will discuss services and endpoints more in the next chapter.

The `startupProbe` will inform the Kubelet whether the application inside the container is started. This probe takes precedent over the others. If a `startupProbe` is defined in the pod spec, all other probes are disabled. Once the `startupProbe` succeeds, the Kubelet will begin running the other probes. But if the startup probe fails, the Kubelet kills the container, and the container executes its restart policy. Like the others, if a `startupProbe` does not exist, the default state is success.

Probe configurable options:

initialDelaySeconds
Amount of seconds after the container starts before liveness or readiness probes are initiated. Default 0; Minimum 0.

periodSeconds

How often probes are performed. Default 10; Minimum 1.

timeoutSeconds

Number of seconds after which the probe times out. Default 1; Minimum 1.

successThreshold

Minimum consecutive successes for the probe to be successful after failing. Default 1; must be 1 for liveness and startup probes; Minimum 1.

failureThreshold

When a probe fails, Kubernetes will try this many times before giving up. Giving up in the case of the liveness probe means the container will restart. For readiness probe, the pod will be marked Unready. Default 3; Minimum 1.

Application developers can also use readiness gates to help determine when the application inside the pod is ready. Available and stable since Kubernetes 1.14, to use readiness gates, manifest writers will add `readiness gates` in the pod's spec to specify a list of additional conditions that the Kubelet evaluates for pod readiness. That is done in the `ConditionType` attribute of the readiness gates in the pod spec. The `Condition Type` is a condition in the pod's condition list with a matching type. Readiness gates are controlled by the current state of `status.condition` fields for the pod, and if the Kubelet cannot find such a condition in the `status.conditions` field of a pod, the status of the condition is defaulted to False.

As you can see in the following example, the `feature-Y` readiness gate is true, while `feature-X` is false, so the pod's status is ultimately false:

```
kind: Pod
...
spec:
  readinessGates:
  - conditionType: www.example.com/feature-X
  - conditionType: www.example.com/feature-Y
...
status:
  conditions:
  - lastProbeTime: null
    lastTransitionTime: 2021-04-25T00:00:00Z
    status: "False"
    type: Ready
  - lastProbeTime: null
    lastTransitionTime: 2021-04-25T00:00:00Z
    status: "False"
    type: www.example.com/feature-X
  - lastProbeTime: null
    lastTransitionTime: 2021-04-25T00:00:00Z
    status: "True"
    type: www.example.com/feature-Y
```

```
containerStatuses:
- containerID: docker://xxxxxxxxxxxxxxxxxxxxxxxxxxxxxx
  ready : true
```

Load balancers like the AWS ALB can use the readiness gate as part of the pod life cycle before sending traffic to it.

The Kubelet must be able to connect to the Kubernetes API server. In Figure 4-5, we can see all the connections made by all the components in a cluster:

CNI
> Network plugin in Kubelet that enables networking to get IPs for pods and services.

gRPC
> API to communicate from the API server to etcd.

Kubelet
> All Kubernetes nodes have a Kubelet that ensures that any pod assigned to it are running and configured in the desired state.

CRI
> The gRPC API compiled in Kubelet, allowing Kubelet to talk to container runtimes using gRPC API. The container runtime provider must adapt it to the CRI API to allow Kubelet to talk to containers using the OCI Standard (runC). CRI consists of protocol buffers and gRPC API and libraries.

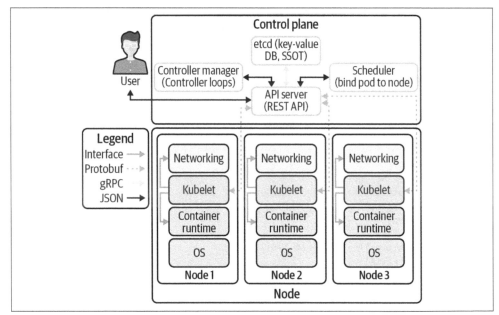

Figure 4-5. Cluster data flow between components

Communication between the pods and the Kubelet is made possible by the CNI. In our next section, we will discuss the CNI specification with examples from several popular CNI projects.

The CNI Specification

The CNI specification itself is quite simple. According to the specification, there are four operations that a CNI plugin must support:

ADD
Add a container to the network.

DEL
Delete a container from the network.

CHECK
Return an error if there is a problem with the container's network.

VERSION
Report version information about the plugin.

> The full CNI spec is available on GitHub (*https://oreil.ly/1uYWl*).

In Figure 4-6, we can see how Kubernetes (or the *runtime*, as the CNI project refers to container orchestrators) invokes CNI plugin operations by executing binaries. Kubernetes supplies any configuration for the command in JSON to `stdin` and receives the command's output in JSON through `stdout`. CNI plugins frequently have very simple binaries, which act as a wrapper for Kubernetes to call, while the binary makes an HTTP or RPC API call to a persistent backend. CNI maintainers have discussed changing this to an HTTP or RPC model, based on performance issues when frequently launching Windows processes.

Kubernetes uses only one CNI plugin at a time, though the CNI specification allows for multiplugin setups (i.e., assigning multiple IP addresses to a container). Multus is a CNI plugin that works around this limitation in Kubernetes by acting as a fan-out to multiple CNI plugins.

> At the time of writing, the CNI spec is at version 0.4. It has not changed drastically over the years and appears unlikely to change in the future—maintainers of the specification plan to release version 1.0 soon.

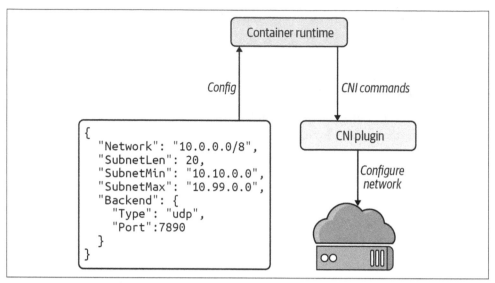

Figure 4-6. CNI configuration

CNI Plugins

The CNI plugin has two primary responsibilities: allocate and assign unique IP addresses for pods and ensure that routes exist within Kubernetes to each pod IP address. These responsibilities mean that the overarching network that the cluster resides in dictates CNI plugin behavior. For example, if there are too few IP addresses or it is not possible to attach sufficient IP addresses to a node, cluster admins will need to use a CNI plugin that supports an overlay network. The hardware stack, or cloud provider used, typically dictates which CNI options are suitable. Chapter 6 will talk about the major cloud platforms and how the network design impacts CNI choice.

To use the CNI, add `--network-plugin=cni` to the Kubelet's startup arguments. By default, the Kubelet reads CNI configuration from the directory /etc/cni/net.d/ and expects to find the CNI binary in /opt/cni/bin/. Admins can override the configuration location with `--cni-config-dir=<directory>`, and the CNI binary directory with `--cni-bin-dir=<directory>`.

> Managed Kubernetes offerings, and many "distros" of Kubernetes, come with a CNI preconfigured.

There are two broad categories of CNI network models: flat networks and overlay networks. In a flat network, the CNI driver uses IP addresses from the cluster's network, which typically requires many IP addresses to be available to the cluster. In an overlay network, the CNI driver creates a secondary network within Kubernetes, which uses the cluster's network (called the *underlay network*) to send packets. Overlay networks create a virtual network within the cluster. In an overlay network, the CNI plugin encapsulates packets. We discussed overlays in greater detail in Chapter 3. Overlay networks add substantial complexity and do not allow hosts on the cluster network to connect directly to pods. However, overlay networks allow the cluster network to be much smaller, as only the nodes must be assigned IP addresses on that network.

CNI plugins also typically need a way to communicate state between nodes. Plugins take very different approaches, such as storing data in the Kubernetes API, in a dedicated database.

The CNI plugin is also responsible for calling IPAM plugins for IP addressing.

The IPAM Interface

The CNI spec has a second interface, the IP Address Management (IPAM) interface, to reduce duplication of IP allocation code in CNI plugins. The IPAM plugin must determine and output the interface IP address, gateway, and routes, as shown in Example 4-2. The IPAM interface is similar to the CNI: a binary with JSON input to `stdin` and JSON output from `stdout`.

Example 4-2. Example IPAM plugin output, from the CNI 0.4 specification docs

```
{
  "cniVersion": "0.4.0",
  "ips": [
      {
          "version": "<4-or-6>",
          "address": "<ip-and-prefix-in-CIDR>",
          "gateway": "<ip-address-of-the-gateway>"  (optional)
      },
      ...
  ],
  "routes": [                                        (optional)
      {
          "dst": "<ip-and-prefix-in-cidr>",
          "gw": "<ip-of-next-hop>"                   (optional)
      },
      ...
  ]
  "dns": {                                           (optional)
    "nameservers": <list-of-nameservers>             (optional)
    "domain": <name-of-local-domain>                 (optional)
```

```
    "search": <list-of-search-domains>              (optional)
    "options": <list-of-options>                    (optional)
  }
}
```

Now we will review several of the options available for cluster administrators to choose from when deploying a CNI.

Popular CNI Plugins

Cilium is open source software for transparently securing network connectivity between application containers. Cilium is an L7/HTTP-aware CNI and can enforce network policies on L3–L7 using an identity-based security model decoupled from the network addressing. The Linux technology eBPF, which we discussed in Chapter 2, is what powers Cilium. Later in this chapter, we will do a deep dive into Network Policy objects; for now know that they are effectively pod-level firewalls.

Flannel focuses on the network and is a simple and easy way to configure a layer 3 network fabric designed for Kubernetes. If a cluster requires functionalities like network policies, an admin must deploy other CNIs, such as Calico. Flannel uses the Kubernetes cluster's existing etcd to store its state information to avoid providing a dedicated data store.

According to Calico, it "combines flexible networking capabilities with run-anywhere security enforcement to provide a solution with native Linux kernel performance and true cloud-native scalability." Calico does not use an overlay network. Instead, Calico configures a layer 3 network that uses the BGP routing protocol to route packets between hosts. Calico can also integrate with Istio, a service mesh, to interpret and enforce policy for workloads within the cluster at the service mesh and network infrastructure layers.

Table 4-2 gives a brief overview of the major CNI plugins to choose from.

Table 4-2. A brief overview of major CNI plugins

Name	NetworkPolicy support	Data storage	Network setup
Cilium	Yes	etcd or consul	Ipvlan(beta), veth, L7 aware
Flannel	No	etcd	Layer 3 IPv4 overlay network
Calico	Yes	etcd or Kubernetes API	Layer 3 network using BGP
Weave Net	Yes	No external cluster store	Mesh overlay network

 Full instructions for running KIND, Helm, and Cilium are in the book's GitHub repo.

Let's deploy Cilium for testing with our Golang web server in Example 4-3. We will need a Kubernetes cluster for deploying Cilium. One of the easiest ways we have found to deploy clusters for testing locally is KIND, which stands for Kubernetes in Docker. It will allow us to create a cluster with a YAML configuration file and then, using Helm, deploy Cilium to that cluster.

Example 4-3. KIND configuration for Cilium local deploy

```
kind: Cluster ❶
apiVersion: kind.x-k8s.io/v1alpha4 ❷
nodes: ❸
- role: control-plane ❹
- role: worker ❺
- role: worker ❻
- role: worker ❼
networking: ❽
disableDefaultCNI: true ❾
```

❶ Specifies that we are configuring a KIND cluster

❷ The version of KIND's config

❸ The list of nodes in the cluster

❹ One control plane node

❺ Worker node 1

❻ Worker node 2

❼ Worker node 3

❽ KIND configuration options for networking

❾ Disables the default networking option so that we can deploy Cilium

> Instructions for configuring a KIND cluster and more can be found in the documentation (*https://oreil.ly/12BRh*).

With the KIND cluster configuration YAML, we can use KIND to create that cluster with the following command. If this is the first time you're running it, it will take some time to download all the Docker images for the working and control plane Docker images:

```
$ kind create cluster --config=kind-config.yaml
Creating cluster "kind" ...
✓ Ensuring node image (kindest/node:v1.18.
2) Preparing nodes
✓ Writing configuration Starting control-plane
Installing StorageClass Joining worker nodes Set kubectl context to "kind-kind"
You can now use your cluster with:

kubectl cluster-info --context kind-kind

Have a question, bug, or feature request?
Let us know! https://kind.sigs.k8s.io/#community †≠---

Always verify that the cluster is up and running with kubectl.

$ kubectl cluster-info --context kind-kind
Kubernetes master -> control plane is running at https://127.0.0.1:59511
KubeDNS is running at
https://127.0.0.1:59511/api/v1/namespaces/kube-system/services/kube-dns:dns/proxy
To further debug and diagnose cluster problems, use 'kubectl cluster-info dump.'
```

 The cluster nodes will remain in state NotReady until Cilium deploys the network. This is normal behavior for the cluster.

Now that our cluster is running locally, we can begin installing Cilium using Helm, a Kubernetes deployment tool. According to its documentation, Helm is the preferred way to install Cilium. First, we need to add the Helm repo for Cilium. Optionally, you can download the Docker images for Cilium and finally instruct KIND to load the Cilium images into the cluster:

```
$ helm repo add cilium https://helm.cilium.io/
# Pre-pulling and loading container images is optional.
$ docker pull cilium/cilium:v1.9.1
kind load docker-image cilium/cilium:v1.9.1
```

Now that the prerequisites for Cilium are completed, we can install it in our cluster with Helm. There are many configuration options for Cilium, and Helm configures options with --set NAME_VAR=VAR:

```
$ helm install cilium cilium/cilium --version 1.10.1 \
  --namespace kube-system

NAME: Cilium
LAST DEPLOYED: Fri Jan  1 15:39:59 2021
NAMESPACE: kube-system
STATUS: deployed
REVISION: 1
TEST SUITE: None
```

```
NOTES:
You have successfully installed Cilium with Hubble.

Your release version is 1.10.1.

For any further help, visit https://docs.cilium.io/en/v1.10/gettinghelp/
```

Cilium installs several pieces in the cluster: the agent, the client, the operator, and the `cilium-cni` plugin:

Agent

The Cilium agent, `cilium-agent`, runs on each node in the cluster. The agent accepts configuration through Kubernetes APIs that describe networking, service load balancing, network policies, and visibility and monitoring requirements.

Client (CLI)

The Cilium CLI client (Cilium) is a command-line tool installed along with the Cilium agent. It interacts with the REST API on the same node. The CLI allows developers to inspect the state and status of the local agent. It also provides tooling to access the eBPF maps to validate their state directly.

Operator

The operator is responsible for managing duties in the cluster, which should be handled per cluster and not per node.

CNI Plugin

The CNI plugin (`cilium-cni`) interacts with the Cilium API of the node to trigger the configuration to provide networking, load balancing, and network policies pods.

We can observe all these components being deployed in the cluster with the `kubectl -n kube-system get pods --watch` command:

```
$ kubectl -n kube-system get pods --watch
NAME                                          READY   STATUS
cilium-65kvp                                  0/1     Init:0/2
cilium-node-init-485lj                        0/1     ContainerCreating
cilium-node-init-79g68                        1/1     Running
cilium-node-init-gfdl8                        1/1     Running
cilium-node-init-jz8qc                        1/1     Running
cilium-operator-5b64c54cd-cgr2b               0/1     ContainerCreating
cilium-operator-5b64c54cd-tblbz               0/1     ContainerCreating
cilium-pg6v8                                  0/1     Init:0/2
cilium-rsnqk                                  0/1     Init:0/2
cilium-vfhrs                                  0/1     Init:0/2
coredns-66bff467f8-dqzql                      0/1     Pending
coredns-66bff467f8-r5nl6                      0/1     Pending
etcd-kind-control-plane                       1/1     Running
kube-apiserver-kind-control-plane             1/1     Running
kube-controller-manager-kind-control-plane    1/1     Running
```

```
kube-proxy-k5zc2                                    1/1    Running
kube-proxy-qzhvq                                    1/1    Running
kube-proxy-v54p4                                    1/1    Running
kube-proxy-xb9tr                                    1/1    Running
kube-scheduler-kind-control-plane                   1/1    Running
cilium-operator-5b64c54cd-tblbz                     1/1    Running
```

Now that we have deployed Cilium, we can run the Cilium connectivity check to ensure it is running correctly:

```
$ kubectl create ns cilium-test
namespace/cilium-test created

$ kubectl apply -n cilium-test \
-f \
https://raw.githubusercontent.com/strongjz/advanced_networking_code_examples/
master/chapter-4/connectivity-check.yaml

deployment.apps/echo-a created
deployment.apps/echo-b created
deployment.apps/echo-b-host created
deployment.apps/pod-to-a created
deployment.apps/pod-to-external-1111 created
deployment.apps/pod-to-a-denied-cnp created
deployment.apps/pod-to-a-allowed-cnp created
deployment.apps/pod-to-external-fqdn-allow-google-cnp created
deployment.apps/pod-to-b-multi-node-clusterip created
deployment.apps/pod-to-b-multi-node-headless created
deployment.apps/host-to-b-multi-node-clusterip created
deployment.apps/host-to-b-multi-node-headless created
deployment.apps/pod-to-b-multi-node-nodeport created
deployment.apps/pod-to-b-intra-node-nodeport created
service/echo-a created
service/echo-b created
service/echo-b-headless created
service/echo-b-host-headless created
ciliumnetworkpolicy.cilium.io/pod-to-a-denied-cnp created
ciliumnetworkpolicy.cilium.io/pod-to-a-allowed-cnp created
ciliumnetworkpolicy.cilium.io/pod-to-external-fqdn-allow-google-cnp created
```

The connectivity test will deploy a series of Kubernetes deployments that will use various connectivity paths. Connectivity paths come with and without service load balancing and in various network policy combinations. The pod name indicates the connectivity variant, and the readiness and liveness gate indicates the success or failure of the test:

```
$ kubectl get pods -n cilium-test -w
NAME                                                READY    STATUS
echo-a-57cbbd9b8b-szn94                             1/1      Running
echo-b-6db5fc8ff8-wkcr6                             1/1      Running
echo-b-host-76d89978c-dsjm8                         1/1      Running
host-to-b-multi-node-clusterip-fd6868749-7zkcr      1/1      Running
```

```
host-to-b-multi-node-headless-54fbc4659f-z4rtd          1/1    Running
pod-to-a-648fd74787-x27hc                               1/1    Running
pod-to-a-allowed-cnp-7776c879f-6rq7z                    1/1    Running
pod-to-a-denied-cnp-b5ff897c7-qp5kp                     1/1    Running
pod-to-b-intra-node-nodeport-6546644d59-qkmck           1/1    Running
pod-to-b-multi-node-clusterip-7d54c74c5f-4j7pm          1/1    Running
pod-to-b-multi-node-headless-76db68d547-fhlz7           1/1    Running
pod-to-b-multi-node-nodeport-7496df84d7-5z872           1/1    Running
pod-to-external-1111-6d4f9d9645-kfl4x                   1/1    Running
pod-to-external-fqdn-allow-google-cnp-5bc496897c-bnlqs  1/1    Running
```

Now that Cilium manages our network for the cluster, we will use it later in this chapter for a `NetworkPolicy` overview. Not all CNI plugins will support `NetworkPolicy`, so that is an important detail when deciding which plugin to use.

kube-proxy

`kube-proxy` is another per-node daemon in Kubernetes, like Kubelet. `kube-proxy` provides basic load balancing functionality within the cluster. It implements services and relies on `Endpoints/EndpointSlices`, two API objects that we will discuss in detail in the next chapter on networking abstractions. It may help to reference that section, but the following is the relevant and quick explanation:

- Services define a load balancer for a set of pods.
- Endpoints (and endpoint slices) list a set of ready pod IPs. They are created automatically from a service, with the same pod selector as the service.

Most types of services have an IP address for the service, called the cluster IP address, which is not routable outside the cluster. `kube-proxy` is responsible for routing requests to a service's cluster IP address to healthy pods. `kube-proxy` is by far the most common implementation for Kubernetes services, but there are alternatives to `kube-proxy`, such as a replacement mode Cilium. A substantial amount of our content on routing in Chapter 2 is applicable to `kube-proxy`, particularly when debugging service connectivity or performance.

Cluster IP addresses are not typically routable from outside a cluster.

`kube-proxy` has four modes, which change its runtime mode and exact feature set: userspace, iptables, ipvs, and kernelspace. You can specify the mode using `--proxy-mode <mode>`. It's worth noting that all modes rely on `iptables` to some extent.

userspace Mode

The first and oldest mode is `userspace` mode. In `userspace` mode, `kube-proxy` runs a web server and routes all service IP addresses to the web server, using `iptables`. The web server terminates connections and proxies the request to a pod in the service's endpoints. `userspace` mode is no longer commonly used, and we suggest avoiding it unless you have a clear reason to use it.

iptables Mode

`iptables` mode uses `iptables` entirely. It is the default mode, and the most commonly used (this may be in part because IPVS mode graduated to GA stability more recently, and `iptables` is a familiar Linux technology).

`iptables` mode performs connection fan-out, instead of true load balancing. In other words, `iptables` mode will route a connection to a backend pod, and all requests made using that connection will go to the same pod, until the connection is terminated. This is simple and has predictable behavior in ideal scenarios (e.g., successive requests in the same connection will be able to benefit from any local caching in backend pods). It can also be unpredictable when dealing with long-lived connections, such as HTTP/2 connections (notably, HTTP/2 is the transport for gRPC). Suppose you have two pods, X and Y, serving a service, and you replace X with Z during a normal rolling update. The older pod Y still has all the existing connections, plus half of the connections that needed to be reestablished when pod X shut down, leading to substantially more traffic being served by pod Y. There are many scenarios like this that lead to unbalanced traffic.

Recall our examples in the "Practical iptables" section in Chapter 2. In it, we showed that `iptables` could be configured with a list of IP addresses and random routing probabilities, such that connections would be made randomly between all IP addresses. Given a service that has healthy backend pods `10.0.0.1`, `10.0.0.2`, `10.0.0.3`, and `10.0.0.4`, `kube-proxy` would create sequential rules that route connections like so:

- 25% of connections go to `10.0.0.1`.
- 33.3% of unrouted connections go to `10.0.0.2`.
- 50% of unrouted connections go to `10.0.0.3`.
- All unrouted connections go to `10.0.0.4`.

This may seem unintuitive and leads some engineers to assume that kube-proxy is misrouting traffic (especially because few people look at kube-proxy when services work as expected). The crucial detail is that each routing rule happens for connections that *haven't* been routed in a prior rule. The final rule routes all connections to 10.0.0.4 (because the connection has to go *somewhere*), the semifinal rule has a 50% chance of routing to 10.0.0.3 as a choice of two IP addresses, and so on. Routing randomness scores are always calculated as 1 / ${remaining number of IP addresses}.

Here are the iptables forwarding rules for the kube-dns service in a cluster. In our example, the kube-dns service's cluster IP address is 10.96.0.10. This output has been filtered and reformatted for clarity:

```
$ sudo iptables -t nat -L KUBE-SERVICES
Chain KUBE-SERVICES (2 references)
target       prot opt source              destination

/* kube-system/kube-dns:dns cluster IP */ udp dpt:domain
KUBE-MARK-MASQ  udp  -- !10.217.0.0/16       10.96.0.10
/* kube-system/kube-dns:dns cluster IP */ udp dpt:domain
KUBE-SVC-TCOU7JCQXEZGVUNU  udp  -- anywhere 10.96.0.10
/* kube-system/kube-dns:dns-tcp cluster IP */ tcp dpt:domain
KUBE-MARK-MASQ  tcp  -- !10.217.0.0/16       10.96.0.10
/* kube-system/kube-dns:dns-tcp cluster IP */ tcp dpt:domain
KUBE-SVC-ERIFXISQEP7F7OF4  tcp  -- anywhere 10.96.0.10 ADDRTYPE
    match dst-type LOCAL
/* kubernetes service nodeports; NOTE: this must be the
    last rule in this chain */
KUBE-NODEPORTS  all  -- anywhere             anywhere
```

There are a pair of UDP and TCP rules for kube-dns. We'll focus on the UDP ones.

The first UDP rule marks any connections to the service that *aren't* originating from a pod IP address (10.217.0.0/16 is the default pod network CIDR) for masquerading.

The next UDP rule has the chain KUBE-SVC-TCOU7JCQXEZGVUNU as its target. Let's take a closer look:

```
$ sudo iptables -t nat -L KUBE-SVC-TCOU7JCQXEZGVUNU
Chain KUBE-SVC-TCOU7JCQXEZGVUNU (1 references)
target       prot opt source              destination

/* kube-system/kube-dns:dns */
KUBE-SEP-OCPCMVGPKTDWRD3C  all -- anywhere anywhere  statistic mode
    random probability 0.50000000000
/* kube-system/kube-dns:dns */
KUBE-SEP-VFGOVXCRCJYSGAY3  all -- anywhere anywhere
```

Here we see a chain with a 50% chance of executing, and the chain that will execute otherwise. If we check the first of those chains, we see it routes to 10.0.1.141, one of our two CoreDNS pods' IPs:

```
$ sudo iptables -t nat -L KUBE-SEP-OCPCMVGPKTDWRD3C
Chain KUBE-SEP-OCPCMVGPKTDWRD3C (1 references)
target       prot opt source              destination

/* kube-system/kube-dns:dns */
KUBE-MARK-MASQ  all  -- 10.0.1.141            anywhere
/* kube-system/kube-dns:dns */ udp to:10.0.1.141:53
DNAT         udp  -- anywhere              anywhere
```

ipvs Mode

ipvs mode uses IPVS, covered in Chapter 2, instead of iptables, for connection load balancing. ipvs mode supports six load balancing modes, specified with --ipvs-scheduler:

- rr: Round-robin
- lc: Least connection
- dh: Destination hashing
- sh: Source hashing
- sed: Shortest expected delay
- nq: Never queue

Round-robin (rr) is the default load balancing mode. It is the closest analog to ipta bles mode's behavior (in that connections are made fairly evenly regardless of pod state), though iptables mode does not actually perform round-robin routing.

kernelspace Mode

kernelspace is the newest, Windows-only mode. It provides an alternative to userspace mode for Kubernetes on Windows, as iptables and ipvs are specific to Linux.

Now that we've covered the basics of pod-to-pod traffic in Kubernetes, let's take a look at NetworkPolicy and securing pod-to-pod traffic.

NetworkPolicy

Kubernetes' default behavior is to allow traffic between any two pods in the cluster network. This behavior is a deliberate design choice for ease of adoption and flexibility of configuration, but it is highly undesirable in practice. Allowing any system to make (or receive) arbitrary connections creates risk. An attacker can probe systems and can potentially exploit captured credentials or find weakened or missing authentication. Allowing arbitrary connections also makes it easier to exfiltrate data from a system through a compromised workload. All in all, we *strongly* discourage running real clusters without `NetworkPolicy`. Since all pods can communicate with all other pods, we strongly recommend that application owners use `NetworkPolicy` objects along with other application-layer security measures, such as authentication tokens or mutual Transport Layer Security (mTLS), for any network communication.

`NetworkPolicy` is a resource type in Kubernetes that contains allow-based firewall rules. Users can add `NetworkPolicy` objects to restrict connections to and from pods. The `NetworkPolicy` resource acts as a configuration for CNI plugins, which themselves are responsible for ensuring connectivity between pods. The Kubernetes API declares that `NetworkPolicy` support is optional for CNI drivers, which means that some CNI drivers do not support network policies, as shown in Table 4-3. If a developer creates a `NetworkPolicy` when using a CNI driver that does not support `NetworkPolicy` objects, it does not affect the pod's network security. Some CNI drivers, such as enterprise products or company-internal CNI drivers, may introduce their equivalent of a `NetworkPolicy`. Some CNI drivers may also have slightly different "interpretations" of the `NetworkPolicy` spec.

Table 4-3. Common CNI plugins and NetworkPolicy support

CNI plugin	NetworkPolicy supported
Calico	Yes, and supports additional plugin-specific policies
Cilium	Yes, and supports additional plugin-specific policies
Flannel	No
Kubenet	No

Example 4-4 details a `NetworkPolicy` object, which contains a pod selector, ingress rules, and egress rules. The policy will apply to all pods in the same namespace as the `NetworkPolicy` that matches the selector label. This use of selector labels is consistent with other Kubernetes APIs: a spec identifies pods by their labels rather than their names or parent objects.

Example 4-4. The broad structure of a `NetworkPolicy`

```
apiVersion: networking.k8s.io/v1
kind: NetworkPolicy
metadata:
  name: demo
  namespace: default
spec:
  podSelector:
    matchLabels:
      app: demo
  policyTypes:
  - Ingress
  - Egress
  ingress: []NetworkPolicyIngressRule # Not expanded
  egress: []NetworkPolicyEgressRule # Not expanded
```

Before getting deep into the API, let's walk through a simple example of creating a `NetworkPolicy` to reduce the scope of access for some pods. Let's assume we have two distinct components: `demo` and `demo-DB`. As we have no existing `NetworkPolicy` in Figure 4-7, all pods can communicate with all other pods (including hypothetically unrelated pods, not shown).

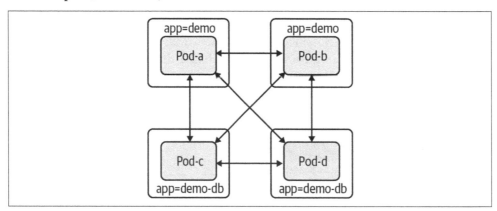

Figure 4-7. Pods without `NetworkPolicy` objects

Let's restrict `demo-DB`'s access level. If we create the following `NetworkPolicy` that selects `demo-DB` pods, `demo-DB` pods will be unable to send or receive any traffic:

```
apiVersion: networking.k8s.io/v1
kind: NetworkPolicy
metadata:
  name: demo-db
  namespace: default
spec:
  podSelector:
    matchLabels:
```

```
    app: demo-db
policyTypes:
- Ingress
- Egress
```

In Figure 4-8, we can now see that pods with the label `app=demo` can no longer create or receive connections.

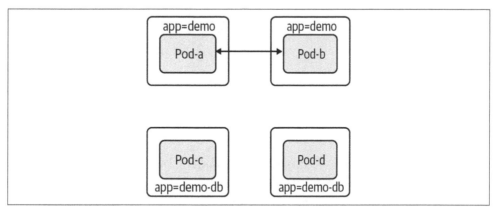

Figure 4-8. Pods with the app:demo-db label cannot receive or send traffic

Having no network access is undesirable for most workloads, including our example database. Our `demo-db` should (only) be able to receive connections from `demo` pods. To do that, we must add an ingress rule to the `NetworkPolicy`:

```
apiVersion: networking.k8s.io/v1
kind: NetworkPolicy
metadata:
  name: demo-db
  namespace: default
spec:
  podSelector:
    matchLabels:
      app: demo-db
  policyTypes:
  - Ingress
  - Egress
  ingress:
  - from:
    - podSelector:
        matchLabels:
          app: demo
```

Now `demo-db` pods can receive connections only from `demo` pods. Moreover, `demo-db` pods cannot make connections (as shown in Figure 4-9).

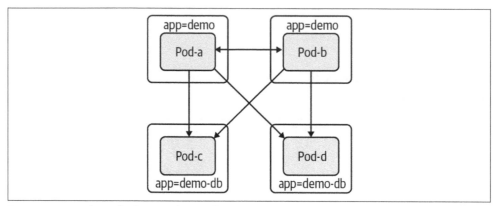

Figure 4-9. Pods with the app:demo-db label cannot create connections, and they can only receive connections from the app:demo pods

 If users can unwittingly or maliciously change labels, they can change how NetworkPolicy objects apply to all pods. In our prior example, if an attacker was able to edit the app: demo-DB label on a pod in that same namespace, the NetworkPolicy that we created would no longer apply to that pod. Similarly, an attacker could gain access from another pod in that namespace if they could add the label app: demo to their compromised pod.

The previous example is just an example; with Cilium we can create these NetworkPolicy objects for our Golang web server.

NetworkPolicy Example with Cilium

Our Golang web server now connects to a Postgres database with no TLS. Also, with no NetworkPolicy objects in place, any pod on the network can sniff traffic between the Golang web server and the database, which is a potential security risk. The following is going to deploy our Golang web application and its database and then deploy NetworkPolicy objects that will only allow connectivity to the database from the web server. Using the same KIND cluster from the Cilium install, let's deploy the Postgres database with the following YAML and kubectl commands:

```
$ kubectl apply -f database.yaml
service/postgres created
configmap/postgres-config created
statefulset.apps/postgres created
```

Here we deploy our web server as a Kubernetes deployment to our KIND cluster:

```
$ kubectl apply -f web.yaml
deployment.apps/app created
```

To run connectivity tests inside the cluster network, we will deploy and use a dnsu tils pod that has basic networking tools like ping and curl:

```
$ kubectl apply -f dnsutils.yaml
pod/dnsutils created
```

Since we are not deploying a service with an ingress, we can use kubectl port-forward to test connectivity to our web server:

```
kubectl port-forward app-5878d69796-j889q 8080:8080
```

 More information about kubectl port-forward can be found in the documentation (*https://oreil.ly/Ac6jk*).

Now from our local terminal, we can reach our API:

```
$ curl localhost:8080/
Hello
$ curl localhost:8080/healthz
Healthy
$ curl localhost:8080/data
Database Connected
```

Let's test connectivity to our web server inside the cluster from other pods. To do that, we need to get the IP address of our web server pod:

```
$ kubectl get pods -l app=app -o wide
NAME                  READY  STATUS   RESTARTS  AGE  IP            NODE
app-5878d69796-j889q  1/1    Running  0         87m  10.244.1.188  kind-worker3
```

Now we can test L4 and L7 connectivity to the web server from the dnsutils pod:

```
$ kubectl exec dnsutils -- nc -z -vv 10.244.1.188 8080
10.244.1.188 (10.244.1.188:8080) open
sent 0, rcvd 0
```

From our dnsutils, we can test the layer 7 HTTP API access:

```
$ kubectl exec dnsutils -- wget -qO- 10.244.1.188:8080/
Hello

$ kubectl exec dnsutils -- wget -qO- 10.244.1.188:8080/data
Database Connected

$ kubectl exec dnsutils -- wget -qO- 10.244.1.188:8080/healthz
Healthy
```

We can also test this on the database pod. First, we have to retrieve the IP address of the database pod, 10.244.2.189. We can use kubectl with a combination of labels and options to get this information:

```
$ kubectl get pods -l app=postgres -o wide
NAME        READY   STATUS    RESTARTS   AGE   IP             NODE
postgres-0  1/1     Running   0          98m   10.244.2.189   kind-worker
```

Again, let's use `dnsutils` pod to test connectivity to the Postgres database over its default port 5432:

```
$ kubectl exec dnsutils -- nc -z -vv 10.244.2.189 5432
10.244.2.189 (10.244.2.189:5432) open
sent 0, rcvd 0
```

The port is open for all to use since no network policies are in place. Now let's restrict this with a Cilium network policy. The following commands deploy the network policies so that we can test the secure network connectivity. Let's first restrict access to the database pod to only the web server. Apply the network policy that only allows traffic from the web server pod to the database:

```
$ kubectl apply -f layer_3_net_pol.yaml
ciliumnetworkpolicy.cilium.io/l3-rule-app-to-db created
```

The Cilium deploy of Cilium objects creates resources that can be retrieved just like pods with `kubectl`. With `kubectl describe ciliumnetworkpolicies.cilium.io l3-rule-app-to-db`, we can see all the information about the rule deployed via the YAML:

```
$ kubectl describe ciliumnetworkpolicies.cilium.io l3-rule-app-to-db
Name:          l3-rule-app-to-db
Namespace:     default
Labels:        <none>
Annotations:   API Version:  cilium.io/v2
Kind:          CiliumNetworkPolicy
Metadata:
Creation Timestamp:  2021-01-10T01:06:13Z
Generation:          1
Managed Fields:
API Version:  cilium.io/v2
Fields Type:  FieldsV1
fieldsV1:
f:metadata:
f:annotations:
.:
f:kubectl.kubernetes.io/last-applied-configuration:
f:spec:
.:
f:endpointSelector:
.:
f:matchLabels:
.:
f:app:
f:ingress:
Manager:       kubectl
Operation:     Update
```

```
Time:                2021-01-10T01:06:13Z
Resource Version:    47377
Self Link:
/apis/cilium.io/v2/namespaces/default/ciliumnetworkpolicies/l3-rule-app-to-db
UID:           71ee6571-9551-449d-8f3e-c177becda35a
Spec:
Endpoint Selector:
Match Labels:
App:   postgres
Ingress:
From Endpoints:
Match Labels:
App:   app
Events:          <none>
```

With the network policy applied, the dnsutils pod can no longer reach the database pod; we can see this in the timeout trying to reach the DB port from the dnsutils pods:

```
$ kubectl exec dnsutils -- nc -z -vv -w 5 10.244.2.189 5432
nc: 10.244.2.189 (10.244.2.189:5432): Operation timed out
sent 0, rcvd 0
command terminated with exit code 1
```

While the web server pod is still connected to the database pod, the /data route connects the web server to the database and the NetworkPolicy allows it:

```
$ kubectl exec dnsutils -- wget -qO- 10.244.1.188:8080/data
Database Connected

$ curl localhost:8080/data
Database Connected
```

Now let's apply the layer 7 policy. Cilium is layer 7 aware so that we can block or allow a specific request on the HTTP URI paths. In our example policy, we allow HTTP GETs on / and /data but do not allow them on /healthz; let's test that:

```
$ kubectl apply -f layer_7_netpol.yml
ciliumnetworkpolicy.cilium.io/l7-rule created
```

We can see the policy applied just like any other Kubernetes objects in the API:

```
$ kubectl get ciliumnetworkpolicies.cilium.io
NAME      AGE
l7-rule   6m54s

$ kubectl describe ciliumnetworkpolicies.cilium.io l7-rule
Name:         l7-rule
Namespace:    default
Labels:       <none>
Annotations:  API Version:  cilium.io/v2
Kind:         CiliumNetworkPolicy
Metadata:
```

```
Creation Timestamp:   2021-01-10T00:49:34Z
Generation:           1
Managed Fields:
  API Version:  cilium.io/v2
  Fields Type:  FieldsV1
  fieldsV1:
    f:metadata:
      f:annotations:
        .:
        f:kubectl.kubernetes.io/last-applied-configuration:
    f:spec:
      .:
      f:egress:
      f:endpointSelector:
        .:
        f:matchLabels:
          .:
          f:app:
  Manager:            kubectl
  Operation:          Update
  Time:               2021-01-10T00:49:34Z
  Resource Version:   43869
  Self Link:/apis/cilium.io/v2/namespaces/default/ciliumnetworkpolicies/l7-rule
  UID:                0162c16e-dd55-4020-83b9-464bb625b164
Spec:
  Egress:
    To Ports:
      Ports:
        Port:       8080
        Protocol:   TCP
      Rules:
        Http:
          Method:   GET
          Path:     /
          Method:   GET
          Path:     /data
  Endpoint Selector:
    Match Labels:
      App:   app
Events:        <none>
```

As we can see, / and /data are available but not /healthz, precisely what we expect from the NetworkPolicy:

```
$ kubectl exec dnsutils -- wget -qO- 10.244.1.188:8080/data
Database Connected

$kubectl exec dnsutils -- wget -qO- 10.244.1.188:8080/
Hello

$ kubectl exec dnsutils -- wget -qO- -T 5 10.244.1.188:8080/healthz
wget: error getting response
command terminated with exit code 1
```

These small examples show how powerful the Cilium network policies can enforce network security inside the cluster. We highly recommend that administrators select a CNI that supports network policies and enforce developers' use of network policies. Network policies are namespaced, and if teams have similar setups, cluster administrators can and should enforce that developers define network policies for added security.

We used two aspects of the Kubernetes API, labels and selectors; in our next section, we will provide more examples of how they are used inside a cluster.

Selecting Pods

Pods are unrestricted until they are *selected* by a `NetworkPolicy`. If selected, the CNI plugin allows pod ingress or egress only when a matching rule allows it. A `NetworkPolicy` has a `spec.policyTypes` field containing a list of policy types (ingress or egress). For example, if we select a pod with a `NetworkPolicy` that has ingress listed but not egress, then ingress will be restricted, and egress will not.

The `spec.podSelector` field will dictate which pods to apply the `NetworkPolicy` to. An empty `label selector.` (`podSelector: {}`) will select all pods in the namespace. We will discuss label selectors in more detail shortly.

`NetworkPolicy` objects are *namespaced* objects, which means they exist in and apply to a specific namespace. The `spec .podSelector` field can select pods only when they are in the same namespace as the `NetworkPolicy`. This means selecting `app: demo` will apply only in the current namespace, and any pods in another namespace with the label `app: demo` will be unaffected.

There are multiple workarounds to achieve firewalled-by-default behavior, including the following:

- Creating a blanket deny-all `NetworkPolicy` object for every namespace, which will require developers to add additional `NetworkPolicy` objects to allow desired traffic.
- Adding a custom CNI plugin that deliberately violates the default-open API behavior. Multiple CNI plugins have an additional configuration that exposes this kind of behavior.
- Creating admission policies to require that workloads have a `NetworkPolicy`.

`NetworkPolicy` objects rely heavily on labels and selectors; for that reason, let's dive into more complex examples.

The LabelSelector type

This is the first time in this book that we see a `LabelSelector` in a resource. It is a ubiquitous configuration element in Kubernetes and will come up many times in the next chapter, so when you get there, it may be helpful to look back at this section as a reference.

Every object in Kubernetes has a `metadata` field, with the type `ObjectMeta`. That gives every type the same metadata fields, like labels. Labels are a map of key-value string pairs:

```
metadata:
  labels:
    colour: purple
    shape: square
```

A `LabelSelector` identifies a group of resources by the present labels (or absent). Very few resources in Kubernetes will refer to other resources by name. Instead, most resources (`NetworkPolicy` objects, services, deployments, and other Kubernetes objects). use label matching with a `LabelSelector`. `LabelSelectors` can also be used in API and `kubectl` calls and avoid returning irrelevant objects. A `LabelSelector` has two fields: `matchExpressions` and `matchLabels`. The normal behavior for an empty `LabelSelector` is to select all objects in scope, e.g., all pods in the same namespace as a `NetworkPolicy`. `matchLabels` is the simpler of the two. `matchLabels` contains a map of key-value pairs. For an object to match, each key must be present on the object, and that key must have the corresponding value. `matchLabels`, often with a single key (e.g., `app=example-thing`), is usually sufficient for a selector.

In Example 4-5, we can see a match object that has both the label `colour=purple` and the label `shape=square`.

Example 4-5. `matchLabels` example

```
matchLabels:
  colour: purple
  shape: square
```

`matchExpressions` is more powerful but more complicated. It contains a list of `Label SelectorRequirements`. All requirements must be true in order for an object to match. Table 4-4 shows all the required fields for a `matchExpressions`.

Table 4-4. LabelSelectorRequirement fields

Field	Description
key	The label key this requirement compares against.
operator	One of Exists, DoesNotExist, In, NotIn. Exists: Matches an object if there is a label with the key, regardless of the value. NotExists: Matches an object if there is no label with the key. In: Matches an object if there is a label with the key, and the value is one of the provided values. NotIn: Matches an object if there is no label with the key, *or* the key's value is not one of the provided values.
values	A list of string values for the key in question. It must be empty when the operator is In or NotIn. It may not be empty when the operator is Exists or NotExists.

Let's look at two brief examples of matchExpressions.

The matchExpressions equivalent of our prior matchLabels example is shown in Example 4-6.

Example 4-6. matchExpressions example 1

```
matchExpressions:
  - key: colour
    operator: In
    values:
      - purple
  - key: shape
    operator: In
    values:
      - square
```

matchExpressions in Example 4-7, will match objects with a color not equal to red, orange, or yellow, and with a shape label.

Example 4-7. matchExpressions example 2

```
matchExpressions:
  - key: colour
    operator: NotIn
    values:
      - red
      - orange
      - yellow
  - key: shape
    operator: Exists
```

Now that we have labels covered, we can discuss rules. Rules will enforce our network policies after a match has been identified.

Rules

`NetworkPolicy` objects contain distinct ingress and egress configuration sections, which contain a list of ingress rules and egress rules, respectively. `NetworkPolicy` rules act as exceptions, or an "allow list," to the default block caused by selecting pods in a policy. Rules cannot block access; they can only add access. If multiple `NetworkPolicy` objects select a pod, all rules in each of those `NetworkPolicy` objects apply. It may make sense to use multiple `NetworkPolicy` objects for the same set of pods (for example, declaring application allowances in one policy and infrastructure allowances like telemetry exporting in another). However, keep in mind that they do not *need* to be separate `NetworkPolicy` objects, and with too many `NetworkPolicy` objects it can become hard to reason.

To support health checks and liveness checks from the Kubelet, the CNI plugin must always allow traffic from a pod's node.

It is possible to abuse labels if an attacker has access to the node (even without admin privileges). Attackers can spoof a node's IP and deliver packets with the node's IP address as the source.

Ingress rules and egress rules are discrete types in the `NetworkPolicy` API (`NetworkPolicyIngressRule` and `NetworkPolicyEgressRule`). However, they are functionally structured the same way. Each `NetworkPolicyIngressRule`/`NetworkPolicyEgressRule` contains a list of ports and a list of `NetworkPolicyPeers`.

A `NetworkPolicyPeer` has four ways for rules to refer to networked entities: `ipBlock`, `namespaceSelector`, `podSelector`, and a combination.

`ipBlock` is useful for allowing traffic to and from external systems. It can be used only on its own in a rule, without a `namespaceSelector` or `podSelector`. `ipBlock` contains a CIDR and an optional `except` CIDR. The `except` CIDR will exclude a sub-CIDR (it must be within the CIDR range). In Example 4-8, we allow traffic from all IP addresses in the range `10.0.0.0` to `10.0.0.255`, excluding `10.0.0.10`. Example 4-9 allows traffic from all pods in any namespace labeled `group:x`.

Example 4-8. Allow traffic example 1

```
from:
  - ipBlock:
    - cidr: "10.0.0.0/24"
    - except: "10.0.0.10"
```

Example 4-9. Allow traffic example 2

```
#
from:
  - namespaceSelector:
    - matchLabels:
      group: x
```

In Example 4-10, we allow traffic from all pods in any namespace labeled `service:`
`x..` `podSelector` behaves like the `spec.podSelector` field that we discussed earlier.
If there is no `namespaceSelector`, it selects pods in the same namespace as the
`NetworkPolicy`.

Example 4-10. Allow traffic example 3

```
from:
  - podSelector:
    - matchLabels:
      service: y
```

If we specify a `namespaceSelector` and a `podSelector`, the rule selects all pods with
the specified pod label in all namespaces with the specified namespace label. It is
common and highly recommended by security experts to keep the scope of a namespace small; typical namespace scopes are per an app or service group or team. There
is a fourth option shown in Example 4-11 with a namespace *and* pod selector. This
selector behaves like an AND condition for the namespace and pod selector: pods
must have the matching label and be in a namespace with the matching label.

Example 4-11. Allow traffic example 4

```
from:
  - namespaceSelector:
    - matchLabels:
      group: monitoring
    podSelector:
    - matchLabels:
      service: logscraper
```

Be aware this is a distinct type in the API, although the YAML syntax looks *extremely*
similar. As `to` and `from` sections can have multiple selectors, a single character can
make the difference between an `AND` and an `OR`, so be careful when writing policies.

Our earlier security warning about API access also applies here. If a user can customize the labels on their namespace, they can make a `NetworkPolicy` in another namespace apply to their namespace in a way not intended. In our previous selector
example, if a user can set the label `group:` `monitoring` on an arbitrary namespace,

they can potentially send or receive traffic that they are not supposed to. If the Net
workPolicy in question has only a namespace selector, then that namespace label is
sufficient to match the policy. If there is also a pod label in the NetworkPolicy selector, the user will need to set pod labels to match the policy selection. However, in a
typical setup, the service owners will grant create/update permissions on pods in that
service's namespace (directly on the pod resource or indirectly via a resource like a
deployment, which can define pods).

A typical NetworkPolicy could look something like this:

```
apiVersion: networking.k8s.io/v1
kind: NetworkPolicy
metadata:
  name: store-api
  namespace: store
spec:
  podSelector:
    matchLabels: {}
  policyTypes:
  - Ingress
  - Egress
  ingress:
  - from:
    - namespaceSelector:
        matchLabels:
          app: frontend
      podSelector:
        matchLabels:
          app: frontend
    ports:
    - protocol: TCP
      port: 8080
  egress:
  - to:
    - namespaceSelector:
        matchLabels:
          app: downstream-1
      podSelector:
        matchLabels:
          app: downstream-1
    - namespaceSelector:
        matchLabels:
          app: downstream-2
      podSelector:
        matchLabels:
          app: downstream-2
    ports:
    - protocol: TCP
      port: 8080
```

In this example, all pods in our store namespace can receive connections only from pods labeled app: frontend in a namespace labeled app: frontend. Those pods can only create connections to pods in namespaces where the pod and namespace both have app: downstream-1 or app: downstream-2. In each of these cases, only traffic to port 8080 is allowed. Finally, remember that this policy does not guarantee a matching policy for downstream-1 or downstream-2 (see the next example). Accepting these connections does not preclude other policies against pods in our namespace, adding additional exceptions:

```
apiVersion: networking.k8s.io/v1
kind: NetworkPolicy
metadata:
  name: store-to-downstream-1
  namespace: downstream-1
spec:
  podSelector:
    app: downstream-1
  policyTypes:
  - Ingress
  ingress:
  - from:
    - namespaceSelector:
        matchLabels:
          app: store
    ports:
    - protocol: TCP
      port: 8080
```

Although they are a "stable" resource (i.e., part of the networking/v1 API), we believe NetworkPolicy objects are still an early version of network security in Kubernetes. The user experience of configuring NetworkPolicy objects is somewhat rough, and the default open behavior is highly undesirable. There is currently a working group to discuss the future of NetworkPolicy and what a v2 API would contain.

CNIs and those who deploy them use labels and selectors to determine which pods are subject to network restrictions. As we have seen in many of the previous examples, they are an essential part of the Kubernetes API, and developers and administrators alike must have a thorough knowledge of how to use them.

NetworkPolicy objects are an important tool in the cluster administrator's toolbox. They are the only tool available for controlling internal cluster traffic, native to the Kubernetes API. We discuss service meshes, which will add further tools for admins to secure and control workloads, in "Service Meshes" on page 229.

Next we will discuss another important tool so administrators can understand how it works inside the cluster: the Domain Name System (DNS).

DNS

DNS is a critical piece of infrastructure for any network. In Kubernetes, this is no different, so a brief overview is warranted. In the following "Services" sections, we will see how much they depend on DNS and why a Kubernetes distribution cannot declare that it is a conforming Kubernetes distribution without providing a DNS service that follows the specification. But first, let's review how DNS works inside Kubernetes.

 We will not outline the entire specification in this book. If readers are interested in reading more about it, it is available on GitHub (*https://oreil.ly/tiB8V*).

KubeDNS was used in earlier versions of Kubernetes. KubeDNS had several containers within a single pod: kube-dns, dnsmasq, and sidecar. The kube-dns container watches the Kubernetes API and serves DNS records based on the Kubernetes DNS specification, dnsmasq provides caching and stub domain support, and sidecar provides metrics and health checks. Versions of Kubernetes after 1.13 now use the separate component CoreDNS.

There are several differences between CoreDNS and KubeDNS:

- For simplicity, CoreDNS runs as a single container.
- CoreDNS is a Go process that replicates and enhances the functionality of Kube-DNS.
- CoreDNS is designed to be a general-purpose DNS server that is backward compatible with Kubernetes, and its extendable plugins can do more than is provided in the Kubernetes DNS specification.

Figure 4-10 shows the components of CoreDNS. It runs a deployment with a default replica of 2, and for it to run, CoreDNS needs access to the API server, a ConfigMap to hold its Corefile, a service to make DNS available to the cluster, and a deployment to launch and manage its pods. All of this also runs in the kube-system namespace along with other critical components in the cluster.

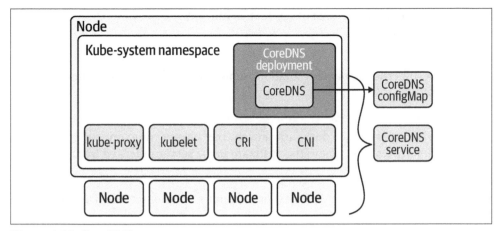

Figure 4-10. CoreDNS components

Like most configuration options, how the pod does DNS queries is in the pod spec under the dnsPolicy attribute.

Outlined in Example 4-12, the pod spec has ClusterFirstWithHostNet as dnsPolicy.

Example 4-12. Pod spec with DNS configuration

```
apiVersion: v1
kind: Pod
metadata:
  name: busybox
  namespace: default
spec:
  containers:
  - image: busybox:1.28
    command:
      - sleep
      - "3600"
    imagePullPolicy: IfNotPresent
    name: busybox
  restartPolicy: Always
  hostNetwork: true
  dnsPolicy: ClusterFirstWithHostNet
```

There are four options for `dnsPolicy` that significantly affect how DNS resolutions work inside a pod:

Default
> The pod inherits the name resolution configuration from the node that the pods run on.

ClusterFirst
> Any DNS query that does not match the cluster domain suffix, such as www.kubernetes.io, is sent to the upstream name server inherited from the node.

ClusterFirstWithHostNet
> For pods running with `hostNetwork`, admins should set the DNS policy to `ClusterFirstWithHostNet`.

None
> All DNS settings use the `dnsConfig` field in the pod spec.

If `none`, developers will have to specify name servers in the pod spec. `nameservers:` is a list of IP addresses that the pod will use as DNS servers. There can be at most three IP addresses specified. `searches:` is a list of DNS search domains for hostname lookup in the pod. Kubernetes allows for at most six search domains. The following is such an example spec:

```
apiVersion: v1
kind: Pod
metadata:
  namespace: default
  name: busybox
spec:
  containers:
  - image: busybox:1.28
    command:
      - sleep
      - "3600"
    imagePullPolicy: IfNotPresent
    name: busybox
  dnsPolicy: "None"
  dnsConfig:
    nameservers:
      - 1.1.1.1
    searches:
      - ns1.svc.cluster-domain.example
      - my.dns.search.suffix
```

Others are in the `options` field, which is a list of objects where each object may have a `name` property and a `value` property (optional).

All of these generated properties merge with `resolv.conf` from the DNS policy. Regular query options have CoreDNS going through the following search path:

```
<service>.default.svc.cluster.local
                ↓
       svc.cluster.local
                ↓
         cluster.local
                ↓
     The host search path
```

The host search path comes from the pod DNS policy or CoreDNS policy.

Querying a DNS record in Kubernetes can result in many requests and increase latency in applications waiting on DNS requests to be answered. CoreDNS has a solution for this called Autopath. Autopath allows for server-side search path completion. It short circuits the client's search path resolution by stripping the cluster search domain and performing the lookups on the CoreDNS server; when it finds an answer, it stores the result as a CNAME and returns with one query instead of five.

Using Autopath does increase the memory usage on CoreDNS, however. Make sure to scale the CoreDNS replica's memory with the cluster's size. Make sure to set the requests for memory and CPU for the CoreDNS pods appropriately. To monitor CoreDNS, it exports several metrics it exposes, listed here:

coredns build info
    Info about CoreDNS itself

dns request count total
    Total query count

dns request duration seconds
    Duration to process each query

dns request size bytes
    The size of the request in bytes

coredns plugin enabled
    Indicates whether a plugin is enabled on per server and zone basis

By combining the pod metrics along with CoreDNS metrics, plugin administrators will ensure that CoreDNS stays healthy and running inside your cluster.

This is only a brief overview of the metrics available. The entire list is available (*https://oreil.ly/gm8IO*).

Autopath and other metrics are enabled via plugins. This allows CoreDNS to focus on its one task, DNS, but still be extensible through the plugin framework, much like the CNI pattern. In Table 4-5, we see a list of the plugins currently available. Being an open source project, anyone can contribute a plugin. There are several cloud-specific ones like router53 that enable serving zone data from AWS route53 service.

Table 4-5. CoreDNS plugins

Name	Description
auto	Enables serving zone data from an RFC 1035-style master file, which is automatically picked up from disk.
autopath	Allows for server-side search path completion. autopath [ZONE...] RESOLV-CONF.
bind	Overrides the host to which the server should bind.
cache	Enables a frontend cache. cache [TTL] [ZONES...].
chaos	Allows for responding to TXT queries in the CH class.
debug	Disables the automatic recovery upon a crash so that you'll get a nice stack trace. text2pcap.
dnssec	Enables on-the-fly DNSSEC signing of served data.
dnstap	Enables logging to dnstap. *http://dnstap.info* golang: go get -u -v github.com/dnstap/golang-dnstap/dnstap.
erratic	A plugin useful for testing client behavior.
errors	Enables error logging.
etcd	Enables reading zone data from an etcd version 3 instance.
federation	Enables federated queries to be resolved via the kubernetes plugin.
file	Enables serving zone data from an RFC 1035-style master file.
forward	Facilitates proxying DNS messages to upstream resolvers.
health	Enables a health check endpoint.
host	Enables serving zone data from a /etc/hosts style file.
kubernetes	Enables the reading zone data from a Kubernetes cluster.
loadbalancer	Randomizes the order of A, AAAA, and MX records.
log enables	Queries logging to standard output.
loop detect	Simple forwarding loops and halt the server.
metadata	Enables a metadata collector.
metrics	Enables Prometheus metrics.
nsid	Adds an identifier of this server to each reply. RFC 5001.
pprof	Publishes runtime profiling data at endpoints under /debug/pprof.
proxy	Facilitates both a basic reverse proxy and a robust load balancer.
reload	Allows automatic reload of a changed Corefile. Graceful reload.
rewrite	Performs internal message rewriting. rewrite name foo.example.com foo.default.svc.cluster.local.
root	Simply specifies the root of where to find zone files.
router53	Enables serving zone data from AWS route53.
secondary	Enables serving a zone retrieved from a primary server.
template	Dynamic responses based on the incoming query.

Name	Description
tls	Configures the server certificates for TLS and gRPC servers.
trace	Enables OpenTracing-based tracing of DNS requests.
whoami	Returns resolver's local IP address, port, and transport.

> A comprehensive list of CoreDNS plugins is available (*https://oreil.ly/rlXRO*).

CoreDNS is exceptionally configurable and compatible with the Kubernetes model. We have only scratched the surface of what CoreDNS is capable of; if you would like to learn more about CoreDNS, we highly recommend reading *Learning CoreDNS* (*https://oreil.ly/O7Xuh*) by John Belamaric Cricket Liu (O'Reilly).

CoreDNS allows pods to figure out the IP addresses to use to reach applications and servers internal and external to the cluster. In our next section, we will discuss more in depth how IPv4 and 6 are managed in a cluster.

IPv4/IPv6 Dual Stack

Kubernetes has still-evolving support for running in IPv4/IPv6 "dual-stack" mode, which allows a cluster to use both IPv4 and IPv6 addresses. Kubernetes has existing stable support for running clusters in IPv6-only mode; however, running in IPv6-only mode is a barrier to communicating with clients and hosts that support only IPv4. The dual-stack mode is a critical bridge to allowing IPv6 adoption. We will attempt to describe the current state of dual-stack networking in Kubernetes as of Kubernetes 1.20, but be aware that it is liable to change substantially in subsequent releases. The full Kubernetes enhancement proposal (KEP) for dual-stack support is on GitHub (*https://oreil.ly/T83u5*).

> In Kubernetes, a feature is "alpha" if the design is not finalized, if the scalability/test coverage/reliability is insufficient, or if it merely has not proven itself sufficiently in the real world yet. Kubernetes Enhancement Proposals (KEPs) set the bar for an individual feature to graduate to beta and then be stable. Like all alpha features, Kubernetes disables dual-stack support by default, and the feature must be explicitly enabled.

IPv4/IPv6 features enable the following features for pod networking:

- A single IPv4 and IPv6 address per pod
- IPv4 and IPv6 services
- Pod cluster egress routing via IPv4 and IPv6 interfaces

Being an alpha feature, administrators must enable IPv4/IPv6 dual-stack; to do so, the `IPv6DualStack` feature gate for the network components must be configured for your cluster. Here is a list of those dual-stack cluster network options:

`kube-apiserver`
- `feature-gates="IPv6DualStack=true"`
- `service-cluster-ip-range=<IPv4 CIDR>,<IPv6 CIDR>`

`kube-controller-manager`
- `feature-gates="IPv6DualStack=true"`
- `cluster-cidr=<IPv4 CIDR>,<IPv6 CIDR>`
- `service-cluster-ip-range=<IPv4 CIDR>,<IPv6 CIDR>`
- `node-cidr-mask-size-ipv4|--node-cidr-mask-size-ipv6` defaults to /24 for IPv4 and /64 for IPv6

`kubelet`
- `feature-gates="IPv6DualStack=true"`

`kube-proxy`
- `cluster-cidr=<IPv4 CIDR>,<IPv6 CIDR>`
- `feature-gates="IPv6DualStack=true"`

When IPv4/IPv6 is on in a cluster, services now have an extra field in which developers can choose the `ipFamilyPolicy` to deploy for their application:

`SingleStack`
: Single-stack service. The control plane allocates a cluster IP for the service, using the first configured service cluster IP range.

`PreferDualStack`
: Used only if the cluster has dual stack enabled. This setting will use the same behavior as `SingleStack`.

`RequireDualStack`
: Allocates service cluster IP addresses from both IPv4 and IPv6 address ranges.

`ipFamilies`

> An array that defines which IP family to use for a single stack or defines the order of IP families for dual stack; you can choose the address families by setting this field on the service. The allowed values are `["IPv4"]`, `["IPv6"]`, and `["IPv4","IPv6"]` (dual stack).

 Starting in 1.21, IPv4/IPv6 dual stack defaults to enabled.

Here is an example service manifest that has PreferDualStack set to PreferDualStack:

```
apiVersion: v1
kind: Service
metadata:
  name: my-service
  labels:
    app: MyApp
spec:
  ipFamilyPolicy: PreferDualStack
  selector:
    app: MyApp
  ports:
    - protocol: TCP
      port: 80
```

Conclusion

The Kubernetes networking model is the basis for how networking is designed to work inside a cluster. The CNI running on the nodes implements the principles set forth in the Kubernetes network model. The model does not define network security; the extensibility of Kubernetes allows the CNI to implement network security through network policies.

CNI, DNS, and network security are essential parts of the cluster network; they bridge the gap between Linux networking, covered in Chapter 2, and container and Kubernetes networking, covered in Chapters 3 and 5, respectively.

Choosing the right CNI requires an evaluation from both the developers' and administrators' perspectives. Requirements need to be laid out and CNIs tested. It is our opinion that a cluster is not complete without a discussion about network security and CNI that supports it.

DNS is essential; a complete setup and a smooth-running network require network and cluster administrators to be proficient at scaling CoreDNS in their clusters. An exceptional number of Kubernetes issues stem from DNS and the misconfiguration of CoreDNS.

The information in this chapter will be important when discussing cloud networking in Chapter 6 and what options administrators have when designing and deploying their production cluster networks.

In our next chapter, we will dive into how Kubernetes uses all of this to power its abstractions.

Kubernetes Networking Abstractions

Previously, we covered a swath of networking fundamentals and how traffic in Kubernetes gets from A to B. In this chapter, we will discuss networking abstractions in Kubernetes, primarily service discovery and load balancing. Most notably, this is the chapter on services and ingresses. Both resources are notoriously complex, due to the large number of options, as they attempt to solve numerous use cases. They are the most visible part of the Kubernetes network stack, as they define basic network characteristics of workloads on Kubernetes. This is where developers interact with the networking stack for their applications deployed on Kubernetes.

This chapter will cover fundamental examples of Kubernetes networking abstractions and the details on\f how they work. To follow along, you will need the following tools:

- Docker
- KIND
- Linkerd

You will need to be familiar with the `kubectl exec` and `Docker exec` commands. If you are not, our code repo will have any and all the commands we discuss, so don't worry too much. We will also make use of `ip` and `netns` from Chapters 2 and 3. Note that most of these tools are for debugging and showing implementation details; you will not necessarily need them during normal operations.

Docker, KIND, and Linkerd installs are available on their respective sites, and we've provided more information in the book's code repository as well.

kubectl is a key tool in this chapter's examples, and it's the standard for operators to interact with clusters and their networks. You should be familiar with the kubectl create, apply, get, delete, and exec commands. Learn more in the Kubernetes documentation (*https://oreil.ly/H8bTU*) or run kubectl [command] --help.

This chapter will explore these Kubernetes networking abstractions:

- StatefulSets
- Endpoints
  - Endpoint slices
- Services
  - NodePort
  - Cluster
  - Headless
  - External
  - LoadBalancer
- Ingress
  - Ingress controller
  - Ingress rules
- Service meshes
  - Linkerd

To explore these abstractions, we will deploy the examples to our Kubernetes cluster with the following steps:

1. Deploy a KIND cluster with ingress enabled.
2. Explore StatefulSets.
3. Deploy Kubernetes services.
4. Deploy an ingress controller.
5. Deploy a Linkerd service mesh.

These abstractions are at the heart of what the Kubernetes API provides to developers and administrators to programmatically control the flow of communications into and out of the cluster. Understanding and mastering how to deploy these abstractions is crucial for the success of any workload inside a cluster. After working through these examples, you will understand which abstractions to use in certain situations for your applications.

With the KIND cluster configuration YAML, we can use KIND to create that cluster with the command in the next section. If this is the first time running it, it will take some time to download all the Docker images for the working and control plane Docker images.

 The following examples assume that you still have the local KIND cluster running from the previous chapter, along with the Golang web server and the dnsutils images for testing.

StatefulSets

StatefulSets are a workload abstraction in Kubernetes to manage pods like you would a deployment. Unlike a deployment, StatefulSets add the following features for applications that require them:

- Stable, unique network identifiers
- Stable, persistent storage
- Ordered, graceful deployment and scaling
- Ordered, automated rolling updates

The deployment resource is better suited for applications that do not have these requirements (for example, a service that stores data in an external database).

Our database for the Golang minimal web server uses a StatefulSet. The database has a service, a ConfigMap for the Postgres username, a password, a test database name, and a StatefulSet for the containers running Postgres.

Let's deploy it now:

```
kubectl apply -f database.yaml
service/postgres created
configmap/postgres-config created
statefulset.apps/postgres created
```

Let's examine the DNS and network ramifications of using a StatefulSet.

To test DNS inside the cluster, we can use the dnsutils image; this image is gcr .io/ kubernetes-e2e-test-images/dnsutils:1.3 and is used for Kubernetes testing:

```
kubectl apply -f dnsutils.yaml

pod/dnsutils created

kubectl get pods
NAME        READY   STATUS    RESTARTS   AGE
dnsutils    1/1     Running   0          9s
```

With the replica configured with two pods, we see the StatefulSet deploy `postgres-0` and `postgres-1`, in that order, a feature of StatefulSets with IP address 10.244.1.3 and 10.244.2.3, respectively:

```
kubectl get pods -o wide
NAME        READY  STATUS   RESTARTS  AGE  IP          NODE
dnsutils    1/1    Running  0         15m  10.244.3.2  kind-worker3
postgres-0  1/1    Running  0         15m  10.244.1.3  kind-worker2
postgres-1  1/1    Running  0         14m  10.244.2.3  kind-worker
```

Here is the name of our headless service, Postgres, that the client can use for queries to return the endpoint IP addresses:

```
kubectl get svc postgres
NAME      TYPE       CLUSTER-IP   EXTERNAL-IP  PORT(S)   AGE
postgres  ClusterIP               <none>       5432/TCP  23m
```

Using our `dnsutils` image, we can see that the DNS names for the StatefulSets will return those IP addresses along with the cluster IP address of the Postgres service:

```
kubectl exec dnsutils -- host postgres-0.postgres.default.svc.cluster.local.
postgres-0.postgres.default.svc.cluster.local has address 10.244.1.3

kubectl exec dnsutils -- host postgres-1.postgres.default.svc.cluster.local.
postgres-1.postgres.default.svc.cluster.local has address 10.244.2.3

kubectl exec dnsutils -- host postgres
postgres.default.svc.cluster.local has address 10.105.214.153
```

StatefulSets attempt to mimic a fixed group of persistent machines. As a generic solution for stateful workloads, specific behavior may be frustrating in specific use cases.

A common problem that users encounter is an update requiring manual intervention to fix when using `.spec .updateStrategy.type: RollingUpdate`, and `.spec.podMa nagementPolicy: OrderedReady`, both of which are default settings. With these settings, a user must manually intervene if an updated pod never becomes ready.

Also, StatefulSets require a service, preferably headless, to be responsible for the network identity of the pods, and end users are responsible for creating this service.

Statefulsets have many configuration options, and many third-party alternatives exist (both generic stateful workload controllers and software-specific workload controllers).

StatefulSets offer functionality for a specific use case in Kubernetes. They should not be used for everyday application deployments. Later in this section, we will discuss more appropriate networking abstractions for run-of-the-mill deployments.

In our next section, we will explore endpoints and endpoint slices, the backbone of Kubernetes services.

Endpoints

Endpoints help identify what pods are running for the service it powers. Endpoints are created and managed by services. We will discuss services on their own later, to avoid covering too many new things at once. For now, let's just say that a service contains a standard label selector (introduced in Chapter 4), which defines which pods are in the endpoints.

In Figure 5-1, we can see traffic being directed to an endpoint on node 2, pod 5.

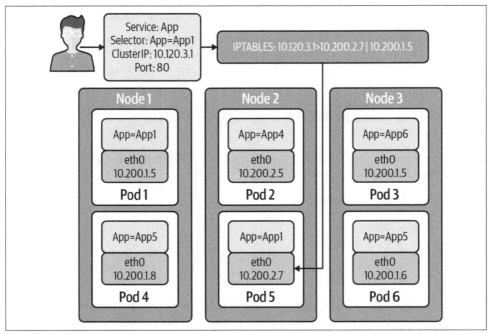

Figure 5-1. Endpoints in a service

Let's discuss how this endpoint is created and maintained in the cluster.

Each endpoint contains a list of ports (which apply to all pods) and two lists of addresses: ready and unready:

```
apiVersion: v1
kind: Endpoints
metadata:
  labels:
    name: demo-endpoints
subsets:
- addresses:
  - ip: 10.0.0.1
- notReadyAddresses:
  - ip: 10.0.0.2
```

```
    ports:
    - port: 8080
      protocol: TCP
```

Addresses are listed in `.addresses` if they are passing pod readiness checks. Addresses are listed in `.notReadyAddresses` if they are not. This makes endpoints a *service discovery* tool, where you can watch an `Endpoints` object to see the health and addresses of all pods:

```
kubectl get endpoints clusterip-service
NAME                   ENDPOINTS
clusterip-service      10.244.1.5:8080,10.244.2.7:8080,10.244.2.8:8080 + 1 more...
```

We can get a better view of all the addresses with `kubectl describe`:

```
kubectl describe endpoints clusterip-service
Name:          clusterip-service
Namespace:     default
Labels:        app=app
Annotations:   endpoints.kubernetes.io/last-change-trigger-time:
2021-01-30T18:51:36Z
Subsets:
  Addresses:           10.244.1.5,10.244.2.7,10.244.2.8,10.244.3.9
  NotReadyAddresses:   <none>
  Ports:
    Name      Port  Protocol
    ----      ----  --------
    <unset>   8080  TCP


Events:
  Type     Reason          Age    From          Message
  ----     ------          ----   ----          -------
```

Let's remove the app label and see how Kubernetes responds. In a separate terminal, run this command. This will allow us to see changes to the pods in real time:

```
kubectl get pods -w
```

In another separate terminal, let's do the same thing with endpoints:

```
kubectl get endpoints -w
```

We now need to get a pod name to remove from the `Endpoints` object:

```
kubectl get pods -l app=app -o wide
NAME                     READY  STATUS   RESTARTS  AGE  IP           NODE
app-5586fc9d77-7frts     1/1    Running  0         19m  10.244.1.5   kind-worker2
app-5586fc9d77-mxhgw     1/1    Running  0         19m  10.244.3.9   kind-worker3
app-5586fc9d77-qpxwk     1/1    Running  0         20m  10.244.2.7   kind-worker
app-5586fc9d77-tpz8q     1/1    Running  0         19m  10.244.2.8   kind-worker
```

With `kubectl label`, we can alter the pod's `app-5586fc9d77-7frts` app=app label:

```
kubectl label pod app-5586fc9d77-7frts app=nope --overwrite
pod/app-5586fc9d77-7frts labeled
```

Both watch commands on endpoints and pods will see some changes for the same reason: removal of the label on the pod. The endpoint controller will notice a change to the pods with the label `app=app` and so did the deployment controller. So Kubernetes did what Kubernetes does: it made the real state reflect the desired state:

```
kubectl get pods -w
NAME                      READY   STATUS             RESTARTS   AGE
app-5586fc9d77-7frts      1/1     Running            0          21m
app-5586fc9d77-mxhgw      1/1     Running            0          21m
app-5586fc9d77-qpxwk      1/1     Running            0          22m
app-5586fc9d77-tpz8q      1/1     Running            0          21m
dnsutils                  1/1     Running            3          3h1m
postgres-0                1/1     Running            0          3h
postgres-1                1/1     Running            0          3h
app-5586fc9d77-7frts      1/1     Running            0          22m
app-5586fc9d77-7frts      1/1     Running            0          22m
app-5586fc9d77-6dcg2      0/1     Pending            0          0s
app-5586fc9d77-6dcg2      0/1     Pending            0          0s
app-5586fc9d77-6dcg2      0/1     ContainerCreating  0          0s
app-5586fc9d77-6dcg2      0/1     Running            0          2s
app-5586fc9d77-6dcg2      1/1     Running            0          7s
```

The deployment has four pods, but our relabeled pod still exists: `app-5586fc9d77-7frts`:

```
kubectl get pods
NAME                      READY   STATUS     RESTARTS   AGE
app-5586fc9d77-6dcg2      1/1     Running    0          4m51s
app-5586fc9d77-7frts      1/1     Running    0          27m
app-5586fc9d77-mxhgw      1/1     Running    0          27m
app-5586fc9d77-qpxwk      1/1     Running    0          28m
app-5586fc9d77-tpz8q      1/1     Running    0          27m
dnsutils                  1/1     Running    3          3h6m
postgres-0                1/1     Running    0          3h6m
postgres-1                1/1     Running    0          3h6m
```

The pod `app-5586fc9d77-6dcg2` now is part of the deployment and endpoint object with IP address `10.244.1.6`:

```
kubectl get pods app-5586fc9d77-6dcg2 -o wide
NAME                    READY   STATUS    RESTARTS   AGE    IP           NODE
app-5586fc9d77-6dcg2    1/1     Running   0          3m6s   10.244.1.6   kind-worker2
```

As always, we can see the full picture of details with `kubectl describe`:

```
kubectl describe endpoints clusterip-service
Name:          clusterip-service
Namespace:     default
Labels:        app=app
Annotations:   endpoints.kubernetes.io/last-change-trigger-time:
2021-01-30T19:14:23Z
Subsets:
  Addresses:             10.244.1.6,10.244.2.7,10.244.2.8,10.244.3.9
```

```
NotReadyAddresses:   <none>
Ports:
  Name      Port  Protocol
  ----      ----  --------
  <unset>   8080  TCP

Events:
  Type      Reason                Age   From            Message
  ----      ------                ----  ----            -------
```

For large deployments, that endpoint object can become very large, so much so that it can actually slow down changes in the cluster. To solve that issue, the Kubernetes maintainers have come up with endpoint slices.

Endpoint Slices

You may be asking, how are they different from endpoints? This is where we *really* start to get into the weeds of Kubernetes networking.

In a typical cluster, Kubernetes runs kube-proxy on every node. kube-proxy is responsible for the per-node portions of making services work, by handling routing and *outbound* load balancing to all the pods in a service. To do that, kube-proxy watches all endpoints in the cluster so it knows all applicable pods that all services should route to.

Now, imagine we have a *big* cluster, with thousands of nodes, and tens of thousands of pods. That means thousands of kube-proxies are watching endpoints. When an address changes in an Endpoints object (say, from a rolling update, scale up, eviction, health-check failure, or any number of reasons), the updated Endpoints object is pushed to all listening kube-proxies. It is made worse by the number of pods, since more pods means larger Endpoints objects, and more frequent changes. This eventually becomes a strain on etcd, the Kubernetes API server, and the network itself. Kubernetes scaling limits are complex and depend on specific criteria, but endpoints watching is a common problem in clusters that have thousands of nodes. Anecdotally, many Kubernetes users consider endpoint watches to be the ultimate bottleneck of cluster size.

This problem is a function of kube-proxy's design and the expectation that any pod should be immediately able to route to any service with no notice. Endpoint slices are an approach that allows kube-proxy's fundamental design to continue, while drastically reducing the watch bottleneck in large clusters where large services are used.

Endpoint slices have similar contents to Endpoints objects but also include an array of endpoints:

```
apiVersion: discovery.k8s.io/v1beta1
kind: EndpointSlice
metadata:
  name: demo-slice-1
  labels:
    kubernetes.io/service-name: demo
addressType: IPv4
ports:
  - name: http
    protocol: TCP
    port: 80
endpoints:
  - addresses:
      - "10.0.0.1"
    conditions:
      ready: true
```

The meaningful difference between endpoints and endpoint slices is not the schema, but how Kubernetes treats them. With "regular" endpoints, a Kubernetes service creates one endpoint for all pods in the service. A service creates *multiple* endpoint slices, each containing a *subset* of pods; Figure 5-2 depicts this subset. The union of all endpoint slices for a service contains all pods in the service. This way, an IP address change (due to a new pod, a deleted pod, or a pod's health changing) will result in a much smaller data transfer to watchers. Because Kubernetes doesn't have a transactional API, the same address may appear temporarily in multiple slices. Any code consuming endpoint slices (such as kube-proxy) must be able to account for this.

The maximum number of addresses in an endpoint slice is set using the --max-endpoints-per-slice kube-controller-manager flag. The current default is 100, and the maximum is 1000. The endpoint slice controller attempts to fill existing endpoint slices before creating new ones, but does not rebalance endpoint slice.

The endpoint slice controller mirrors endpoints to endpoint slice, to allow systems to continue writing endpoints while treating endpoint slice as the source of truth. The exact future of this behavior, and endpoints in general, has not been finalized (however, as a v1 resource, endpoints would be sunset with substantial notice). There are four exceptions that will prevent mirroring:

- There is no corresponding service.
- The corresponding service resource selects pods.
- The Endpoints object has the label endpointslice.kubernetes.io/skip-mirror: true.
- The Endpoints object has the annotation control-plane.alpha.kubernetes .io/leader.

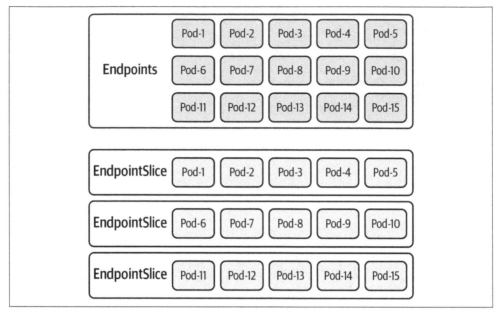

Figure 5-2. Endpoints versus EndpointSlice objects

You can fetch all endpoint slices for a specific service by fetching endpoint slices filtered to the desired name in .metadata.labels."kubernetes.io/service-name".

 Endpoint slices have been in beta state since Kubernetes 1.17. This is still the case in Kubernetes 1.20, the current version at the time of writing. Beta resources typically don't see major changes, and eventually graduate to stable APIs, but that is not guaranteed. If you directly use endpoint slices, be aware that a future Kubernetes release may make a breaking change without much warning, or the behaviors described here may change.

Let's see some endpoints running in the cluster with kubectl get endpointslice:

```
kubectl get endpointslice
NAME                      ADDRESSTYPE   PORTS   ENDPOINTS
clusterip-service-l2n9q   IPv4          8080    10.244.2.7,10.244.2.8,10.244.1.5
+ 1 more...
```

If we want more detail about the endpoint slices `clusterip-service-l2n9q`, we can use `kubectl describe` on it:

```
kubectl describe endpointslice clusterip-service-l2n9q
Name:          clusterip-service-l2n9q
Namespace:     default
Labels:
endpointslice.kubernetes.io/managed-by=endpointslice-controller.k8s.io
kubernetes.io/service-name=clusterip-service
Annotations:   endpoints.kubernetes.io/last-change-trigger-time:
2021-01-30T18:51:36Z
AddressType:   IPv4
Ports:
  Name      Port  Protocol
  ----      ----  --------
  <unset>   8080  TCP
Endpoints:
  - Addresses:  10.244.2.7
    Conditions:
      Ready:    true
    Hostname:   <unset>
    TargetRef:  Pod/app-5586fc9d77-qpxwk
    Topology:   kubernetes.io/hostname=kind-worker
  - Addresses:  10.244.2.8
    Conditions:
      Ready:    true
    Hostname:   <unset>
    TargetRef:  Pod/app-5586fc9d77-tpz8q
    Topology:   kubernetes.io/hostname=kind-worker
  - Addresses:  10.244.1.5
    Conditions:
      Ready:    true
    Hostname:   <unset>
    TargetRef:  Pod/app-5586fc9d77-7frts
    Topology:   kubernetes.io/hostname=kind-worker2
  - Addresses:  10.244.3.9
    Conditions:
      Ready:    true
    Hostname:   <unset>
    TargetRef:  Pod/app-5586fc9d77-mxhgw
    Topology:   kubernetes.io/hostname=kind-worker3
Events:         <none>
```

In the output, we see the pod powering the endpoint slice from `TargetRef`. The `Top ology` information gives us the hostname of the worker node that the pod is deployed to. Most importantly, the `Addresses` returns the IP address of the endpoint object.

Endpoints and endpoint slices are important to understand because they identify the pods responsible for the services, no matter the type deployed. Later in the chapter, we'll review how to use endpoints and labels for troubleshooting. Next, we will investigate all the Kubernetes service types.

Kubernetes Services

A service in Kubernetes is a load balancing abstraction within a cluster. There are four types of services, specified by the `.spec.Type` field. Each type offers a different form of load balancing or discovery, which we will cover individually. The four types are: ClusterIP, NodePort, LoadBalancer, and ExternalName.

Services use a standard pod selector to match pods. The service includes all matching pods. Services create an endpoint (or endpoint slice) to handle pod discovery:

```
apiVersion: v1
kind: Service
metadata:
  name: demo-service
spec:
  selector:
    app: demo
```

We will use the Golang minimal web server for all the service examples. We have added functionality to the application to display the host and pod IP addresses in the REST request.

Figure 5-3 outlines our pod networking status as a single pod in a cluster. The networking objects we are about to explore will expose our app pods outside the cluster in some instances and in others allow us to scale our application to meet demand. Recall from Chapters 3 and 4 that containers running inside pods share a network namespace. In addition, there is also a pause container that is created for each pod. The pause container manages the namespaces for the pod.

 The pause container is the parent container for all running containers in the pod. It holds and shares all the namespaces for the pod. You can read more about the pause container in Ian Lewis' blog post (*https://oreil.ly/n51eq*).

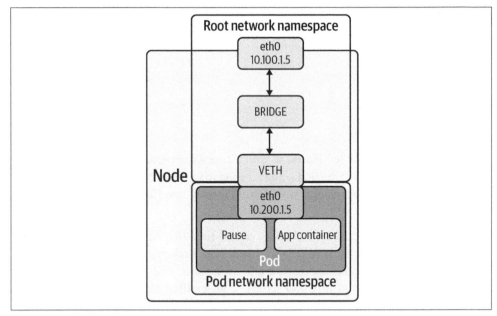

Figure 5-3. Pod on host

Before we deploy the services, we must first deploy the web server that the services will be routing traffic to, if we have not already:

```
 kubectl apply -f web.yaml
deployment.apps/app created

kubectl get pods -o wide
NAME                  READY  STATUS   RESTARTS  AGE  IP          NODE
app-9cc7d9df8-ffsm6   1/1    Running  0         49s  10.244.1.4  kind-worker2
dnsutils              1/1    Running  0         49m  10.244.3.2  kind-worker3
postgres-0            1/1    Running  0         48m  10.244.1.3  kind-worker2
postgres-1            1/1    Running  0         48m  10.244.2.3  kind-worker
```

Let's look at each type of service starting with NodePort.

NodePort

A NodePort service provides a simple way for external software, such as a load balancer, to route traffic to the pods. The software only needs to be aware of node IP addresses, and the service's port(s). A NodePort service exposes a fixed port on all nodes, which routes to applicable pods. A NodePort service uses the .spec.ports.[].nodePort field to specify the port to open on all nodes, for the corresponding port on pods:

```
apiVersion: v1
kind: Service
```

```
metadata:
  name: demo-service
spec:
  type: NodePort
  selector:
    app: demo
  ports:
    - port: 80
      targetPort: 80
      nodePort: 30000
```

The nodePort field can be left blank, in which case Kubernetes automatically selects a unique port. The --service-node-port-range flag in kube-controller-manager sets the valid range for ports, 30000–32767. Manually specified ports must be within this range.

Using a NodePort service, external users can connect to the nodeport on any node and be routed to a pod on a node that has a pod backing that service; Figure 5-4 demonstrates this. The service directs traffic to node 3, and iptables rules forward the traffic to node 2 hosting the pod. This is a bit inefficient, as a typical connection will be routed to a pod on another node.

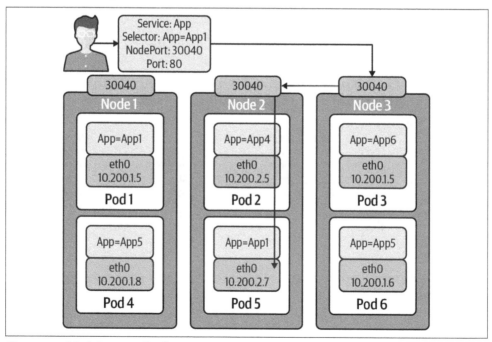

Figure 5-4. NodePort traffic flow

Figure 5-4 requires us to discuss an attribute of services, externalTrafficPolicy. ExternalTrafficPolicy indicates how a service will route external traffic to either node-local or cluster-wide endpoints. Local preserves the client source IP and avoids a second hop for LoadBalancer and NodePort type services but risks potentially imbalanced traffic spreading. Cluster obscures the client source IP and may cause a second hop to another node but should have good overall load-spreading. A Cluster value means that for each worker node, the kube-proxy iptable rules are set up to route the traffic to the pods backing the service anywhere in the cluster, just like we have shown in Figure 5-4.

A Local value means the kube-proxy iptable rules are set up only on the worker nodes with relevant pods running to route the traffic local to the worker node. Using Local also allows application developers to preserve the source IP of the user request. If you set externalTrafficPolicy to the value Local, kube-proxy will proxy requests only to node-local endpoints and will not forward traffic to other nodes. If there are no local endpoints, packets sent to the node are dropped.

Let's scale up the deployment of our web app for some more testing:

```
kubectl scale deployment app --replicas 4
deployment.apps/app scaled

kubectl get pods -l app=app -o wide
NAME                   READY  STATUS    IP          NODE
app-9cc7d9df8-9d5t8    1/1    Running   10.244.2.4  kind-worker
app-9cc7d9df8-ffsm6    1/1    Running   10.244.1.4  kind-worker2
app-9cc7d9df8-srxk5    1/1    Running   10.244.3.4  kind-worker3
app-9cc7d9df8-zrnvb    1/1    Running   10.244.3.5  kind-worker3
```

With four pods running, we will have one pod at every node in the cluster:

```
kubectl get pods -o wide -l app=app
NAME                   READY  STATUS    IP          NODE
app-5586fc9d77-7frts   1/1    Running   10.244.1.5  kind-worker2
app-5586fc9d77-mxhgw   1/1    Running   10.244.3.9  kind-worker3
app-5586fc9d77-qpxwk   1/1    Running   10.244.2.7  kind-worker
app-5586fc9d77-tpz8q   1/1    Running   10.244.2.8  kind-worker
```

Now let's deploy our NodePort service:

```
kubectl apply -f services-nodeport.yaml
service/nodeport-service created

kubectl describe svc nodeport-service
Name:                    nodeport-service
Namespace:               default
Labels:                  <none>
Annotations:             Selector:  app=app
Type:                    NodePort
IP:                      10.101.85.57
Port:                    echo  8080/TCP
TargetPort:              8080/TCP
NodePort:                echo  30040/TCP
```

```
Endpoints:              10.244.1.5:8080,10.244.2.7:8080,10.244.2.8:8080
+ 1 more...
Session Affinity:       None
External Traffic Policy: Cluster
Events:                 <none>
```

To test the NodePort service, we must retrieve the IP address of a worker node:

```
kubectl get nodes -o wide
NAME                STATUS  ROLES    INTERNAL-IP OS-IMAGE
kind-control-plane  Ready   master   172.18.0.5  Ubuntu 19.10
kind-worker         Ready   <none>   172.18.0.3  Ubuntu 19.10
kind-worker2        Ready   <none>   172.18.0.4  Ubuntu 19.10
kind-worker3        Ready   <none>   172.18.0.2  Ubuntu 19.10
```

Communication external to the cluster will use a `NodePort` value of 30040 opened on each worker and the node worker's IP address.

We can see that our pods are reachable on each host in the cluster:

```
kubectl exec -it dnsutils -- wget -q -O-  172.18.0.5:30040/host
NODE: kind-worker2, POD IP:10.244.1.5

kubectl exec -it dnsutils -- wget -q -O-  172.18.0.3:30040/host
NODE: kind-worker, POD IP:10.244.2.8

kubectl exec -it dnsutils -- wget -q -O-  172.18.0.4:30040/host
NODE: kind-worker2, POD IP:10.244.1.5
```

It's important to consider the limitations as well. A NodePort deployment will fail if it cannot allocate the requested port. Also, ports must be tracked across all applications using a NodePort service. Using manually selected ports raises the issue of port collisions (especially when applying a workload to multiple clusters, which may not have the same NodePorts free).

Another downside of using the NodePort service type is that the load balancer or client software must be aware of the node IP addresses. A static configuration (e.g., an operator manually copying node IP addresses) may become too outdated over time (especially on a cloud provider) as IP addresses change or nodes are replaced. A reliable system automatically populates node IP addresses, either by watching which machines have been allocated to the cluster or by listing nodes from the Kubernetes API itself.

NodePorts are the earliest form of services. We will see that other service types use NodePorts as a base structure in their architecture. NodePorts should not be used by themselves, as clients would need to know the IP addresses of hosts and the node for connection requests. We will see how NodePorts are used to enable load balancers later in the chapter when we discuss cloud networks.

Next up is the default type for services, ClusterIP.

ClusterIP

The IP addresses of pods share the life cycle of the pod and thus are not reliable for clients to use for requests. Services help overcome this pod networking design. A ClusterIP service provides an internal load balancer with a single IP address that maps to all matching (and ready) pods.

The service's IP address must be within the CIDR set in `service-cluster-ip-range`, in the API server. You can specify a valid IP address manually, or leave `.spec.clus terIP` unset to have one assigned automatically. The ClusterIP service address is a virtual IP address that is routable only internally.

`kube-proxy` is responsible for making the ClusterIP service address route to all applicable pods. In "normal" configurations, `kube-proxy` performs L4 load balancing, which may not be sufficient. For example, older pods may see more load, due to accumulating more long-lived connections from clients. Or, a few clients making many requests may cause the load to be distributed unevenly.

A particular use case example for ClusterIP is when a workload requires a load balancer within the same cluster.

In Figure 5-5, we can see a ClusterIP service deployed. The service name is App with a selector, or App=App1. There are two pods powering this service. Pod 1 and Pod 5 match the selector for the service.

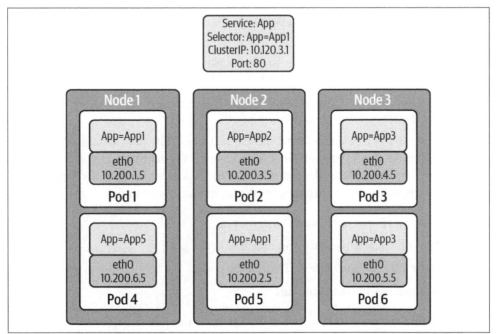

Figure 5-5. Cluster IP example service

Let's dig into an example on the command line with our KIND cluster.

We will deploy a ClusterIP service for use with our Golang web server:

```
kubectl apply -f service-clusterip.yaml
service/clusterip-service created

kubectl describe svc clusterip-service
Name:              clusterip-service
Namespace:         default
Labels:            app=app
Annotations:       Selector:  app=app
Type:              ClusterIP
IP:                10.98.252.195
Port:              <unset>  80/TCP
TargetPort:        8080/TCP
Endpoints:         <none>
Session Affinity:  None
Events:            <none>
```

The ClusterIP service name is resolvable in the network:

```
kubectl exec dnsutils -- host clusterip-service
clusterip-service.default.svc.cluster.local has address 10.98.252.195
```

Now we can reach the host API endpoint with the Cluster IP address 10.98.252.195, with the service name clusterip-service; or directly with the pod IP address 10.244.1.4 and port 8080:

```
kubectl exec dnsutils -- wget -q -O- clusterip-service/host
NODE: kind-worker2, POD IP:10.244.1.4

kubectl exec dnsutils -- wget -q -O- 10.98.252.195/host
NODE: kind-worker2, POD IP:10.244.1.4

kubectl exec dnsutils -- wget -q -O- 10.244.1.4:8080/host
NODE: kind-worker2, POD IP:10.244.1.4
```

The ClusterIP service is the default type for services. With that default status, it is warranted that we should explore what the ClusterIP service abstracted for us. If you recall from Chapters 2 and 3, this list is similar to what is set up with the Docker network, but we now also have iptables for the service across all nodes:

- View the VETH pair and match with the pod.
- View the network namespace and match with the pod.
- Verify the PIDs on the node and match the pods.
- Match services with iptables rules.

To explore this, we need to know what worker node the pod is deployed to, and that is kind-worker2:

```
kubectl get pods -o wide --field-selector spec.nodeName=kind-worker2 -l app=app
NAME               READY   STATUS    RESTARTS   AGE     IP           NODE
app-9cc7d9df8-ffsm6   1/1     Running   0          7m23s   10.244.1.4   kind-worker2
```

 The container IDs and names will be different for you.

Since we are using KIND, we can use docker ps and docker exec to get information out of the running worker node kind-worker-2:

```
docker ps
CONTAINER ID   COMMAND                PORTS                      NAMES
df6df0736958   "/usr/local/bin/entr…"                            kind-worker2
e242f11d2d00   "/usr/local/bin/entr…"                            kind-worker
a76b32f37c0e   "/usr/local/bin/entr…"                            kind-worker3
07ccb63d870f   "/usr/local/bin/entr…"  0.0.0.0:80->80/tcp,       kind-control-plane
                                        0.0.0.0:443->443/tcp,
                                        127.0.0.1:52321->6443/tcp
```

The kind-worker2 container ID is df6df0736958; KIND was *kind* enough to label each container with names, so we can reference each worker node with its name kind-worker2:

Let's see the IP address and route table information of our pod, app-9cc7d9df8-ffsm6:

```
kubectl exec app-9cc7d9df8-ffsm6 ip r
default via 10.244.1.1 dev eth0
10.244.1.0/24 via 10.244.1.1 dev eth0 src 10.244.1.4
10.244.1.1 dev eth0 scope link src 10.244.1.4
```

Our pod's IP address is 10.244.1.4 running on interface eth0@if5 with 10.244.1.1 as its default route. That matches interface 5 on the pod veth45d1f3e8@if5:

```
kubectl exec app-9cc7d9df8-ffsm6 ip a
1: lo: <LOOPBACK,UP,LOWER_UP> mtu 65536 qdisc noqueue state UNKNOWN group default
qlen 1000
    link/loopback 00:00:00:00:00:00 brd 00:00:00:00:00:00
    inet 127.0.0.1/8 scope host lo
       valid_lft forever preferred_lft forever
    inet6 ::1/128 scope host
       valid_lft forever preferred_lft forever
2: tunl0@NONE: <NOARP> mtu 1480 qdisc noop state DOWN
group default qlen 1000
    link/ipip 0.0.0.0 brd 0.0.0.0
3: ip6tnl0@NONE: <NOARP> mtu 1452 qdisc noop state DOWN group default qlen 1000
    link/tunnel6 :: brd ::
5: eth0@if5: <BROADCAST,MULTICAST,UP,LOWER_UP> mtu 1500 qdisc noqueue state UP
group default
    link/ether 3e:57:42:6e:cd:45 brd ff:ff:ff:ff:ff:ff link-netnsid 0
    inet 10.244.1.4/24 brd 10.244.1.255 scope global eth0
       valid_lft forever preferred_lft forever
```

```
inet6 fe80::3c57:42ff:fe6e:cd45/64 scope link
   valid_lft forever preferred_lft forever
```

Let's check the network namespace as well, from the `node ip a` output:

```
docker exec -it kind-worker2 ip a
<trimmerd>
5: veth45d1f3e8@if5: <BROADCAST,MULTICAST,UP,LOWER_UP> mtu 1500 qdisc noqueue
state UP group default
   link/ether 3e:39:16:38:3f:23 brd <>
   link-netns cni-ec37f6e4-a1b5-9bc9-b324-59d612edb4d4
   inet 10.244.1.1/32 brd 10.244.1.1 scope global veth45d1f3e8
      valid_lft forever preferred_lft forever
```

`netns list` confirms that the network namespaces match our pods, interface to the host interface, `cni-ec37f6e4-a1b5-9bc9-b324-59d612edb4d4`:

```
docker exec -it kind-worker2 /usr/sbin/ip netns list
cni-ec37f6e4-a1b5-9bc9-b324-59d612edb4d4 (id: 2)
cni-c18c44cb-6c3e-c48d-b783-e7850d40e01c (id: 1)
```

Let's see what processes run inside that network namespace. For that we will use `docker exec` to run commands inside the node `kind-worker2` hosting the pod and its network namespace:

```
docker exec -it kind-worker2 /usr/sbin/ip netns pid
cni-ec37f6e4-a1b5-9bc9-b324-59d612edb4d4
4687
4737
```

Now we can `grep` for each process ID and inspect what they are doing:

```
docker exec -it kind-worker2 ps aux | grep 4687
root      4687  0.0  0.0    968    4 ?        Ss   17:00   0:00 /pause

docker exec -it kind-worker2 ps aux | grep 4737
root      4737  0.0  0.0 708376 6368 ?       Ssl  17:00   0:00 /opt/web-server
```

4737 is the process ID of our web server container running on `kind-worker2`.

4687 is our pause container holding onto all our namespaces.

Now let's see what will happen to the `iptables` on the worker node:

```
docker exec -it kind-worker2 iptables -L
Chain INPUT (policy ACCEPT)
target                 prot opt source      destination
/* kubernetes service portals */
KUBE-SERVICES          all  --  anywhere    anywhere    ctstate NEW
/* kubernetes externally-visible service portals */
KUBE-EXTERNAL-SERVICES all  --  anywhere    anywhere    ctstate NEW
KUBE-FIREWALL          all  --  anywhere    anywhere

Chain FORWARD (policy ACCEPT)
target         prot opt source      destination
```

```
/* kubernetes forwarding rules */
KUBE-FORWARD  all  --  anywhere    anywhere
/* kubernetes service portals */
KUBE-SERVICES all  --  anywhere    anywhere          ctstate NEW

Chain OUTPUT (policy ACCEPT)
target         prot opt source                destination
/* kubernetes service portals */
KUBE-SERVICES   all  --  anywhere           anywhere          ctstate NEW
KUBE-FIREWALL   all  --  anywhere           anywhere

Chain KUBE-EXTERNAL-SERVICES (1 references)
target    prot opt source              destination

Chain KUBE-FIREWALL (2 references)
target    prot opt source     destination
/* kubernetes firewall for dropping marked packets */
DROP        all  --  anywhere  anywhere   mark match 0x8000/0x8000

Chain KUBE-FORWARD (1 references)
target   prot opt source     destination
DROP     all  --  anywhere  anywhere   ctstate INVALID
/*kubernetes forwarding rules*/
ACCEPT  all  --  anywhere  anywhere     mark match 0x4000/0x4000
/*kubernetes forwarding conntrack pod source rule*/
ACCEPT  all  --  anywhere  anywhere    ctstate RELATED,ESTABLISHED
/*kubernetes forwarding conntrack pod destination rule*/
ACCEPT  all  --  anywhere  anywhere    ctstate RELATED,ESTABLISHED

Chain KUBE-KUBELET-CANARY (0 references)
target    prot opt source                destination

Chain KUBE-PROXY-CANARY (0 references)
target    prot opt source              destination

Chain KUBE-SERVICES (3 references)
target    prot opt source              destination
```

That is a lot of tables being managed by Kubernetes.

We can dive a little deeper to examine the `iptables` responsible for the services we deployed. Let's retrieve the IP address of the `clusterip-service` deployed. We need this to find the matching `iptables` rules:

```
kubectl get svc clusterip-service
NAME              TYPE       CLUSTER-IP      EXTERNAL-IP   PORT(S)   AGE
clusterip-service ClusterIP  10.98.252.195   <none>        80/TCP    57m
```

Now use the clusterIP of the service, `10.98.252.195`, to find our `iptables` rule:

```
docker exec -it  kind-worker2 iptables -L -t nat | grep 10.98.252.195
/* default/clusterip-service: cluster IP */
KUBE-MARK-MASQ  tcp  --  !10.244.0.0/16       10.98.252.195 tcp dpt:80
```

```
/* default/clusterip-service: cluster IP */
KUBE-SVC-V7R3EVKW3DT43QQM  tcp  --  anywhere  10.98.252.195 tcp dpt:80
```

List all the rules on the chain KUBE-SVC-V7R3EVKW3DT43QQM:

```
docker exec -it  kind-worker2 iptables -t nat -L KUBE-SVC-V7R3EVKW3DT43QQM
Chain KUBE-SVC-V7R3EVKW3DT43QQM (1 references)
target      prot opt source             destination
/* default/clusterip-service: */
KUBE-SEP-THJR2P3Q4C2QAEPT  all  --  anywhere             anywhere
```

The KUBE-SEP- will contain the endpoints for the services, KUBE-SEP-THJR2P3Q4C2QAEPT.

Now we can see what the rules for this chain are in iptables:

```
docker exec -it kind-worker2 iptables -L KUBE-SEP-THJR2P3Q4C2QAEPT -t nat
Chain KUBE-SEP-THJR2P3Q4C2QAEPT (1 references)
target          prot opt source         destination
/* default/clusterip-service: */
KUBE-MARK-MASQ  all  --  10.244.1.4       anywhere
/* default/clusterip-service: */
DNAT            tcp  --  anywhere         anywhere    tcp to:10.244.1.4:8080
```

10.244.1.4:8080 is one of the service endpoints, aka a pod backing the service, which is confirmed with the output of kubectl get ep clusterip-service:

```
kubectl get ep clusterip-service
NAME                     ENDPOINTS                        AGE
clusterip-service    10.244.1.4:8080                  62m

kubectl describe ep clusterip-service
Name:         clusterip-service
Namespace:    default
Labels:       app=app
Annotations:  <none>
Subsets:
  Addresses:            10.244.1.4
  NotReadyAddresses:  <none>
  Ports:
    Name      Port  Protocol
    ----      ----  --------
    <unset>   8080  TCP

Events:  <none>
```

Now, let's explore the limitations of the ClusterIP service. The ClusterIP service is for internal traffic to the cluster, and it suffers the same issues as endpoints do. As the service size grows, updates to it will slow. In Chapter 2, we discussed how to mitigate that by using IPVS over iptables as the proxy mode for kube-proxy. We will discuss later in this chapter how to get traffic into the cluster using ingress and the other service type LoadBalancer.

ClusterIP is the default type of service, but there are several other specific types of services such as headless and ExternalName. ExternalName is a specific type of services that helps with reaching services outside the cluster. We briefly touched on headless services with StatefulSets, but let's review those services in depth now.

Headless

A headless service isn't a formal type of service (i.e., there is no `.spec.type: Headless`). A headless service is a service with `.spec.clusterIP: "None"`. This is distinct from merely *not setting* a cluster IP address, which makes Kubernetes automatically assign a cluster IP address.

When ClusterIP is set to None, the service does not support any load balancing functionality. Instead, it only provisions an `Endpoints` object and points the service DNS record at all pods that are selected and ready.

A headless service provides a generic way to watch endpoints, without needing to interact with the Kubernetes API. Fetching DNS records is much simpler than integrating with the Kubernetes API, and it may not be possible with third-party software.

Headless services allow developers to deploy multiple copies of a pod in a deployment. Instead of a single IP address returned, like with the ClusterIP service, all the IP addresses of the endpoint are returned in the query. It then is up to the client to pick which one to use. To see this in action, let's scale up the deployment of our web app:

```
kubectl scale deployment app --replicas 4
deployment.apps/app scaled

kubectl get pods -l app=app -o wide
NAME                    READY   STATUS    IP           NODE
app-9cc7d9df8-9d5t8     1/1     Running   10.244.2.4   kind-worker
app-9cc7d9df8-ffsm6     1/1     Running   10.244.1.4   kind-worker2
app-9cc7d9df8-srxk5     1/1     Running   10.244.3.4   kind-worker3
app-9cc7d9df8-zrnvb     1/1     Running   10.244.3.5   kind-worker3
```

Now let's deploy the headless service:

```
kubectl apply -f service-headless.yml
service/headless-service created
```

The DNS query will return all four of the pod IP addresses. Using our `dnsutils` image, we can verify that is the case:

```
kubectl exec dnsutils -- host -v -t a headless-service
Trying "headless-service.default.svc.cluster.local"
;; ->>HEADER<<- opcode: QUERY, status: NOERROR, id: 45294
;; flags: qr aa rd; QUERY: 1, ANSWER: 4, AUTHORITY: 0, ADDITIONAL: 0
```

```
;; QUESTION SECTION:
;headless-service.default.svc.cluster.local. IN A

;; ANSWER SECTION:
headless-service.default.svc.cluster.local. 30 IN A 10.244.2.4
headless-service.default.svc.cluster.local. 30 IN A 10.244.3.5
headless-service.default.svc.cluster.local. 30 IN A 10.244.1.4
headless-service.default.svc.cluster.local. 30 IN A 10.244.3.4

Received 292 bytes from 10.96.0.10#53 in 0 ms
```

The IP addresses returned from the query also match the endpoints for the service. Using kubectl describe for the endpoint confirms that:

```
 kubectl describe endpoints headless-service
Name:          headless-service
Namespace:     default
Labels:        service.kubernetes.io/headless
Annotations:   endpoints.kubernetes.io/last-change-trigger-time:
2021-01-30T18:16:09Z
Subsets:
  Addresses:          10.244.1.4,10.244.2.4,10.244.3.4,10.244.3.5
  NotReadyAddresses:  <none>
  Ports:
    Name      Port  Protocol
    ----      ----  --------
    <unset>   8080  TCP

Events:  <none>
```

Headless has a specific use case and is not typically used for deployments. As we mentioned in "StatefulSets" on page 191, if developers need to let the client decide which endpoint to use, headless is the appropriate type of service to deploy. Two examples of headless services are clustered databases and applications that have client-side load-balancing logic built into the code.

Our next example is ExternalName, which aids in migrations of services external to the cluster. It also offers other DNS advantages inside cluster DNS.

ExternalName Service

ExternalName is a special type of service that does not have selectors and uses DNS names instead.

When looking up the host ext-service.default.svc.cluster.local, the cluster DNS service returns a CNAME record of database.mycompany.com:

```
apiVersion: v1
kind: Service
metadata:
  name: ext-service
```

```
spec:
  type: ExternalName
  externalName: database.mycompany.com
```

If developers are migrating an application into Kubernetes but its dependencies are staying external to the cluster, ExternalName service allows them to define a DNS record internal to the cluster no matter where the service actually runs.

DNS will try the search as shown in the following example:

```
 kubectl exec -it dnsutils -- host -v -t a github.com
Trying "github.com.default.svc.cluster.local"
Trying "github.com.svc.cluster.local"
Trying "github.com.cluster.local"
Trying "github.com"
;; ->>HEADER<<- opcode: QUERY, status: NOERROR, id: 55908
;; flags: qr rd ra; QUERY: 1, ANSWER: 1, AUTHORITY: 0, ADDITIONAL: 0

;; QUESTION SECTION:
;github.com.                    IN      A

;; ANSWER SECTION:
github.com.            30       IN      A       140.82.112.3

Received 54 bytes from 10.96.0.10#53 in 18 ms
```

As an example, the ExternalName service allows developers to map a service to a DNS name.

Now if we deploy the external service like so:

```
kubectl apply -f service-external.yml
service/external-service created
```

The A record for github.com is returned from the external-service query:

```
kubectl exec -it dnsutils -- host -v -t a external-service
Trying "external-service.default.svc.cluster.local"
;; ->>HEADER<<- opcode: QUERY, status: NOERROR, id: 11252
;; flags: qr aa rd; QUERY: 1, ANSWER: 2, AUTHORITY: 0, ADDITIONAL: 0

;; QUESTION SECTION:
;external-service.default.svc.cluster.local. IN A

;; ANSWER SECTION:
external-service.default.svc.cluster.local. 24 IN CNAME github.com.
github.com.            24       IN      A       140.82.112.3

Received 152 bytes from 10.96.0.10#53 in 0 ms
```

The CNAME for the external service returns github.com:

```
kubectl exec -it dnsutils -- host -v -t cname external-service
Trying "external-service.default.svc.cluster.local"
```

```
;; ->>HEADER<<- opcode: QUERY, status: NOERROR, id: 36874
;; flags: qr aa rd; QUERY: 1, ANSWER: 1, AUTHORITY: 0, ADDITIONAL: 0

;; QUESTION SECTION:
;external-service.default.svc.cluster.local. IN CNAME

;; ANSWER SECTION:
external-service.default.svc.cluster.local. 30 IN CNAME github.com.

Received 126 bytes from 10.96.0.10#53 in 0 ms
```

Sending traffic to a headless service via a DNS record is possible but inadvisable. DNS is a notoriously poor way to load balance, as software takes very different (and often simple or unintuitive) approaches to A or AAAA DNS records that return multiple IP addresses. For example, it is common for software to always choose the first IP address in the response and/or cache and reuse the same IP address indefinitely. If you need to be able to send traffic to the service's DNS address, consider a (standard) ClusterIP or LoadBalancer service.

The "correct" way to use a headless service is to query the service's A/AAAA DNS record and use that data in a server-side or client-side load balancer.

Most of the services we have been discussing are for internal traffic management for the cluster network. In our next sections, will be reviewing how to route requests into the cluster with service type LoadBalancer and ingress.

LoadBalancer

LoadBalancer service exposes services external to the cluster network. They combine the NodePort service behavior with an external integration, such as a cloud provider's load balancer. Notably, LoadBalancer services handle L4 traffic (unlike ingress, which handles L7 traffic), so they will work for any TCP or UDP service, provided the load balancer selected supports L4 traffic.

Configuration and load balancer options are extremely dependent on the cloud provider. For example, some will support .spec.loadBalancerIP (with varying setup required), and some will ignore it:

```
apiVersion: v1
kind: Service
metadata:
  name: demo-service
spec:
  selector:
    app: demo
  ports:
    - protocol: TCP
      port: 80
      targetPort: 8080
```

```
clusterIP: 10.0.5.1
type: LoadBalancer
```

Once the load balancer has been provisioned, its IP address will be written to `.sta`
`tus.loadBalancer.ingress.ip`.

LoadBalancer services are useful for exposing TCP or UDP services to the outside
world. Traffic will come into the load balancer on its public IP address and TCP port
80, defined by `spec.ports[*].port` and routed to the cluster IP address, `10.0.5.1`,
and then to container target port 8080, `spec.ports[*].targetPort`. Not shown in
the example is the `.spec.ports[*].nodePort`; if not specified, Kubernetes will pick
one for the service.

> The service's `spec.ports[*].targetPort` must match your pod's
> container applications `spec.container[*].ports.containerPort`,
> along with the protocol. It's like missing a semicolon in Kubernetes
> networking otherwise.

In Figure 5-6, we can see how a LoadBalancer type builds on the other service types.
The cloud load balancer will determine how to distribute traffic; we will discuss that
in depth in the next chapter.

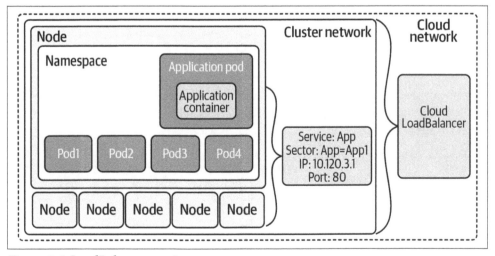

Figure 5-6. LoadBalancer service

Let's continue to extend our Golang web server example with a LoadBalancer service.

Since we are running on our local machine and not in a service provider like AWS,
GCP, or Azure, we can use MetalLB as an example for our LoadBalancer service. The
MetalLB project aims to allow users to deploy bare-metal load balancers for their
clusters.

This example has been modified from the KIND example deployment (*https://oreil.ly/ h8xIt*).

Our first step is to deploy a separate namespace for MetalLB:

```
kubectl apply -f mlb-ns.yaml
namespace/metallb-system created
```

MetalLB members also require a secret for joining the LoadBalancer cluster; let's deploy one now for them to use in our cluster:

```
kubectl create secret generic -n metallb-system memberlist
--from-literal=secretkey="$(openssl rand -base64 128)"
secret/memberlist created
```

Now we can deploy MetalLB!

```
 kubectl apply -f ./metallb.yaml
podsecuritypolicy.policy/controller created
podsecuritypolicy.policy/speaker created
serviceaccount/controller created
serviceaccount/speaker created
clusterrole.rbac.authorization.k8s.io/metallb-system:controller created
clusterrole.rbac.authorization.k8s.io/metallb-system:speaker created
role.rbac.authorization.k8s.io/config-watcher created
role.rbac.authorization.k8s.io/pod-lister created
clusterrolebinding.rbac.authorization.k8s.io/metallb-system:controller created
clusterrolebinding.rbac.authorization.k8s.io/metallb-system:speaker created
rolebinding.rbac.authorization.k8s.io/config-watcher created
rolebinding.rbac.authorization.k8s.io/pod-lister created
daemonset.apps/speaker created
deployment.apps/controller created
```

As you can see, it deploys many objects, and now we wait for the deployment to finish. We can monitor the deployment of resources with the `--watch` option in the `metallb-system` namespace:

```
kubectl get pods -n metallb-system --watch
NAME                          READY  STATUS             RESTARTS  AGE
controller-5df88bd85d-mvgqn   0/1    ContainerCreating  0         10s
speaker-5knqb                 1/1    Running            0         10s
speaker-k79c9                 1/1    Running            0         10s
speaker-pfs2p                 1/1    Running            0         10s
speaker-sl7fd                 1/1    Running            0         10s
controller-5df88bd85d-mvgqn   1/1    Running            0         12s
```

To complete the configuration, we need to provide MetalLB with a range of IP addresses it controls. This range has to be on the Docker KIND network:

```
docker network inspect -f '{{.IPAM.Config}}' kind
[{172.18.0.0/16  172.18.0.1 map[]} {fc00:f853:ccd:e793::/64  fc00:f853:ccd:e793::1 map[]}]
```

`172.18.0.0/16` is our Docker network running locally.

We want our LoadBalancer IP range to come from this subclass. We can configure MetalLB, for instance, to use 172.18.255.200 to 172.18.255.250 by creating the ConfigMap.

The ConfigMap would look like this:

```
apiVersion: v1
kind: ConfigMap
metadata:
  namespace: metallb-system
  name: config
data:
  config: |
    address-pools:
    - name: default
      protocol: layer2
      addresses:
      - 172.18.255.200-172.18.255.250
```

Let's deploy it so we can use MetalLB:

```
kubectl apply -f ./metallb-configmap.yaml
```

Now we deploy a load balancer for our web app:

```
kubectl apply -f services-loadbalancer.yaml
service/loadbalancer-service created
```

For fun let's scale the web app deployment to 10, if you have the resources for it:

```
kubectl scale deployment app --replicas 10
```

```
 kubectl get pods -o wide
NAME                    READY  STATUS   RESTARTS  AGE  IP           NODE
app-7bdb9ffd6c-b5x7m    2/2    Running  0         26s  10.244.3.15  kind-worker
app-7bdb9ffd6c-bqtf8    2/2    Running  0         26s  10.244.2.13  kind-worker2
app-7bdb9ffd6c-fb9sf    2/2    Running  0         26s  10.244.3.14  kind-worker
app-7bdb9ffd6c-hrt7b    2/2    Running  0         26s  10.244.2.7   kind-worker2
app-7bdb9ffd6c-l2794    2/2    Running  0         26s  10.244.2.9   kind-worker2
app-7bdb9ffd6c-l4cfx    2/2    Running  0         26s  10.244.3.11  kind-worker2
app-7bdb9ffd6c-rr4kn    2/2    Running  0         23m  10.244.3.10  kind-worker
app-7bdb9ffd6c-s4k92    2/2    Running  0         26s  10.244.3.13  kind-worker
app-7bdb9ffd6c-shmdt    2/2    Running  0         26s  10.244.1.12  kind-worker3
app-7bdb9ffd6c-v87f9    2/2    Running  0         26s  10.244.1.11  kind-worker3
app2-658bcd97bd-4n888   1/1    Running  0         35m  10.244.2.6   kind-worker3
app2-658bcd97bd-mnpkp   1/1    Running  0         35m  10.244.3.7   kind-worker
app2-658bcd97bd-w2qkl   1/1    Running  0         35m  10.244.3.8   kind-worker
dnsutils                1/1    Running  1         75m  10.244.1.2   kind-worker3
postgres-0              1/1    Running  0         75m  10.244.1.4   kind-worker3
postgres-1              1/1    Running  0         75m  10.244.3.4   kind-worker
```

Now we can test the provisioned load balancer.

With more replicas deployed for our app behind the load balancer, we need the external IP of the load balancer, 172.18.255.200:

```
kubectl get svc loadbalancer-service
NAME                    TYPE           CLUSTER-IP     EXTERNAL-IP
PORT(S)         AGE
loadbalancer-service    LoadBalancer   10.99.24.220   172.18.255.200
80:31276/TCP    52s


kubectl get svc/loadbalancer-service -o=jsonpath='{.status.loadBalancer.ingress[0].ip}'
172.18.255.200
```

Since Docker for Mac or Windows does not expose the KIND network to the host, we cannot directly reach the 172.18.255.200 LoadBalancer IP on the Docker private network.

We can simulate it by attaching a Docker container to the KIND network and cURL-ing the load balancer as a workaround.

 If you would like to read more about this issue, there is a great blog post (*https://oreil.ly/6rTKJ*).

We will use another great networking Docker image called nicolaka/netshoot to run locally, attach to the KIND Docker network, and send requests to our MetalLB load balancer.

If we run it several times, we can see the load balancer is doing its job of routing traffic to different pods:

```
docker run --network kind -a stdin -a stdout -i -t nicolaka/netshoot
curl 172.18.255.200/host
NODE: kind-worker, POD IP:10.244.2.7

docker run --network kind -a stdin -a stdout -i -t nicolaka/netshoot
curl 172.18.255.200/host
NODE: kind-worker, POD IP:10.244.2.9

docker run --network kind -a stdin -a stdout -i -t nicolaka/netshoot
curl 172.18.255.200/host
NODE: kind-worker3, POD IP:10.244.3.11

docker run --network kind -a stdin -a stdout -i -t nicolaka/netshoot
curl 172.18.255.200/host
NODE: kind-worker2, POD IP:10.244.1.6

docker run --network kind -a stdin -a stdout -i -t nicolaka/netshoot
curl 172.18.255.200/host
NODE: kind-worker, POD IP:10.244.2.9
```

With each new request, the metalLB service is sending requests to different pods. LoadBalancer, like other services, uses selectors and labels for the pods, and we can see that in the kubectl describe endpoints loadbalancer-service. The pod IP addresses match our results from the cURL commands:

```
kubectl describe endpoints loadbalancer-service
Name:          loadbalancer-service
Namespace:     default
Labels:        app=app
Annotations:   endpoints.kubernetes.io/last-change-trigger-time:
2021-01-30T19:59:57Z
Subsets:
  Addresses:
  10.244.1.6,
  10.244.1.7,
  10.244.1.8,
  10.244.2.10,
  10.244.2.7,
  10.244.2.8,
  10.244.2.9,
  10.244.3.11,
  10.244.3.12,
  10.244.3.9
  NotReadyAddresses:  <none>
  Ports:
    Name          Port  Protocol
    ----          ----  --------
    service-port  8080  TCP

Events:  <none>
```

It is important to remember that LoadBalancer services require specific integrations and will not work without cloud provider support, or manually installed software such as MetalLB.

They are not (normally) L7 load balancers, and therefore cannot intelligently handle HTTP(S) requests. There is a one-to-one mapping of load balancer to workload, which means that all requests sent to that load balancer must be handled by the same workload.

 While it's not a network service, it is important to mention the Horizontal Pod Autoscaler service, which that will scale pods in a replication controller, deployment, ReplicaSet, or StatefulSet based on CPU utilization.

We can scale our application to the demands of the users, with no need for configuration changes on anyone's part. Kubernetes and the LoadBalancer service take care of all of that for developers, systems, and network administrators.

We will see in the next chapter how we can take that even further using cloud services for autoscaling.

Services Conclusion

Here are some troubleshooting tips if issues arise with the endpoints or services:

- Removing the label on the pod allows it to continue to run while also updating the endpoint and service. The endpoint controller will remove that unlabeled pod from the endpoint objects, and the deployment will deploy another pod; this will allow you to troubleshoot issues with that specific unlabeled pod but not adversely affect the service to end customers. I've used this one countless times during development, and we did so in the previous section's examples.

- There are two probes that communicate the pod's health to the Kubelet and the rest of the Kubernetes environment.

- It is also easy to mess up the YAML manifest, so make sure to compare ports on the service and pods and make sure they match.

- We discussed network policies in Chapter 3, which can also stop pods from communicating with each other and services. If your cluster network is using network policies, ensure that they are set up appropriately for application traffic flow.

- Also remember to use diagnostic tools like the `dnsutils` pod; the `netshoot` pods on the cluster network are helpful debugging tools.

- If endpoints are taking too long to come up in the cluster, there are several options that can be configured on the Kubelet to control how fast it responds to change in the Kubernetes environment:

  `--kube-api-qps`
  > Sets the query-per-second rate the Kubelet will use when communicating with the Kubernetes API server; the default is 5.

  `--kube-api-burst`
  > Temporarily allows API queries to burst to this number; the default is 10.

  `--iptables-sync-period`
  > This is the maximum interval of how often `iptables` rules are refreshed (e.g., 5s, 1m, 2h22m). This must be greater than 0; the default is 30s.

  `--ipvs-sync-period duration`
  > This is the maximum interval of how often IPVS rules are refreshed. This must be greater than 0; the efault is 30s.

- Increasing these options for larger clusters is recommended, but also remember this increases the resources on both the Kubelet and the API server, so keep that in mind.

These tips can help alleviate issues and are good to be aware of as the number of services and pods grow in the cluster.

The various types of services exemplify how powerful the network abstractions are in Kubernetes. We have dug deep into how these work for each layer of the tool chain. Developers looking to deploy applications to Kubernetes now have the knowledge to pick and choose which services are right for their use cases. No longer will network administrators have to manually update load balancers with IP addresses, with Kubernetes managing that for them.

We have just scratched the surface of what is possible with services. With each new version of Kubernetes, there are options to tune and configurations to run services. Test each service for your use cases and ensure you are using the appropriate services to optimize your applications on the Kubernetes network.

The LoadBalancer service type is the only one that allows for traffic into the cluster, exposing HTTP(S) services behind a load balancer for external users to connect to. Ingresses support path-based routing, which allows different HTTP paths to be served by different services. The next section will discuss ingress and how it is an alternative to managing connectivity into the cluster resources.

Ingress

Ingress is a Kubernetes-specific L7 (HTTP) load balancer, which is accessible externally, contrasting with L4 ClusterIP service, which is internal to the cluster. This is the typical choice for exposing an HTTP(S) workload to external users. An ingress can be a single entry point into an API or a microservice-based architecture. Traffic can be routed to services based on HTTP information in the request. Ingress is a configuration spec (with multiple implementations) for routing HTTP traffic to Kubernetes services. Figure 5-7 outlines the ingress components.

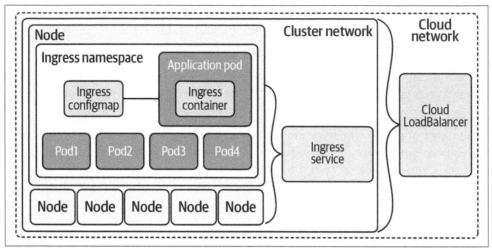

Figure 5-7. Ingress architecture

To manage traffic in a cluster with ingress, there are two components required: the controller and rules. The controller manages ingress pods, and the rules deployed define how the traffic is routed.

Ingress Controllers and Rules

We call ingress implementations ingress *controllers*. In Kubernetes, a controller is software that is responsible for managing a typical resource type and making reality match the desired state.

There are two general kinds of controllers: external load balancer controllers and internal load balancer controllers. External load balancer controllers create a load balancer that exists "outside" the cluster, such as a cloud provider product. Internal load balancer controllers deploy a load balancer that runs within the cluster and do not directly solve the problem of routing consumers to the load balancer. There are a myriad of ways that cluster administrators run internal load balancers, such as running the load balancer on a subset of special nodes, and routing traffic somehow to those nodes. The primary motivation for choosing an internal load balancer is cost reduction. An internal load balancer for ingress can route traffic for multiple ingress objects, whereas an external load balancer controller typically needs one load balancer per ingress. As most cloud providers charge by load balancer, it is cheaper to support a single cloud load balancer that does fan-out within the cluster, than many cloud load balancers. Note that this incurs operational overhead and increased latency and compute costs, so be sure the money you're saving is worth it. Many companies have a bad habit of optimizing on inconsequential cloud spend line items.

Let's look at the spec for an ingress controller. Like LoadBalancer services, most of the spec is universal, but various ingress controllers have different features and accept different configs. We'll start with the basics:

```
apiVersion: networking.k8s.io/v1
kind: Ingress
metadata:
  name: basic-ingress
spec:
  rules:
  - http:
      paths:
      # Send all /demo requests to demo-service.
      - path: /demo
        pathType: Prefix
        backend:
          service:
            name: demo-service
            port:
              number: 80
  # Send all other requests to main-service.
  defaultBackend:
    service:
      name: main-service
      port:
        number: 80
```

The previous example is representative of a typical ingress. It sends traffic to /demo to one service and all other traffic to another. Ingresses have a "default backend" where requests are routed if no rule matches. This can be configured in many ingress controllers in the controller configuration itself (e.g., a generic 404 page), and many support the .spec.defaultBackend field. Ingresses support multiple ways to specify a path. There are currently three:

Exact
> Matches the specific path and only the given path (including trailing / or lack thereof).

Prefix
> Matches all paths that start with the given path.

ImplementationSpecific
> Allows for custom semantics from the current ingress controller.

When a request matches multiple paths, the most specific match is chosen. For example, if there are rules for /first and /first/second, any request starting with /first/second will go to the backend for /first/second. If a path matches an exact path and a prefix path, the request will go to the backend for the exact rule.

Ingresses can also use hostnames in rules:

```
apiVersion: networking.k8s.io/v1
kind: Ingress
metadata:
  name: multi-host-ingress
spec:
  rules:
  - host: a.example.com
    http:
      paths:
      - pathType: Prefix
        path: "/"
        backend:
          service:
            name: service-a
            port:
              number: 80
  - host: b.example.com
    http:
      paths:
      - pathType: Prefix
        path: "/"
        backend:
          service:
            name: service-b
            port:
              number: 80
```

In this example, we serve traffic to a.example.com from one service and traffic to b.example.com from another. This is comparable to virtual hosts in web servers. You may want to use host rules to use a single load balancer and IP to serve multiple unique domains.

Ingresses have basic TLS support:

```
apiVersion: networking.k8s.io/v1
kind: Ingress
metadata:
  name: demo-ingress-secure
spec:
  tls:
  - hosts:
      - https-example.com
    secretName: demo-tls
  rules:
  - host: https-example.com
    http:
      paths:
      - path: /
        pathType: Prefix
        backend:
```

```
        service:
          name: demo-service
          port:
            number: 80
```

The TLS config references a Kubernetes secret by name, in `.spec.tls.[*].secret Name`. Ingress controllers expect the TLS certificate and key to be provided in `.data."tls.crt"` and `.data."tls.key"` respectively, as shown here:

```
apiVersion: v1
kind: Secret
metadata:
  name: demo-tls
type: kubernetes.io/tls
data:
  tls.crt: cert, encoded in base64
  tls.key: key, encoded in base64
```

 If you don't need to manage traditionally issued certificates by hand, you can use cert-manager (*https://oreil.ly/qkN0h*) to automatically fetch and update certs.

We mentioned earlier that ingress is simply a spec, and drastically different implementations exist. It's possible to use multiple ingress controllers in a single cluster, using `IngressClass` settings. An ingress class represents an ingress controller, and therefore a specific ingress implementation.

 Annotations in Kubernetes must be strings. Because `true` and `false` have distinct nonstring meanings, you cannot set an annotation to `true` or `false` without quotes. `"true"` and `"false"` are both valid. This is a long-running bug (*https://oreil.ly/76uSI*), which is often encountered when setting a default priority class.

`IngressClass` was introduced in Kubernetes 1.18. Prior to 1.18, annotating ingresses with `kubernetes.io/ingress.class` was a common convention but relied on all installed ingress controllers to support it. Ingresses can pick an ingress class by setting the class's name in `.spec.ingressClassName`.

 If more than one ingress class is set as default, Kubernetes will not allow you to create an ingress with no ingress class or remove the ingress class from an existing ingress. You can use admission control to prevent multiple ingress classes from being marked as default.

Ingress only supports HTTP(S) requests, which is insufficient if your service uses a different protocol (e.g., most databases use their own protocols). Some ingress controllers, such as the NGINX ingress controller, do support TCP and UDP, but this is not the norm.

Now on to deploying an ingress controller so we can add ingress rules to our Golang web server example.

When we deployed our KIND cluster, we had to add several options to allow us to deploy an ingress controller:

- extraPortMappings allow the local host to make requests to the ingress controller over ports 80/443.

- Node-labels only allow the ingress controller to run on a specific node(s) matching the label selector.

There are many options to choose from with ingress controllers. The Kubernetes system does not start or have a default controller like it does with other pieces. The Kubernetes community does support AWS, GCE, and Nginx ingress controllers. Table 5-1 outlines several options for ingress.

Table 5-1. Brief list of ingress controller options

Name	Commercial support	Engine	Protocol support	SSL termination
Ambassador ingress controller	Yes	Envoy	gRPC, HTTP/2, WebSockets	Yes
Community ingress Nginx	No	NGINX	gRPC, HTTP/2, WebSockets	Yes
NGINX Inc. ingress	Yes	NGINX	HTTP, Websocket, gRPC	Yes
HAProxy ingress	Yes	HAProxy	gRPC, HTTP/2, WebSockets	Yes
Istio Ingress	No	Envoy	HTTP, HTTPS, gRPC, HTTP/2	Yes
Kong ingress controller for Kubernetes	Yes	Lua on top of Nginx	gRPC, HTTP/2	Yes
Traefik Kubernetes ingress	Yes	Traefik	HTTP/2, gRPC, and WebSockets	Yes

Some things to consider when deciding on the ingress for your clusters:

- Protocol support: Do you need more than TCP/UDP, for example gRPC integration or WebSocket?

- Commercial support: Do you need commercial support?

- Advanced features: Are JWT/oAuth2 authentication or circuit breakers requirements for your applications?

- API gateway features: Do you need some API gateway functionalities such as rate-limiting?
- Traffic distribution: Does your application require support for specialized traffic distribution like canary A/B testing or mirroring?

For our example, we have chosen to use the Community version of the NGINX ingress controller.

> For more ingress controllers to choose from, kubernetes.io (*https:// oreil.ly/Lzn5q*) maintains a list.

Let's deploy the NGINX ingress controller into our KIND cluster:

```
kubectl apply -f ingress.yaml
namespace/ingress-nginx created
serviceaccount/ingress-nginx created
configmap/ingress-nginx-controller created
clusterrole.rbac.authorization.k8s.io/ingress-nginx created
clusterrolebinding.rbac.authorization.k8s.io/ingress-nginx created
role.rbac.authorization.k8s.io/ingress-nginx created
rolebinding.rbac.authorization.k8s.io/ingress-nginx created
service/ingress-nginx-controller-admission created
service/ingress-nginx-controller created
deployment.apps/ingress-nginx-controller created
validatingwebhookconfiguration.admissionregistration.k8s.io/
ingress-nginx-admission created
serviceaccount/ingress-nginx-admission created
clusterrole.rbac.authorization.k8s.io/ingress-nginx-admission created
clusterrolebinding.rbac.authorization.k8s.io/ingress-nginx-admission created
role.rbac.authorization.k8s.io/ingress-nginx-admission created
rolebinding.rbac.authorization.k8s.io/ingress-nginx-admission created
job.batch/ingress-nginx-admission-create created
job.batch/ingress-nginx-admission-patch created
```

As with all deployments, we must wait for the controller to be ready before we can use it. With the following command, we can verify if our ingress controller is ready for use:

```
kubectl wait --namespace ingress-nginx \
>    --for=condition=ready pod \
>    --selector=app.kubernetes.io/component=controller \
>    --timeout=90s
pod/ingress-nginx-controller-76b5f89575-zps4k condition met
```

The controller is deployed to the cluster, and now we're ready to write ingress rules for our application.

Deploy ingress rules

Our YAML manifest defines several ingress rules to use with our Golang web server example:

```
kubectl apply -f ingress-rule.yaml
ingress.extensions/ingress-resource created

kubectl get ingress
NAME                  CLASS    HOSTS  ADDRESS  PORTS  AGE
ingress-resource      <none>   *               80     4s
```

With describe we can see all the backends that map to the ClusterIP service and the pods:

```
kubectl describe ingress
Name:              ingress-resource
Namespace:         default
Address:
Default backend:   default-http-backend:80 (<error:
endpoints "default-http-backend" not found>)
Rules:
  Host        Path  Backends
  ----        ----  --------
  *
              /host  clusterip-service:8080 (
10.244.1.6:8080,10.244.1.7:8080,10.244.1.8:8080)
Annotations:  kubernetes.io/ingress.class: nginx
Events:
  Type    Reason  Age   From                      Message
  ----    ------  ----  ----                      -------
  Normal  Sync    17s   nginx-ingress-controller  Scheduled for sync
```

Our ingress rule is only for the /host route and will route requests to our clusterip-service:8080 service.

We can test that with cURL to http://localhost/host:

```
curl localhost/host
NODE: kind-worker2, POD IP:10.244.1.6
curl localhost/healthz
```

Now we can see how powerful ingresses are; let's deploy a second deployment and ClusterIP service.

Our new deployment and service will be used to answer the requests for /data:

```
kubectl apply -f ingress-example-2.yaml
deployment.apps/app2 created
service/clusterip-service-2 configured
ingress.extensions/ingress-resource-2 configured
```

Now both the /host and /data work but are going to separate services:

```
curl localhost/host
NODE: kind-worker2, POD IP:10.244.1.6

curl localhost/data
Database Connected
```

Since ingress works on layer 7, there are many more options to route traffic with, such as host header and URI path.

For more advanced traffic routing and release patterns, a service mesh is required to be deployed in the cluster network. Let's dig into that next.

Service Meshes

A new cluster with the default options has some limitations. So, let's get an understanding for what those limitations are and how a service mesh can resolve some of those limitations. A *service mesh* is an API-driven infrastructure layer for handling service-to-service communication.

From a security point of view, all traffic inside the cluster is unencrypted between pods, and each application team that runs a service must configure monitoring separately for each service. We have discussed the service types, but we have not discussed how to update deployments of pods for them. Service meshes support more than the basic deployment type; they support rolling updates and re-creations, like Canary does. From a developer's perspective, injecting faults into the network is useful, but also not directly supported in default Kubernetes network deployments. With service meshes, developers can add fault testing, and instead of just killing pods, you can use service meshes to inject delays—again, each application would have to build in fault testing or circuit breaking.

There are several pieces of functionality that a service mesh enhances or provides in a default Kubernetes cluster network:

Service Discovery
> Instead of relying on DNS for service discovery, the service mesh manages service discovery, and removes the need for it to be implemented in each individual application.

Load Balancing
> The service mesh adds more advanced load balancing algorithms such as least request, consistent hashing, and zone aware.

Communication Resiliency
> The service mesh can increase communication resilience for applications by not having to implement retries, timeouts, circuit breaking, or rate limiting in application code.

Security
> A service mesh can provide the folllowing: * End-to-end encryption with mTLS between services * Authorization policies, which authorize what services can communicate with each other, not just at the layer 3 and 4 levels like in Kubernetes network polices.

Observability
> Service meshes add in observability by enriching the layer 7 metrics and adding tracing and alerting.

Routing Control
> Traffic shifting and mirroring in the cluster.

API
> All of this can be controlled via an API provided by the service mesh implementation.

Let's walk through several components of a service mesh in Figure 5-8.

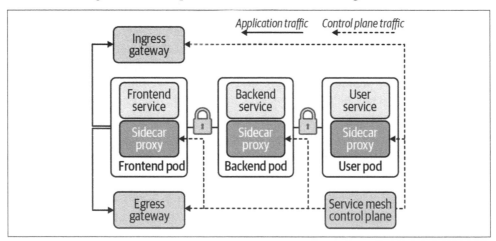

Figure 5-8. Service mesh components

Traffic is handled differently depending on the component or destination of traffic. Traffic into and out of the cluster is managed by the gateways. Traffic between the frontend, backend, and user service is all encrypted with Mutual TLS (mTLS) and is handled by the service mesh. All the traffic to the frontend, backend, and user pods in the service mesh is proxied by the sidecar proxy deployed within the pods. Even if the control plane is down and updates cannot be made to the mesh, the service and application traffic are not affected.

There are several options to use when deploying a service mesh; here are highlights of just a few:

- Istio
  - Uses a Go control plane with an Envoy proxy.
  - This is a Kubernetes-native solution that was initially released by Lyft.
- Consul
  - Uses HashiCorp Consul as the control plane.
  - Consul Connect uses an agent installed on every node as a DaemonSet, which communicates with the Envoy sidecar proxies that handle routing and forwarding of traffic.
- AWS App Mesh
  - Is an AWS-managed solution that implements its own control plane.
  - Does not have mTLS or traffic policy.
  - Uses the Envoy proxy for the data plane.
- Linkerd
  - Also uses Go for the control plane with the Linkerd proxy.
  - No traffic shifting and no distributed tracing.
  - Is a Kubernetes-only solution, which results in fewer moving pieces and means that Linkerd has less complexity overall.

It is our opinion that the best use case for a service mesh is mTLS between services. Other higher-level use cases for developers include circuit breaking and fault testing for APIs. For network administrators, advanced routing policies and algorithms can be deployed with service meshes.

Let's look at a service mesh example. The first thing you need to do if you haven't already is install the Linkerd CLI (*https://oreil.ly/jVaPm*).

Your choices are cURL, bash, or brew if you're on a Mac:

```
curl -sL https://run.linkerd.io/install | sh

OR

brew install linkerd

linkerd version
```

```
Client version: stable-2.9.2
Server version: unavailable
```

This preflight checklist will verify that our cluster can run Linkerd:

```
 linkerd check --pre
kubernetes-api
--------------
√ can initialize the client
√ can query the Kubernetes API

kubernetes-version
------------------
√ is running the minimum Kubernetes API version
√ is running the minimum kubectl version

pre-kubernetes-setup
--------------------
√ control plane namespace does not already exist
√ can create non-namespaced resources
√ can create ServiceAccounts
√ can create Services
√ can create Deployments
√ can create CronJobs
√ can create ConfigMaps
√ can create Secrets
√ can read Secrets
√ can read extension-apiserver-authentication configmap
√ no clock skew detected

pre-kubernetes-capability
-------------------------
√ has NET_ADMIN capability
√ has NET_RAW capability

linkerd-version
---------------
√ can determine the latest version
√ cli is up-to-date

Status check results are √
```

The Linkerd CLI tool can install Linkerd for us onto our KIND cluster:

```
linkerd install | kubectl apply -f -
namespace/linkerd created
clusterrole.rbac.authorization.k8s.io/linkerd-linkerd-identity created
clusterrolebinding.rbac.authorization.k8s.io/linkerd-linkerd-identity created
serviceaccount/linkerd-identity created
clusterrole.rbac.authorization.k8s.io/linkerd-linkerd-controller created
clusterrolebinding.rbac.authorization.k8s.io/linkerd-linkerd-controller created
serviceaccount/linkerd-controller created
clusterrole.rbac.authorization.k8s.io/linkerd-linkerd-destination created
clusterrolebinding.rbac.authorization.k8s.io/linkerd-linkerd-destination created
```

```
serviceaccount/linkerd-destination created
role.rbac.authorization.k8s.io/linkerd-heartbeat created
rolebinding.rbac.authorization.k8s.io/linkerd-heartbeat created
serviceaccount/linkerd-heartbeat created
role.rbac.authorization.k8s.io/linkerd-web created
rolebinding.rbac.authorization.k8s.io/linkerd-web created
clusterrole.rbac.authorization.k8s.io/linkerd-linkerd-web-check created
clusterrolebinding.rbac.authorization.k8s.io/linkerd-linkerd-web-check created
clusterrolebinding.rbac.authorization.k8s.io/linkerd-linkerd-web-admin created
serviceaccount/linkerd-web created
customresourcedefinition.apiextensions.k8s.io/serviceprofiles.linkerd.io created
customresourcedefinition.apiextensions.k8s.io/trafficsplits.split.smi-spec.io
created
clusterrole.rbac.authorization.k8s.io/linkerd-linkerd-proxy-injector created
clusterrolebinding.rbac.authorization.k8s.io/linkerd-linkerd-proxy-injector
created
serviceaccount/linkerd-proxy-injector created
secret/linkerd-proxy-injector-k8s-tls created
mutatingwebhookconfiguration.admissionregistration.k8s.io
 /linkerd-proxy-injector-webhook-config created
clusterrole.rbac.authorization.k8s.io/linkerd-linkerd-sp-validator created
clusterrolebinding.rbac.authorization.k8s.io/linkerd-linkerd-sp-validator
created
serviceaccount/linkerd-sp-validator created
secret/linkerd-sp-validator-k8s-tls created
validatingwebhookconfiguration.admissionregistration.k8s.io
 /linkerd-sp-validator-webhook-config created
clusterrole.rbac.authorization.k8s.io/linkerd-linkerd-tap created
clusterrole.rbac.authorization.k8s.io/linkerd-linkerd-tap-admin created
clusterrolebinding.rbac.authorization.k8s.io/linkerd-linkerd-tap created
clusterrolebinding.rbac.authorization.k8s.io/linkerd-linkerd-tap-auth-delegator
created
serviceaccount/linkerd-tap created
rolebinding.rbac.authorization.k8s.io/linkerd-linkerd-tap-auth-reader created
secret/linkerd-tap-k8s-tls created
apiservice.apiregistration.k8s.io/v1alpha1.tap.linkerd.io created
podsecuritypolicy.policy/linkerd-linkerd-control-plane created
role.rbac.authorization.k8s.io/linkerd-psp created
rolebinding.rbac.authorization.k8s.io/linkerd-psp created
configmap/linkerd-config created
secret/linkerd-identity-issuer created
service/linkerd-identity created
service/linkerd-identity-headless created
deployment.apps/linkerd-identity created
service/linkerd-controller-api created
deployment.apps/linkerd-controller created
service/linkerd-dst created
service/linkerd-dst-headless created
deployment.apps/linkerd-destination created
cronjob.batch/linkerd-heartbeat created
service/linkerd-web created
deployment.apps/linkerd-web created
```

```
deployment.apps/linkerd-proxy-injector created
service/linkerd-proxy-injector created
service/linkerd-sp-validator created
deployment.apps/linkerd-sp-validator created
service/linkerd-tap created
deployment.apps/linkerd-tap created
serviceaccount/linkerd-grafana created
configmap/linkerd-grafana-config created
service/linkerd-grafana created
deployment.apps/linkerd-grafana created
clusterrole.rbac.authorization.k8s.io/linkerd-linkerd-prometheus created
clusterrolebinding.rbac.authorization.k8s.io/linkerd-linkerd-prometheus created
serviceaccount/linkerd-prometheus created
configmap/linkerd-prometheus-config created
service/linkerd-prometheus created
deployment.apps/linkerd-prometheus created
secret/linkerd-config-overrides created
```

As with the ingress controller and MetalLB, we can see that a lot of components are installed in our cluster.

Linkerd can validate the installation with the `linkerd check` command.

It will validate a plethora of checks for the Linkerd install, included but not limited to the Kubernetes API version, controllers, pods, and configs to run Linkerd, as well as all the services, versions, and APIs needed to run Linkerd:

```
linkerd check
kubernetes-api
--------------
√ can initialize the client
√ can query the Kubernetes API

kubernetes-version
------------------
√ is running the minimum Kubernetes API version
√ is running the minimum kubectl version

linkerd-existence
-----------------
√ 'linkerd-config' config map exists
√ heartbeat ServiceAccount exists
√ control plane replica sets are ready
√ no unschedulable pods
√ controller pod is running
√ can initialize the client
√ can query the control plane API

linkerd-config
--------------
√ control plane Namespace exists
√ control plane ClusterRoles exist
√ control plane ClusterRoleBindings exist
```

```
√ control plane ServiceAccounts exist
√ control plane CustomResourceDefinitions exist
√ control plane MutatingWebhookConfigurations exist
√ control plane ValidatingWebhookConfigurations exist
√ control plane PodSecurityPolicies exist

linkerd-identity
----------------
√ certificate config is valid
√ trust anchors are using supported crypto algorithm
√ trust anchors are within their validity period
√ trust anchors are valid for at least 60 days
√ issuer cert is using supported crypto algorithm
√ issuer cert is within its validity period
√ issuer cert is valid for at least 60 days
√ issuer cert is issued by the trust anchor

linkerd-webhooks-and-apisvc-tls
-------------------------------
√ tap API server has valid cert
√ tap API server cert is valid for at least 60 days
√ proxy-injector webhook has valid cert
√ proxy-injector cert is valid for at least 60 days
√ sp-validator webhook has valid cert
√ sp-validator cert is valid for at least 60 days

linkerd-api
-----------
√ control plane pods are ready
√ control plane self-check
√ [kubernetes] control plane can talk to Kubernetes
√ [prometheus] control plane can talk to Prometheus
√ tap api service is running

linkerd-version
---------------
√ can determine the latest version
√ cli is up-to-date

control-plane-version
---------------------
√ control plane is up-to-date
√ control plane and cli versions match

linkerd-prometheus
------------------
√ prometheus add-on service account exists
√ prometheus add-on config map exists
√ prometheus pod is running

linkerd-grafana
---------------
```

```
√ grafana add-on service account exists
√ grafana add-on config map exists
√ grafana pod is running

Status check results are √
```

Now that everything looks good with our install of Linkerd, we can add our application to the service mesh:

```
kubectl -n linkerd get deploy
NAME                     READY  UP-TO-DATE  AVAILABLE  AGE
linkerd-controller       1/1    1           1          3m17s
linkerd-destination      1/1    1           1          3m17s
linkerd-grafana          1/1    1           1          3m16s
linkerd-identity         1/1    1           1          3m17s
linkerd-prometheus       1/1    1           1          3m16s
linkerd-proxy-injector   1/1    1           1          3m17s
linkerd-sp-validator     1/1    1           1          3m17s
linkerd-tap              1/1    1           1          3m17s
linkerd-web              1/1    1           1          3m17s
```

Let's pull up the Linkerd console to investigate what we have just deployed. We can start the console with `linkerd dashboard &`.

This will proxy the console to our local machine available at `http://localhost:50750`:

```
linkerd viz install | kubectl apply -f -
linkerd viz dashboard
Linkerd dashboard available at:
http://localhost:50750
Grafana dashboard available at:
http://localhost:50750/grafana
Opening Linkerd dashboard in the default browser
```

 If you're having issues with reaching the dashboard, you can run `linkerd viz check` and find more help in the Linkerd documentation (*https://oreil.ly/MqgAp*).

We can see all our deployed objects from the previous exercises in Figure 5-9.

Our ClusterIP service is not part of the Linkerd service mesh. We will need to use the proxy injector to add our service to the mesh. It accomplishes this by watching for a specific annotation that can be added either with Linkerd `inject` or by hand to the pod's spec.

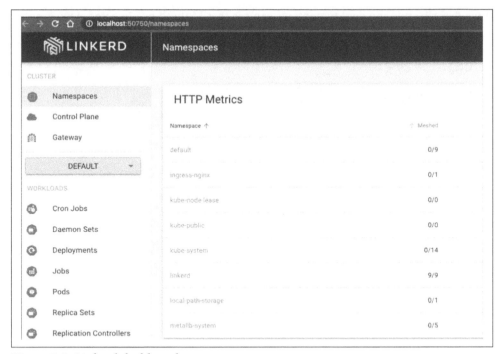

Figure 5-9. Linkerd dashboard

Let's remove some older exercises' resources for clarity:

```
kubectl delete -f ingress-example-2.yaml
deployment.apps "app2" deleted
service "clusterip-service-2" deleted
ingress.extensions "ingress-resource-2" deleted

kubectl delete pods app-5586fc9d77-7frts
pod "app-5586fc9d77-7frts" deleted

kubectl delete -f ingress-rule.yaml
ingress.extensions "ingress-resource" deleted
```

We can use the Linkerd CLI to inject the proper annotations into our deployment spec, so that will become part of the mesh.

We first need to get our application manifest, `cat web.yaml`, and use Linkerd to inject the annotations, `linkerd inject -`, then apply them back to the Kubernetes API with `kubectl apply -f -`:

```
cat web.yaml | linkerd inject - | kubectl apply -f -

deployment "app" injected

deployment.apps/app configured
```

If we describe our app deployment, we can see that Linkerd has injected new annotations for us, Annotations: `linkerd.io/inject: enabled`:

```
kubectl describe deployment app
Name:                   app
Namespace:              default
CreationTimestamp:      Sat, 30 Jan 2021 13:48:47 -0500
Labels:                 <none>
Annotations:            deployment.kubernetes.io/revision: 3
Selector:               app=app
Replicas:               1 desired | 1 updated | 1 total | 1 available |
0 unavailable
StrategyType:           RollingUpdate
MinReadySeconds:        0
RollingUpdateStrategy:  25% max unavailable, 25% max surge
Pod Template:
  Labels:       app=app
  Annotations:  linkerd.io/inject: enabled
  Containers:
   go-web:
    Image:      strongjz/go-web:v0.0.6
    Port:       8080/TCP
    Host Port:  0/TCP
    Liveness:   http-get http://:8080/healthz delay=5s timeout=1s period=5s
    Readiness:  http-get http://:8080/ delay=5s timeout=1s period=5s
    Environment:
      MY_NODE_NAME:              (v1:spec.nodeName)
      MY_POD_NAME:               (v1:metadata.name)
      MY_POD_NAMESPACE:          (v1:metadata.namespace)
      MY_POD_IP:                 (v1:status.podIP)
      MY_POD_SERVICE_ACCOUNT:    (v1:spec.serviceAccountName)
      DB_HOST:                   postgres
      DB_USER:                   postgres
      DB_PASSWORD:               mysecretpassword
      DB_PORT:                   5432
    Mounts:                      <none>
  Volumes:                       <none>
Conditions:
  Type           Status   Reason
  ----           ------   ------
  Available      True     MinimumReplicasAvailable
  Progressing    True     NewReplicaSetAvailable
OldReplicaSets:  <none>
NewReplicaSet:   app-78dfbb4854 (1/1 replicas created)
Events:
  Type   Reason            Age    From                    Message
  ----   ------            ----   ----                    -------
  Normal ScalingReplicaSet 4m4s   deployment-controller   Scaled down app-5586fc9d77
  Normal ScalingReplicaSet 4m4s   deployment-controller   Scaled up app-78dfbb4854
  Normal Injected          4m4s   linkerd-proxy-injector  Linkerd sidecar injected
  Normal ScalingReplicaSet 3m54s  deployment-controller   Scaled app-5586fc9d77
```

If we navigate to the app in the dashboard, we can see that our deployment is part of the Linkerd service mesh now, as shown in Figure 5-10.

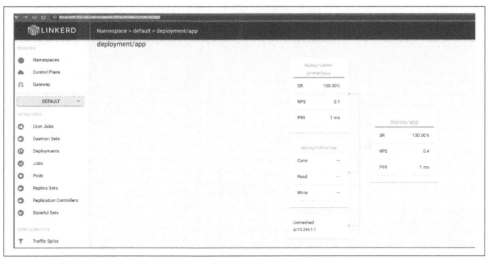

Figure 5-10. Web app deployment linkerd dashboard

The CLI can also display our stats for us:

```
linkerd stat deployments -n default
NAME   MESHED   SUCCESS     RPS LATENCY_P50 LATENCY_P95 LATENCY_P99 TCP_CONN
app       1/1   100.00% 0.4rps        1ms         1ms         1ms            1
```

Again, let's scale up our deployment:

```
kubectl scale deploy app --replicas 10
deployment.apps/app scaled
```

In Figure 5-11, we navigate to the web browser and open this link (*https://oreil.ly/ qQx9T*) so we can watch the stats in real time. Select the default namespaces, and in Resources select our deployment/app. Then click "start for the web" to start displaying the metrics.

In a separate terminal let's use the netshoot image, but this time running inside our KIND cluster:

```
kubectl run tmp-shell --rm -i --tty --image nicolaka/netshoot -- /bin/bash
If you don't see a command prompt, try pressing enter.
bash-5.0#
```

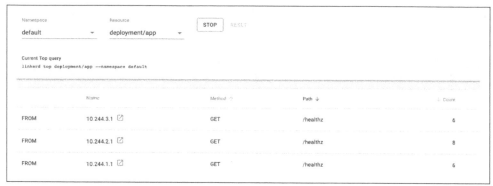

Figure 5-11. Web app dashboard

Let's send a few hundred queries and see the stats:

```
bash-5.0#for i in `seq 1 100`;
do curl http://clusterip-service/host && sleep 2;
done
```

In our terminal we can see all the liveness and readiness probes as well as our /host requests.

tmp-shell is our netshoot bash terminal with our for loop running.

10.244.2.1, 10.244.3.1, and 10.244.2.1 are the Kubelets of the hosts running our probes for us:

```
linkerd viz stat deploy
NAME   MESHED   SUCCESS    RPS   LATENCY_P50   LATENCY_P95   LATENCY_P99   TCP_CONN
app      1/1    100.00%  0.7rps          1ms           1ms           1ms          3
```

Our example showed the observability functionality for a service mesh only. Linkerd, Istio, and the like have many more options available for developers and network administrators to control, monitor, and troubleshoot services running inside their cluster network. As with the ingress controller, there are many options and features available. It is up to you and your teams to decide what functionality and features are important for your networks.

Conclusion

The Kubernetes networking world is feature rich with many options for teams to deploy, test, and manage with their Kubernetes cluster. Each new addition will add complexity and overhead to the cluster operations. We have given developers, network administrators, and system administrators a view into the abstractions that Kubernetes offers.

From internal traffic to external traffic to the cluster, teams must choose what abstractions work best for their workloads. This is no small task, and now you are armed with the knowledge to begin those discussions.

In our next chapter, we take our Kubernetes services and network learnings to the cloud! We will explore the network services offered by each cloud provider and how they are integrated into their Kubernetes managed service offering.

Kubernetes and Cloud Networking

The use of the cloud and its service offerings has grown tremendously: 77% of enterprises are using the public cloud in some capacity, and 81% can innovate more quickly with the public cloud than on-premise. With the popularity and innovation available in the cloud, it follows that running Kubernetes in the cloud is a logical step. Each major cloud provider has its own managed service offering for Kubernetes using its cloud network services.

In this chapter, we'll explore the network services offered by the major cloud providers AWS, Azure, and GCP with a focus on how they affect the networking needed to run a Kubernetes cluster inside that specific cloud. All the providers also have a CNI project that makes running a Kubernetes cluster smoother from an integration perspective with their cloud network APIs, so an exploration of the CNIs is warranted. After reading this chapter, administrators will understand how cloud providers implement their managed Kubernetes on top of their cloud network services.

Amazon Web Services

Amazon Web Services (AWS) has grown its cloud service offerings from Simple Queue Service (SQS) and Simple Storage Service (S3) to well over 200 services. Gartner Research positions AWS in the Leaders quadrant of its 2020 Magic Quadrant for Cloud Infrastructure & Platform Services. Many services are built atop of other foundational services. For example, Lambda uses S3 for code storage and DynamoDB for metadata. AWS CodeCommit uses S3 for code storage. EC2, S3, and CloudWatch are integrated into the Amazon Elastic MapReduce service, creating a managed data platform. The AWS networking services are no different. Advanced services such as peering and endpoints use building blocks from core networking fundamentals. Understanding those fundamentals, which enable AWS to build a comprehensive Kubernetes service, is needed for administrators and developers.

AWS Network Services

AWS has many services that allow users to extend and secure their cloud networks. Amazon Elastic Kubernetes Service (EKS) makes extensive use of those network components available in the AWS cloud. We will discuss the basics of AWS networking components and how they are related to deploying an EKS cluster network. This section will also discuss several other open source tools that make managing a cluster and application deployments simple. The first is `eksctl`, a CLI tool that deploys and manages EKS clusters. As we have seen from previous chapters, there are many components needed to run a cluster, and that is also true on the AWS network. `eksctl` will deploy all the components in AWS for cluster and network administrators. Then, we will discuss the AWS VPC CNI, which allows the cluster to use native AWS services to scale pods and manage their IP address space. Finally, we will examine the AWS Application Load Balancer ingress controller, which automates, manages, and simplifies deployments of application load balancers and ingresses for developers running applications on the AWS network.

Virtual private cloud

The basis of the AWS network is the virtual private cloud (VPC). A majority of AWS resources will work inside the VPC. VPC networking is an isolated virtual network defined by administrators for only their account and its resources. In Figure 6-1, we can see a VPC defined with a single CIDR of `192.168.0.0/16`. All resources inside the VPC will use that range for private IP addresses. AWS is constantly enhancing its service offerings; now, network administrators can use multiple nonoverlapping CIDRs in a VPC. The pod IP addresses will also come from VPC CIDR and host IP addressing; more on that in "AWS VPC CNI" on page 263. A VPC is set up per AWS region; you can have multiple VPCs per region, but a VPC is defined in only one.

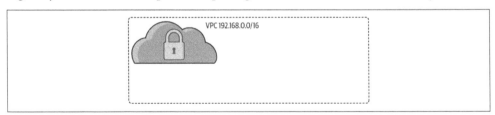

Figure 6-1. AWS virtual private cloud

Region and availability zones

Resources are defined by boundaries in AWS, such as global, region, or availability zone. AWS networking comprises multiple regions; each AWS region consists of multiple isolated and physically separate availability zones (AZs) within a geographic area. An AZ can contain multiple data centers, as shown in Figure 6-2. Some regions can contain six AZs, while newer regions could contain only two. Each AZ is directly connected to the others but is isolated from the failures of another AZ. This design is important to understand for multiple reasons: high availability, load balancing, and subnets are all affected. In one region a load balancer will route traffic over multiple AZs, which have separate subnets and thus enable HA for applications.

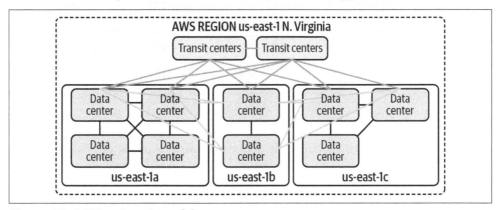

Figure 6-2. AWS region network layout

An up-to-date list of AWS regions and AZs is available in the documentation (*https://oreil.ly/gppRp*).

Subnet

A VPC is compromised of multiple subnets from the CIDR range and deployed to a single AZ. Applications that require high availability should run in multiple AZs and be load balanced with any one of the load balancers available, as discussed in "Region and availability zones" on page 244.

A subnet is public if the routing table has a route to an internet gateway. In Figure 6-3, there are three public and private subnets. Private subnets have no direct route to the internet. These subnets are for internal network traffic, such as databases. The size of your VPC CIDR range and the number of public and private subnets are a design consideration when deploying your network architecture. Recent improvements to VPC like allowing multiple CIDR ranges help lessen the ramification of poor design choices, since now network engineers can simply add another CIDR range to a provisioned VPC.

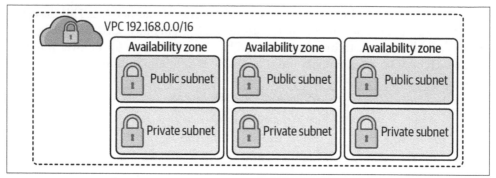

Figure 6-3. VPC subnets

Let's discuss those components that help define if a subnet is public or private.

Routing tables

Each subnet has exactly one route table associated with it. If one is not explicitly associated with it, the main route table is the default one. Network connectivity issues can manifest here; developers deploying applications inside a VPC must know to manipulate route tables to ensure traffic flows where it's intended.

The following are rules for the main route table:

- The main route table cannot be deleted.
- A gateway route table cannot be set as the main.
- The main route table can be replaced with a custom route table.
- Admins can add, remove, and modify routes in the main route table.
- The local route is the most specific.
- Subnets can explicitly associate with the main route table.

There are route tables with specific goals in mind; here is a list of them and a description of how they are different:

Main route table
   This route table automatically controls routing for all subnets that are not explicitly associated with any other route table.

Custom route table
   A route table network engineers create and customize for specific application traffic flow.

Edge association
   A routing table to route inbound VPC traffic to an edge appliance.

Subnet route table
A route table that's associated with a subnet.

Gateway route table
A route table that's associated with an internet gateway or virtual private gateway.

Each route table has several components that determine its responsibilities:

Route table association
The association between a route table and a subnet, internet gateway, or virtual private gateway.

Rules
A list of routing entries that define the table; each rule has a destination, target, status, and propagated flag.

Destination
The range of IP addresses where you want traffic to go (destination CIDR).

Target
The gateway, network interface, or connection through which to send the destination traffic; for example, an internet gateway.

Status
The state of a route in the route table: active or blackhole. The blackhole state indicates that the route's target isn't available.

Propagation
Route propagation allows a virtual private gateway to automatically propagate routes to the route tables. This flag lets you know if it was added via propagation.

Local route
A default route for communication within the VPC.

In Figure 6-4, there are two routes in the route table. Any traffic destined for `11.0.0.0/16` stays on the local network inside the VPC. All other traffic, `0.0.0.0/0`, goes to the internet gateway, `igw-f43c4690`, making it a public subnet.

Destination	Target	Status	Propagated
11.0.0.0/16	local	Active	No
0.0.0.0/0	igw-f43c4690	Active	No

Figure 6-4. Route table

Elastic network interface

An elastic network interface (ENI) is a logical networking component in a VPC that is equivalent to a virtual network card. ENIs contain an IP address, for the instance, and they are elastic in the sense that they can be associated and disassociated to an instance while retaining its properties.

ENIs have these properties:

- Primary private IPv4 address
- Secondary private IPv4 addresses
- One elastic IP (EIP) address per private IPv4 address
- One public IPv4 address, which can be auto-assigned to the network interface for eth0 when you launch an instance
- One or more IPv6 addresses
- One or more security groups
- MAC address
- Source/destination check flag
- Description

A common use case for ENIs is the creation of management networks that are accessible only from a corporate network. AWS services like Amazon WorkSpaces use ENIs to allow access to the customer VPC and the AWS-managed VPC. Lambda can reach resources, like databases, inside a VPC by provisioning and attaching to an ENI.

Later in the section we will see how the AWS VPC CNI uses and manages ENIs along with IP addresses for pods.

Elastic IP address

An EIP address is a static public IPv4 address used for dynamic network addressing in the AWS cloud. An EIP is associated with any instance or network interface in any VPC. With an EIP, application developers can mask an instance's failures by remapping the address to another instance.

An EIP address is a property of an ENI and is associated with an instance by updating the ENI attached to the instance. The advantage of associating an EIP with the ENI rather than directly to the instance is that all the network interface attributes move from one instance to another in a single step.

The following rules apply:

- An EIP address can be associated with either a single instance or a network interface at a time.
- An EIP address can migrate from one instance or network interface to another.
- There is a (soft) limit of five EIP addresses.
- IPv6 is not supported.

Services like NAT and internet gateway use EIPs for consistency between the AZ. Other gateway services like a bastion can benefit from using an EIP. Subnets can automatically assign public IP addresses to EC2 instances, but that address could change; using an EIP would prevent that.

Security controls

There are two fundamental security controls within AWS networking: security groups and network access control lists (NACLs). In our experience, lots of issues arise from misconfigured security groups and NACLs. Developers and network engineers need to understand the differences between the two and the impacts of changes on them.

Security groups. Security groups operate at the instance or network interface level and act as a firewall for those devices associated with them. A security group is a group of network devices that require common network access to each other and other devices on the network. In Figure 6-5 ,we can see that security works across AZs. Security groups have two tables, for inbound and outbound traffic flow. Security groups are stateful, so if traffic is allowed on the inbound flow, the outgoing traffic is allowed. Each security group has a list of rules that define the filter for traffic. Each rule is evaluated before a forwarding decision is made.

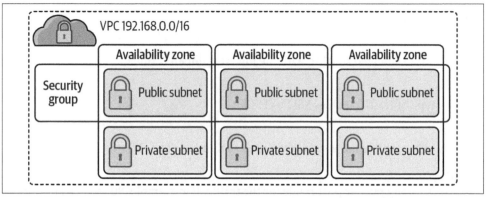

Figure 6-5. Security group

The following is a list of components of security group rules:

Source/destination
> Source (inbound rules) or destination (outbound rules) of the traffic inspected:
>
> - Individual or range of IPv4 or IPv6 addresses
> - Another security group
> - Other ENIs, gateways, or interfaces

Protocol
> Which layer 4 protocol being filtered, 6 (TCP), 17 (UDP), and 1 (ICMP)

Port range
> Specific ports for the protocol being filtered

Description
> User-defined field to inform others of the intent of the security group

Security groups are similar to the Kubernetes network policies we discussed in earlier chapters. They are a fundamental network technology and should always be used to secure your instances in the AWS VPC. EKS deploys several security groups for communication between the AWS-managed data plane and your worker nodes.

Network access control lists. Network access control lists operate similarly to how they do in other firewalls so that network engineers will be familiar with them. In Figure 6-6, you can see each subnet has a default NACL associated with it and is bounded to an AZ, unlike the security group. Filter rules must be defined explicitly in both directions. The default rules are quite permissive, allowing all traffic in both directions. Users can define their own NACLs to use with a subnet for an added security layer if the security group is too open. By default, custom NACLs deny all traffic, and therefore add rules when deployed; otherwise, instances will lose connectivity.

Here are the components of an NACL:

Rule number
> Rules are evaluated starting with the lowest numbered rule.

Type
> The type of traffic, such as SSH or HTTP.

Protocol
> Any protocol that has a standard protocol number: TCP/UDP or ALL.

Port range
> The listening port or port range for the traffic. For example, 80 for HTTP traffic.

Source
    Inbound rules only; the CIDR range source of the traffic.

Destination
    Outbound rules only; the destination for the traffic.

Allow/Deny
    Whether to allow or deny the specified traffic.

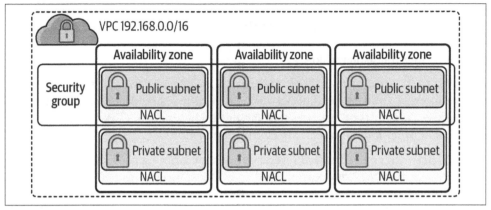

Figure 6-6. NACL

NACLs add an extra layer of security for subnets that may protect from lack or misconfiguration of security groups.

Table 6-1 summarizes the fundamental differences between security groups and network ACLs.

Table 6-1. Security and NACL comparison table

Security group	Network ACL
Operates at the instance level.	Operates at the subnet level.
Supports allow rules only.	Supports allow rules and deny rules.
Stateful: Return traffic is automatically allowed, regardless of any rules.	Stateless: Return traffic must be explicitly allowed by rules.
All rules are evaluated before a forwarding decision is made.	Rules are processed in order, starting with the lowest numbered rule.
Applies to an instance or network interface.	All rules apply to all instances in the subnets that it's associated with.

It is crucial to understand the differences between NACL and security groups. Network connectivity issues often arise due to a security group not allowing traffic on a specific port or someone not adding an outbound rule on an NACL. When troubleshooting issues with AWS networking, developers and network engineers alike should add checking these components to their troubleshooting list.

All the components we have discussed thus far manage traffic flow inside the VPC. The following services manage traffic into the VPC from client requests and ultimately to applications running inside a Kubernetes cluster: network address translation devices, internet gateway, and load balancers. Let's dig into those a little more.

Network address translation devices

Network address translation (NAT) devices are used when instances inside a VPC require internet connectivity, but network connections should not be made directly to instances. Examples of instances that should run behind a NAT device are database instances or other middleware needed to run applications.

In AWS, network engineers have several options for running NAT devices. They can manage their own NAT devices deployed as EC2 instances or use the AWS Managed Service NAT gateway (NAT GW). Both require public subnets deployed in multiple AZs for high availability and EIP. A restriction of a NAT GW is that the IP address of it cannot change after you deploy it. Also, that IP address will be the source IP address used to communicate with the internet gateway.

In the VPC route table in Figure 6-7, we can see how the two route tables exist to establish a connection to the internet. The main route table has two rules, a local route for the inter-VPC and a route for `0.0.0.0/0` with a target of the NAT GW ID. The private subnet's database servers will route traffic to the internet via that NAT GW rule in their route tables.

Pods and instances in EKS will need to egress the VPC, so a NAT device must be deployed. Your choice of NAT device will depend on the operational overhead, cost, or availability requirements for your network design.

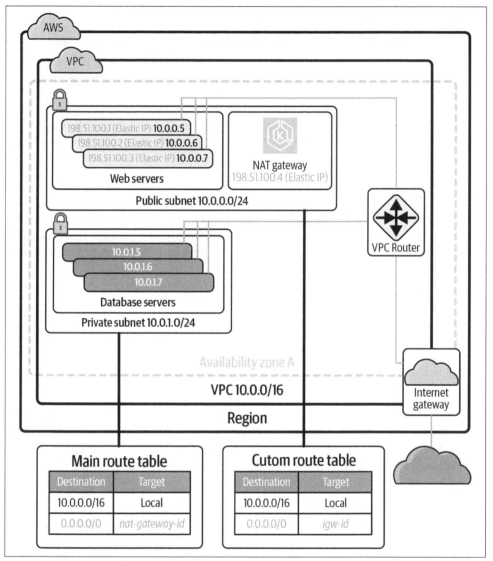

The following text appears within the figure:

AWS

VPC

198.51.100.1 (Elastic IP) **10.0.0.5**
198.51.100.2 (Elastic IP) **10.0.0.6**
198.51.100.3 (Elastic IP) **10.0.0.7**
Web servers

NAT gateway
198.51.100.4 (Elastic IP)

Public subnet 10.0.0.0/24

VPC Router

10.0.1.5
10.0.1.6
10.0.1.7
Database servers

Private subnet 10.0.1.0/24

Availability zone A

VPC 10.0.0/16

Internet gateway

Region

Main route table	
Destination	Target
10.0.0.0/16	Local
0.0.0.0/0	nat-gateway-id

Cutom route table	
Destination	Target
10.0.0.0/16	Local
0.0.0.0/0	igw-id

Figure 6-7. VPC routing diagram

Internet gateway

The internet gateway is an AWS-managed service and device in the VPC network that allows connectivity to the internet for all devices in the VPC. Here are the steps to ensure access to or from the internet in a VPC:

1. Deploy and attach an IGW to the VPC.

2. Define a route in the subnet's route table that directs internet-bound traffic to the IGW.

3. Verify NACLs and security group rules allow the traffic to flow to and from instances.

All of this is shown in the VPC routing from Figure 6-7. We see the IGW deploy for the VPC, a custom route table setup that routes all traffic, `0.0.0.0/0`, to the IGW. The web instances have an IPv4 internet routable address, `198.51.100.1-3`.

Elastic load balancers

Now that traffic flows from the internet and clients can request access to applications running inside a VPC, we will need to scale and distribute the load for requests. AWS has several options for developers, depending on the type of application load and network traffic requirements needed.

The elastic load balancer has four options:

Classic
> A classic load balancer provides fundamental load balancing of EC2 instances. It operates at the request and the connection level. Classic load balancers are limited in functionality and are not to be used with containers.

Application
> Application load balancers are layer 7 aware. Traffic routing is made with request-specific information like HTTP headers or HTTP paths. The application load balancer is used with the application load balancer controller. The ALB controller allows devs to automate the deployment and ALB without using the console or API, instead just a few YAML lines.

Network
> The network load balancer operates at layer 4. Traffic can be routed based on incoming TCP/UDP ports to individual hosts running services on that port. The network load balancer also allows admins to deploy then with an EIP, a feature unique to the network load balancer.

Gateway
> The gateway load balancer manages traffic for appliances at the VPC level. Such network devices like deep packet inspection or proxies can be used with a gateway load balancer. The gateway load balancer is added here to complete the AWS service offering but is not used within the EKS ecosystem.

AWS load balancers have several attributes that are important to understand when working with not only containers but other workloads inside the VPC:

Rule
> (ALB only) The rules that you define for your listener determine how the load balancer routes all requests to the targets in the target groups.

Listener
> Checks for requests from clients. They support HTTP and HTTPS on ports 1–65535.

Target
> An EC2 instance, IP address, pods, or lambda running application code.

Target Group
> Used to route requests to a registered target.

Health Check
> Test to ensure targets are still able to accept client requests.

Each of these components of an ALB is outlined in Figure 6-8. When a request comes into the load balancer, a listener is continually checking for requests that match the protocol and port defined for it. Each listener has a set of rules that define where to direct the request. The rule will have an action type to determine how to handle the request:

authenticate-cognito
> (HTTPS listeners) Use Amazon Cognito to authenticate users.

authenticate-oidc
> (HTTPS listeners) Use an identity provider that is compliant with OpenID Connect to authenticate users.

fixed-response
> Returns a custom HTTP response.

forward
> Forward requests to the specified target groups.

redirect
> Redirect requests from one URL to another.

The action with the lowest order value is performed first. Each rule must include exactly one of the following actions: forward, redirect, or fixed-response. In Figure 6-8, we have target groups, which will be the recipient of our forward rules. Each target in the target group will have health checks so the load balancer will know which instances are healthy and ready to receive requests.

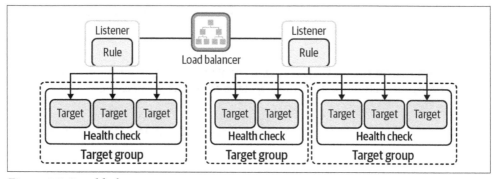

Figure 6-8. Load balancer components

Now that we have a basic understanding of how AWS structures its networking components, we can begin to see how EKS leverages these components to the network and secure the managed Kubernetes cluster and network.

Amazon Elastic Kubernetes Service

Amazon Elastic Kubernetes Service (EKS) is AWS's managed Kubernetes service. It allows developers, cluster administrators, and network administrators to quickly deploy a production-scale Kubernetes cluster. Using the scaling nature of the cloud and AWS network services, with one API request, many services are deployed, including all the components we reviewed in the previous sections.

How does EKS accomplish this? Like with any new service AWS releases, EKS has gotten significantly more feature-rich and easier to use. EKS now supports on-prem deploys with EKS Anywhere, serverless with EKS Fargate, and even Windows nodes. EKS clusters can be deployed traditionally with the AWS CLI or console. `eksctl` is a command-line tool developed by Weaveworks, and it is by far the easiest way to date to deploy all the components needed to run EKS. Our next section will detail the requirements to run an EKS cluster and how `eksctl` accomplishes this for cluster admins and devs.

Let's discuss the components of EKS cluster networking.

EKS nodes

Workers nodes in EKS come in three flavors: EKS-managed node groups, self-managed nodes, and AWS Fargate. The choice for the administrator is how much control and operational overhead they would like to accrue.

Managed node group
Amazon EKS managed node groups create and manage EC2 instances for you. All managed nodes are provisioned as part of an EC2 Auto Scaling group that's managed by Amazon EKS as well. All resources including EC2 instances and

Auto Scaling groups run within your AWS account. A managed-node group's Auto Scaling group spans all the subnets that you specify when you create the group.

Self-managed node group

Amazon EKS nodes run in your AWS account and connect to your cluster's control plane via the API endpoint. You deploy nodes into a node group. A node group is a collection of EC2 instances that are deployed in an EC2 Auto Scaling group. All instances in a node group must do the following:

- Be the same instance type
- Be running the same Amazon Machine Image
- Use the same Amazon EKS node IAM role

Fargate

Amazon EKS integrates Kubernetes with AWS Fargate by using controllers that are built by AWS using the upstream, extensible model provided by Kubernetes. Each pod running on Fargate has its own isolation boundary and does not share the underlying kernel, CPU, memory, or elastic network interface with another pod. You also cannot use security groups for pods with pods running on Fargate.

The instance type also affects the cluster network. In EKS the number of pods that can run on the nodes is defined by the number of IP addresses that instance can run. We discuss this further in "AWS VPC CNI" on page 263 and "eksctl" on page 261.

Nodes must be able to communicate with the Kubernetes control plane and other AWS services. The IP address space is crucial to run an EKS cluster. Nodes, pods, and all other services will use the VPC CIDR address ranges for components. The EKS VPC requires a NAT gateway for private subnets and that those subnets be tagged for use with EKS:

```
Key - kubernetes.io/cluster/<cluster-name>
Value - shared
```

The placement of each node will determine the network "mode" that EKS operates; this has design considerations for your subnets and Kubernetes API traffic routing.

EKS mode

Figure 6-9 outlines EKS components. The Amazon EKS control plane creates up to four cross-account elastic network interfaces in your VPC for each cluster. EKS uses two VPCs, one for the Kubernetes control plane, including the Kubernetes API masters, API loadbalancer, and etcd depending on the networking model; the other is the customer VPC where the EKS worker nodes run your pods. As part of the boot process for the EC2 instance, the Kubelet is started. The node's Kubelet reaches out to the Kubernetes cluster endpoint to register the node. It connects either to the public endpoint outside the VPC or to the private endpoint within the VPC. kubectl commands reach out to the API endpoint in the EKS VPC. End users reach applications running in the customer VPC.

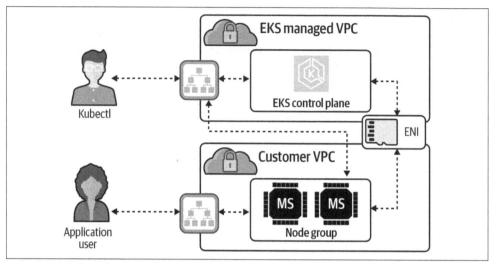

Figure 6-9. EKS communication path

There are three ways to configure cluster control traffic and the Kubernetes API endpoint for EKS, depending on where the control and data planes of the Kubernetes components run.

The networking modes are as follows:

Public-only
Everything runs in a public subnet, including worker nodes.

Private-only
Runs solely in a private subnet, and Kubernetes cannot create internet-facing load balancers.

Mixed
Combo of public and private.

The public endpoint is the default option; it is public because the load balancer for the API endpoint is on a public subnet, as shown in Figure 6-10. Kubernetes API requests that originate from within the cluster's VPC, like when the worker node reaches out to the control plane, leave the customer VPC, but not the Amazon network. One security concern to consider when using a public endpoint is that the API endpoints are on a public subnet and reachable on the internet.

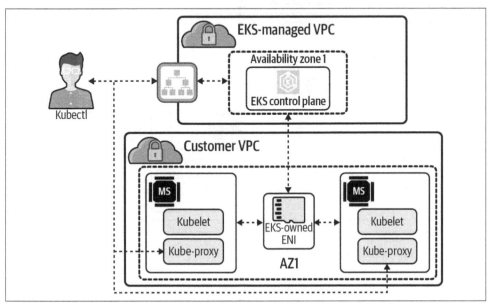

Figure 6-10. EKS public-only network mode

Figure 6-11 shows the private endpoint mode; all traffic to your cluster API must come from within your cluster's VPC. There's no internet access to your API server; any kubectl commands must come from within the VPC or a connected network. The cluster's API endpoint is resolved by public DNS to a private IP address in the VPC.

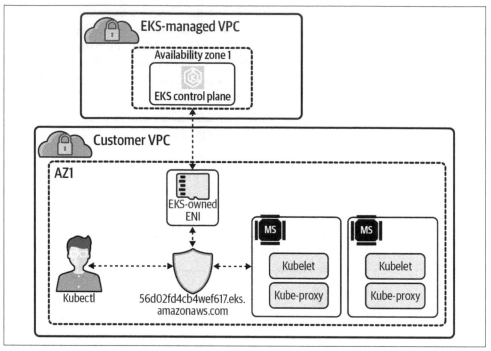

Figure 6-11. EKS private-only network mode

When both public and private endpoints are enabled, any Kubernetes API requests from within the VPC communicate to the control plane by the EKS-managed ENIs within the customer VPC, as demonstrated in Figure 6-12. The cluster API is still accessible from the internet, but it can be limited using security groups and NACLs.

> Please see the AWS documentation (*https://oreil.ly/mW7ii*) for more ways to deploy an EKS.

Determining what mode to operate in is a critical decision administrators will make. It will affect the application traffic, the routing for load balancers, and the security of the cluster. There are many other requirements when deploying a cluster in EKS as well. eksctl is one tool to help manage all those requirements. But how does eksctl accomplish that?

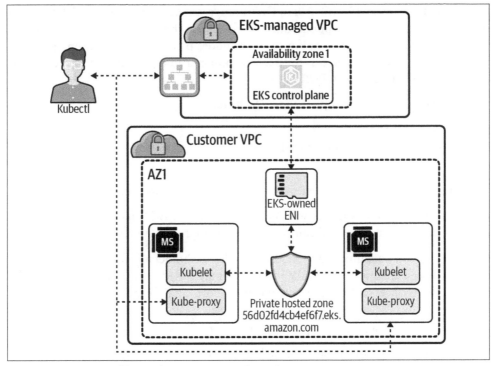

Figure 6-12. EKS public and private network mode

eksctl

eksctl is a command-line tool developed by Weaveworks, and it is by far the easiest way to deploy all the components needed to run EKS.

 All the information about eksctl is available on its website (*https:// eksctl.io*).

eksctl defaults to creating a cluster with the following default parameters:

- An autogenerated cluster name
- Two m5.large worker nodes
- Use of the official AWS EKS AMI
- Us-west-2 default AWS region
- A dedicated VPC

A dedicated VPC with 192.168.0.0/16 CIDR range, eksctl will create by default 8 /19 subnets: three private, three public, and two reserved subnets. eksctl will also deploy a NAT GW that allows for communication of nodes placed in private subnets and an internet gateway to enable access for needed container images and communication to the Amazon S3 and Amazon ECR APIs.

Two security groups are set up for the EKS cluster:

Ingress inter node group SG
    Allows nodes to communicate with each other on all ports

Control plane security group
    Allows communication between the control plane and worker node groups

Node groups in public subnets will have SSH disabled. EC2 instances in the initial node group get a public IP and can be accessed on high-level ports.

One node group containing two m5.large nodes is the default for eksctl. But how many pods can that node run? AWS has a formula based on the node type and the number of interfaces and IP addresses it can support. That formula is as follows:

```
(Number of network interfaces for the instance type ×
(the number of IP addresses per network interface - 1)) + 2
```

Using the preceding formula and the default instance size on eksctl, an m5.large can support a maximum of 29 pods.

System pods count toward the maximum pods. The CNI plugin and kube-proxy pods run on every node in a cluster, so you're only able to deploy 27 additional pods to an m5.large instance. Core-DNS runs on nodes in the cluster, which further decrements the maximum number of pods a node can run.

Teams running clusters must decide on cluster sizing and instance types to ensure no deployment issues with hitting node and IP limitations. Pods will sit in the "waiting" state if there are no nodes available with the pod's IP address. Scaling events for the EKS node groups can also hit EC2 instance type limits and cause cascading issues.

All of these networking options are configurable via the eksctl config file.

eksctl VPC options are available in the eksctl documentation (*https://oreil.ly/m2Nqc*).

We have discussed how the size node is important for pod IP addressing and the number of them we can run. Once the node is deployed, the AWS VPC CNI manages pod IP addressing for nodes. Let's dive into the inner workings of the CNI.

AWS VPC CNI

AWS has its open source implementation of a CNI. AWS VPC CNI for the Kubernetes plugin offers high throughput and availability, low latency, and minimal network jitter on the AWS network. Network engineers can apply existing AWS VPC networking and security best practices for building Kubernetes clusters on AWS. It includes using native AWS services like VPC flow logs, VPC routing policies, and security groups for network traffic isolation.

> The open source for AWS VPC CNI is on GitHub (*https://oreil.ly/ akwqx*).

There are two components to the AWS VPC CNI:

CNI plugin
  The CNI plugin is responsible for wiring up the host's and pod's network stack when called. It also configures the interfaces and virtual Ethernet pairs.

ipamd
  A long-running node-local IPAM daemon is responsible for maintaining a warm pool of available IP addresses and assigning an IP address to a pod.

Figure 6-13 demonstrates what the VPC CNI will do for nodes. A customer VPC with a subnet 10.200.1.0/24 in AWS gives us 250 usable addresses in this subnet. There are two nodes in our cluster. In EKS, the managed nodes run with the AWS CNI as a daemon set. In our example, each node has only one pod running, with a secondary IP address on the ENI, `10.200.1.6` and `10.200.1.8`, for each pod. When a worker node first joins the cluster, there is only one ENI and all its addresses in the ENI. When pod three gets scheduled to node 1, ipamd assigns the IP address to the ENI for that pod. In this case, `10.200.1.7` is the same thing on node 2 with pod 4.

When a worker node first joins the cluster, there is only one ENI and all of its addresses in the ENI. Without any configuration, `ipamd` always tries to keep one extra ENI. When several pods running on the node exceeds the number of addresses on a single ENI, the CNI backend starts allocating a new ENI. The CNI plugin works by allocating multiple ENIs to EC2 instances and then attaches secondary IP addresses to these ENIs. This plugin allows the CNI to allocate as many IPs per instance as possible.

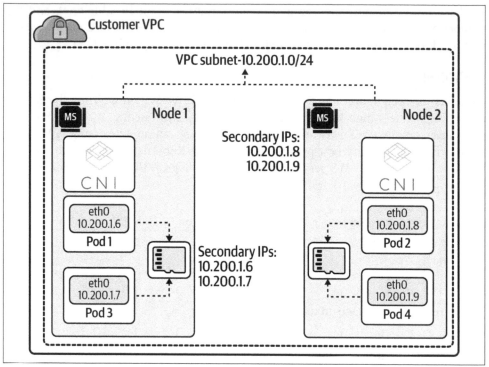

Figure 6-13. AWS VPC CNI example

The AWS VPC CNI is highly configurable. This list includes just a few options:

AWS_VPC_CNI_NODE_PORT_SUPPORT
Specifies whether NodePort services are enabled on a worker node's primary network interface. This requires additional `iptables` rules and that the kernel's reverse path filter on the primary interface is set to loose.

AWS_VPC_K8S_CNI_CUSTOM_NETWORK_CFG
Worker nodes can be configured in public subnets, so you need to configure pods to be deployed in private subnets, or if pods' security requirement needs are different from others running on the node, setting this to `true` will enable that.

AWS_VPC_ENI_MTU
Default: 9001. Used to configure the MTU size for attached ENIs. The valid range is from 576 to 9001.

WARM_ENI_TARGET
Specifies the number of free elastic network interfaces (and all of their available IP addresses) that the `ipamd` daemon should attempt to keep available for pod assignment on the node. By default, `ipamd` attempts to keep one elastic network

interface and all of its IP addresses available for pod assignment. The number of IP addresses per network interface varies by instance type.

AWS_VPC_K8S_CNI_EXTERNALSNAT

Specifies whether an external NAT gateway should be used to provide SNAT of secondary ENI IP addresses. If set to `true`, the SNAT `iptables` rule and external VPC IP rule are not applied, and these rules are removed if they have already been applied. Disable SNAT if you need to allow inbound communication to your pods from external VPNs, direct connections, and external VPCs, and your pods do not need to access the internet directly via an internet gateway.

For example, if your pods with a private IP address need to communicate with others' private IP address spaces, you enable `AWS_VPC_K8S_CNI_EXTERNALSNAT` by using this command:

```
kubectl set env daemonset
-n kube-system aws-node AWS_VPC_K8S_CNI_EXTERNALSNAT=true
```

> All the information for EKS pod networking can be found in the EKS documentation (*https://oreil.ly/RAVVY*).

The AWS VPC CNI allows for maximum control over the networking options on EKS in the AWS network.

There is also the AWS ALB ingress controller that makes managing and deploying applications on the AWS cloud network smooth and automated. Let's dig into that next.

AWS ALB ingress controller

Let's walk through the example in Figure 6-14 of how the AWS ALB works with Kubernetes. For a review of what an ingress controller is, please check out Chapter 5.

Let's discuss all the moving parts of ALB Ingress controller:

1. The ALB ingress controller watches for ingress events from the API server. When requirements are met, it will start the creation process of an ALB.

2. An ALB is created in AWS for the new ingress resource. Those resources can be internal or external to the cluster.

3. Target groups are created in AWS for each unique Kubernetes service described in the ingress resource.

4. Listeners are created for every port detailed in your ingress resource annotations. Default ports for HTTP and HTTPS traffic are set up if not specified. NodePort services for each service create the node ports that are used for our health checks.

5. Rules are created for each path specified in your ingress resource. This ensures traffic to a specific path is routed to the correct Kubernetes service.

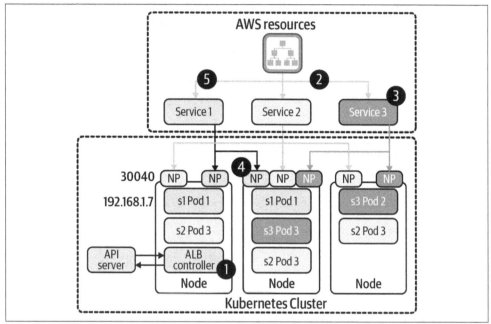

Figure 6-14. AWS ALB example

How traffic reaches nodes and pods is affected by one of two modes the ALB can run:

Instance mode
    Ingress traffic starts at the ALB and reaches the Kubernetes nodes through each service's NodePort. This means that services referenced from ingress resources must be exposed by type:NodePort to be reached by the ALB.

IP mode
    Ingress traffic starts at the ALB and reaches directly to the Kubernetes pods. CNIs must support a directly accessible pod IP address via secondary IP addresses on ENI.

The AWS ALB ingress controller allows developers to manage their network needs like their application components. There is no need for other tool sets in the pipeline.

The AWS networking components are tightly integrated with EKS. Understanding the basic options of how they work is fundamental for all those looking to scale their applications on Kubernetes on AWS using EKS. The size of your subnets, the placements of the nodes in those subnets, and of course the size of nodes will affect how large of a network of pods and services you can run on the AWS network. Using a managed service such as EKS, with open source tools like `eksctl`, will greatly reduce the operational overhead of running an AWS Kubernetes cluster.

Deploying an Application on an AWS EKS Cluster

Let's walk through deploying an EKS cluster to manage our Golang web server:

1. Deploy the EKS cluster.

2. Deploy the web server Application and LoadBalancer.

3. Verify.

4. Deploy ALB Ingress Controller and Verify.

5. Clean up.

Deploy EKS cluster

Let's deploy an EKS cluster, with the current and latest version EKS supports, 1.20:

```
export CLUSTER_NAME=eks-demo
eksctl create cluster -N 3 --name ${CLUSTER_NAME} --version=1.20
eksctl version 0.54.0
using region us-west-2
setting availability zones to [us-west-2b us-west-2a us-west-2c]
subnets for us-west-2b - public:192.168.0.0/19 private:192.168.96.0/19
subnets for us-west-2a - public:192.168.32.0/19 private:192.168.128.0/19
subnets for us-west-2c - public:192.168.64.0/19 private:192.168.160.0/19
nodegroup "ng-90b7a9a5" will use "ami-0a1abe779ecfc6a3e" [AmazonLinux2/1.20]
using Kubernetes version 1.20
creating EKS cluster "eks-demo" in "us-west-2" region with un-managed nodes
will create 2 separate CloudFormation stacks for cluster itself and the initial
nodegroup
if you encounter any issues, check CloudFormation console or try
'eksctl utils describe-stacks --region=us-west-2 --cluster=eks-demo'
CloudWatch logging will not be enabled for cluster "eks-demo" in "us-west-2"
you can enable it with
'eksctl utils update-cluster-logging --enable-types={SPECIFY-YOUR-LOG-TYPES-HERE
(e.g. all)} --region=us-west-2 --cluster=eks-demo'
Kubernetes API endpoint access will use default of
{publicAccess=true, privateAccess=false} for cluster "eks-demo" in "us-west-2"
2 sequential tasks: { create cluster control plane "eks-demo",
3 sequential sub-tasks: { wait for control plane to become ready, 1 task:
{ create addons }, create nodegroup "ng-90b7a9a5" } }
building cluster stack "eksctl-eks-demo-cluster"
deploying stack "eksctl-eks-demo-cluster"
waiting for CloudFormation stack "eksctl-eks-demo-cluster"
```

```
<truncate>
building nodegroup stack "eksctl-eks-demo-nodegroup-ng-90b7a9a5"
--nodes-min=3 was set automatically for nodegroup ng-90b7a9a5
deploying stack "eksctl-eks-demo-nodegroup-ng-90b7a9a5"
waiting for CloudFormation stack "eksctl-eks-demo-nodegroup-ng-90b7a9a5"
<truncated>
waiting for the control plane availability...
saved kubeconfig as "/Users/strongjz/.kube/config"
no tasks
all EKS cluster resources for "eks-demo" have been created
adding identity
"arn:aws:iam::1234567890:role/
eksctl-eks-demo-nodegroup-ng-9-NodeInstanceRole-TLKVDDVTW2TZ" to auth ConfigMap
nodegroup "ng-90b7a9a5" has 0 node(s)
waiting for at least 3 node(s) to become ready in "ng-90b7a9a5"
nodegroup "ng-90b7a9a5" has 3 node(s)
node "ip-192-168-31-17.us-west-2.compute.internal" is ready
node "ip-192-168-58-247.us-west-2.compute.internal" is ready
node "ip-192-168-85-104.us-west-2.compute.internal" is ready
kubectl command should work with "/Users/strongjz/.kube/config",
try 'kubectl get nodes'
EKS cluster "eks-demo" in "us-west-2" region is ready
```

In the output we can see that EKS creating a nodegroup, `eksctl-eks-demo-nodegroup-ng-90b7a9a5`, with three nodes:

```
ip-192-168-31-17.us-west-2.compute.internal
ip-192-168-58-247.us-west-2.compute.internal
ip-192-168-85-104.us-west-2.compute.internal
```

They are all inside a VPC with three public and three private subnets across three AZs:

```
public:192.168.0.0/19 private:192.168.96.0/19
public:192.168.32.0/19 private:192.168.128.0/19
public:192.168.64.0/19 private:192.168.160.0/19
```

We used the default settings of eksctl, and it deployed the k8s API as a public endpoint, {publicAccess=true, privateAccess=false}.

Now we can deploy our Golang web application in the cluster and expose it with a LoadBalancer service.

Deploy test application

You can deploy applications individually or all together. *dnsutils.yml* is our `dnsutils` testing pod, *database.yml* is the Postgres database for pod connectivity testing, *web.yml* is the Golang web server and the LoadBalancer service:

```
kubectl apply -f dnsutils.yml,database.yml,web.yml
```

Let's run a kubectl get pods to see if all the pods are running fine:

```
kubectl get pods -o wide
NAME                    READY   STATUS    IP               NODE
app-6bf97c555d-5mzfb    1/1     Running   192.168.15.108   ip-192-168-0-94
app-6bf97c555d-76fgm    1/1     Running   192.168.52.42    ip-192-168-63-151
app-6bf97c555d-gw4k9    1/1     Running   192.168.88.61    ip-192-168-91-46
dnsutils                1/1     Running   192.168.57.174   ip-192-168-63-151
postgres-0              1/1     Running   192.168.70.170   ip-192-168-91-46
```

Now check on the LoadBalancer service:

```
kubectl get svc clusterip-service
NAME               TYPE           CLUSTER-IP
EXTERNAL-IP                                                              PORT(S)       AGE
clusterip-service  LoadBalancer   10.100.159.28
a76d1c69125e543e5b67c899f5e45284-593302470.us-west-2.elb.amazonaws.com   80:32671/TCP  29m
```

The service has endpoints as well:

```
kubectl get endpoints clusterip-service
NAME               ENDPOINTS                                                      AGE
clusterip-service  192.168.15.108:8080,192.168.52.42:8080,192.168.88.61:8080      58m
```

We should verify the application is reachable inside the cluster, with the ClusterIP and port, 10.100.159.28:8080; service name and port, clusterip-service:80; and finally pod IP and port, 192.168.15.108:8080:

```
kubectl exec dnsutils -- wget -qO- 10.100.159.28:80/data
Database Connected

kubectl exec dnsutils -- wget -qO- 10.100.159.28:80/host
NODE: ip-192-168-63-151.us-west-2.compute.internal, POD IP:192.168.52.42

kubectl exec dnsutils -- wget -qO- clusterip-service:80/host
NODE: ip-192-168-91-46.us-west-2.compute.internal, POD IP:192.168.88.61

kubectl exec dnsutils -- wget -qO- clusterip-service:80/data
Database Connected

kubectl exec dnsutils -- wget -qO- 192.168.15.108:8080/data
Database Connected

kubectl exec dnsutils -- wget -qO- 192.168.15.108:8080/host
NODE: ip-192-168-0-94.us-west-2.compute.internal, POD IP:192.168.15.108
```

The database port is reachable from dnsutils, with the pod IP and port 192.168.70.170:5432, and the service name and port - postgres:5432:

```
kubectl exec dnsutils -- nc -z -vv -w 5 192.168.70.170 5432
192.168.70.170 (192.168.70.170:5432) open
sent 0, rcvd 0
```

```
kubectl exec dnsutils -- nc -z -vv -w 5 postgres 5432
postgres (10.100.106.134:5432) open
sent 0, rcvd 0
```

The application inside the cluster is up and running. Let's test it from external to the cluster.

Verify LoadBalancer services for Golang web server

`kubectl` will return all the information we will need to test, the ClusterIP, the external IP, and all the ports:

```
kubectl get svc clusterip-service
NAME               TYPE           CLUSTER-IP
EXTERNAL-IP                                                        PORT(S)      AGE
clusterip-service  LoadBalancer   10.100.159.28
a76d1c69125e543e5b67c899f5e45284-593302470.us-west-2.elb.amazonaws.com  80:32671/TCP  29m
```

Using the external IP of the load balancer:

```
wget -q0-
a76d1c69125e543e5b67c899f5e45284-593302470.us-west-2.elb.amazonaws.com/data
Database Connected
```

Let's test the load balancer and make multiple requests to our backends:

```
wget -q0-
a76d1c69125e543e5b67c899f5e45284-593302470.us-west-2.elb.amazonaws.com/host
NODE: ip-192-168-63-151.us-west-2.compute.internal, POD IP:192.168.52.42

wget -q0-
a76d1c69125e543e5b67c899f5e45284-593302470.us-west-2.elb.amazonaws.com/host
NODE: ip-192-168-91-46.us-west-2.compute.internal, POD IP:192.168.88.61

wget -q0-
a76d1c69125e543e5b67c899f5e45284-593302470.us-west-2.elb.amazonaws.com/host
NODE: ip-192-168-0-94.us-west-2.compute.internal, POD IP:192.168.15.108

wget -q0-
a76d1c69125e543e5b67c899f5e45284-593302470.us-west-2.elb.amazonaws.com/host
NODE: ip-192-168-0-94.us-west-2.compute.internal, POD IP:192.168.15.108
```

`kubectl get pods -o wide` again will verify our pod information matches the load-balancer requests:

```
kubectl get pods -o wide
NAME                   READY  STATUS   IP               NODE
app-6bf97c555d-5mzfb   1/1    Running  192.168.15.108   ip-192-168-0-94
app-6bf97c555d-76fgm   1/1    Running  192.168.52.42    ip-192-168-63-151
app-6bf97c555d-gw4k9   1/1    Running  192.168.88.61    ip-192-168-91-46
dnsutils               1/1    Running  192.168.57.174   ip-192-168-63-151
postgres-0             1/1    Running  192.168.70.170   ip-192-168-91-46
```

We can also check the nodeport, since `dnsutils` is running inside our VPC, on an EC2 instance; it can do a DNS lookup on the private host, `ip-192-168-0-94.us-west-2.compute.internal`, and the `kubectl get service` command gave us the node port, 32671:

```
kubectl exec dnsutils -- wget -q0-
ip-192-168-0-94.us-west-2.compute.internal:32671/host
NODE: ip-192-168-0-94.us-west-2.compute.internal, POD IP:192.168.15.108
```

Everything seems to running just fine externally and locally in our cluster.

Deploy ALB ingress and verify

For some sections of the deployment, we will need to know the AWS account ID we are deploying. Let's put that into an environment variable. To get your account ID, you can run the following:

```
aws sts get-caller-identity
{
    "UserId": "AIDA2RZMTHAQTEUI3Z537",
    "Account": "1234567890",
    "Arn": "arn:aws:iam::1234567890:user/eks"
}

export ACCOUNT_ID=1234567890
```

If it is not set up for the cluster already, we will have to set up an OIDC provider with the cluster.

This step is needed to give IAM permissions to a pod running in the cluster using the IAM for SA:

```
eksctl utils associate-iam-oidc-provider \
--region ${AWS_REGION} \
--cluster ${CLUSTER_NAME}  \
--approve
```

For the SA role, we will need to create an IAM policy to determine the permissions for the ALB controller in AWS:

```
aws iam create-policy \
--policy-name AWSLoadBalancerControllerIAMPolicy \
--policy-document iam_policy.json
```

Now we need to create the SA and attach it to the IAM role we created:

```
eksctl create iamserviceaccount \
> --cluster ${CLUSTER_NAME} \
> --namespace kube-system \
> --name aws-load-balancer-controller \
> --attach-policy-arn
arn:aws:iam::${ACCOUNT_ID}:policy/AWSLoadBalancerControllerIAMPolicy \
> --override-existing-serviceaccounts \
```

```
> --approve
eksctl version 0.54.0
using region us-west-2
1 iamserviceaccount (kube-system/aws-load-balancer-controller) was included
(based on the include/exclude rules)
metadata of serviceaccounts that exist in Kubernetes will be updated,
as --override-existing-serviceaccounts was set
1 task: { 2 sequential sub-tasks: { create IAM role for serviceaccount
"kube-system/aws-load-balancer-controller", create serviceaccount
"kube-system/aws-load-balancer-controller" } }
building iamserviceaccount stack
deploying stack
waiting for CloudFormation stack
waiting for CloudFormation stack
waiting for CloudFormation stack
created serviceaccount "kube-system/aws-load-balancer-controller"
```

We can see all the details of the SA with the following:

```
kubectl get sa aws-load-balancer-controller -n kube-system -o yaml
apiVersion: v1
kind: ServiceAccount
metadata:
annotations:
eks.amazonaws.com/role-arn:
arn:aws:iam::1234567890:role/eksctl-eks-demo-addon-iamserviceaccount-Role1
creationTimestamp: "2021-06-27T18:40:06Z"
labels:
app.kubernetes.io/managed-by: eksctl
name: aws-load-balancer-controller
namespace: kube-system
resourceVersion: "16133"
uid: 30281eb5-8edf-4840-bc94-f214c1102e4f
secrets:
- name: aws-load-balancer-controller-token-dtq48
```

The `TargetGroupBinding` CRD allows the controller to bind a Kubernetes service endpoint to an AWS `TargetGroup`:

```
kubectl apply -f crd.yml
customresourcedefinition.apiextensions.k8s.io/ingressclassparams.elbv2.k8s.aws
configured
customresourcedefinition.apiextensions.k8s.io/targetgroupbindings.elbv2.k8s.aws
configured
```

Now we're ready to the deploy the ALB controller with Helm.

Set the version environment to deploy:

```
export ALB_LB_VERSION="v2.2.0"
```

Now deploy it, add the eks Helm repo, get the VPC ID the cluster is running in, and finally deploy via Helm.

```
helm repo add eks https://aws.github.io/eks-charts

export VPC_ID=$(aws eks describe-cluster \
--name ${CLUSTER_NAME} \
--query "cluster.resourcesVpcConfig.vpcId" \
--output text)

helm upgrade -i aws-load-balancer-controller \
eks/aws-load-balancer-controller \
-n kube-system \
--set clusterName=${CLUSTER_NAME} \
--set serviceAccount.create=false \
--set serviceAccount.name=aws-load-balancer-controller \
--set image.tag="${ALB_LB_VERSION}" \
--set region=${AWS_REGION} \
--set vpcId=${VPC_ID}

Release "aws-load-balancer-controller" has been upgraded. Happy Helming!
NAME: aws-load-balancer-controller
LAST DEPLOYED: Sun Jun 27 14:43:06 2021
NAMESPACE: kube-system
STATUS: deployed
REVISION: 2
TEST SUITE: None
NOTES:
AWS Load Balancer controller installed!
```

We can watch the deploy logs here:

```
kubectl logs -n kube-system -f deploy/aws-load-balancer-controller
```

Now to deploy our ingress with ALB:

```
kubectl apply -f alb-rules.yml
ingress.networking.k8s.io/app configured
```

With the kubectl describe ing app output, we can see the ALB has been deployed.

We can also see the ALB public DNS address, the rules for the instances, and the endpoints backing the service.

```
kubectl describe ing app
Name:           app
Namespace:      default
Address:
k8s-default-app-d5e5a26be4-2128411681.us-west-2.elb.amazonaws.com
Default backend:  default-http-backend:80
(<error: endpoints "default-http-backend" not found>)
Rules:
Host       Path  Backends
 ----       ----  --------
*
         /data   clusterip-service:80 (192.168.3.221:8080,
192.168.44.165:8080,
```

```
         192.168.89.224:8080)
                  /host   clusterip-service:80 (192.168.3.221:8080,
         192.168.44.165:8080,
         192.168.89.224:8080)
         Annotations:  alb.ingress.kubernetes.io/scheme: internet-facing
         kubernetes.io/ingress.class: alb
         Events:
         Type     Reason                Age              From
         Message
         ----     ------                ----             ----
         -------
         Normal   SuccessfullyReconciled  4m33s (x2 over 5m58s)   ingress
         Successfully reconciled
```

It's time to test our ALB!

```
wget -qO- k8s-default-app-d5e5a26be4-2128411681.us-west-2.elb.amazonaws.com/data
Database Connected

wget -qO- k8s-default-app-d5e5a26be4-2128411681.us-west-2.elb.amazonaws.com/host
NODE: ip-192-168-63-151.us-west-2.compute.internal, POD IP:192.168.44.165
```

Cleanup

Once you are done working with EKS and testing, make sure to delete the applications pods and the service to ensure that everything is deleted:

```
kubectl delete -f dnsutils.yml,database.yml,web.yml
```

Clean up the ALB:

```
kubectl delete -f alb-rules.yml
```

Remove the IAM policy for ALB controller:

```
aws iam  delete-policy
--policy-arn arn:aws:iam::${ACCOUNT_ID}:policy/AWSLoadBalancerControllerIAMPolicy
```

Verify there are no leftover EBS volumes from the PVCs for test application. Delete any EBS volumes found for the PVC's for the Postgres test database:

```
aws ec2 describe-volumes --filters
Name=tag:kubernetes.io/created-for/pv/name,Values=*
--query "Volumes[].{ID:VolumeId}"
```

Verify there are no load balancers running, ALB or otherwise:

```
aws elbv2 describe-load-balancers --query "LoadBalancers[].LoadBalancerArn"
```

```
aws elb describe-load-balancers --query "LoadBalancerDescriptions[].DNSName"
```

Let's make sure we delete the cluster, so you don't get charged for a cluster doing nothing:

```
eksctl delete cluster --name ${CLUSTER_NAME}
```

We deployed a service load balancer that will for each service deploy a classical ELB into AWS. The ALB controller allows developers to use ingress with ALB or NLBs to expose the application externally. If we were to scale our application to multiple back-end services, the ingress allows us to use one load balancer and route based on layer 7 information.

In the next section, we will explore GCP in the same manner we just did for AWS.

Google Compute Cloud (GCP)

In 2008, Google announced App Engine, a platform as a service to deploy Java, Python, Ruby, and Go applications. Like its competitors, GCP has extended its service offerings. Cloud providers work to distinguish their offerings, so no two products are ever the same. Nonetheless, many products do have a lot in common. For instance, GCP Compute Engine is an infrastructure as a service to run virtual machines. The GCP network consists of 25 cloud regions, 76 zones, and 144 network edge locations. Utilizing both the scale of the GCP network and Compute Engine, GCP has released Google Kubernetes Engine, its container as a service platform.

GCP Network Services

Managed and unmanaged Kubernetes clusters on GCP share the same networking principles. Nodes in either managed or unmanaged clusters run as Google Compute Engine instances. Networks in GCP are VPC networks. GCP VPC networks, like in AWS, contain functionality for IP management, routing, firewalling, and peering.

The GCP network is divided into tiers for customers to choose from; there are premium and standard tiers. They differ in performance, routing, and functionality, so network engineers must decide which is suitable for their workloads. The premium tier is the highest performance for your workloads. All the traffic between the internet and instances in the VPC network is routed within Google's network as far as possible. If your services need global availability, you should use premium. Make sure to remember that the premium tier is the default unless you make configuration changes.

The standard tier is a cost-optimized tier where traffic between the internet and VMs in the VPC network is routed over the internet in general. Network engineers should pick this tier for services that are going to be hosted entirely within a region. The standard tier cannot guarantee performance as it is subject to the same performance that all workloads share on the internet.

The GCP network differs from the other providers by having what is called *global* resources. Global because users can access them in any zone within the same project. These resources include such things as VPC, firewalls, and their routes.

See the GCP documentation (*https://oreil.ly/mzgG2*) for a more comprehensive overview of the network tiers.

Regions and zones

Regions are independent geographic areas that contain multiple zones. Regional resources offer redundancy by being deployed across multiple zones for that region. Zones are deployment areas for resources within a region. One zone is typically a data center within a region, and administrators should consider them a single fault domain. In fault-tolerant application deployments, the best practice is to deploy applications across multiple zones within a region, and for high availability, you should deploy applications across various regions. If a zone becomes unavailable, all the zone resources will be unavailable until owners restore services.

Virtual private cloud

A VPC is a virtual network that provides connectivity for resources within a GCP project. Like accounts and subscriptions, projects can contain multiple VPC networks, and by default, new projects start with a default auto-mode VPC network that also includes one subnet in each region. Custom-mode VPC networks can contain no subnets. As stated earlier, VPC networks are global resources and are not associated with any particular region or zone.

A VPC network contains one or more regional subnets. Subnets have a region, CIDR, and globally unique name. You can use any CIDR for a subnet, including one that overlaps with another private address space. The specific choice of subnet CIDR impacts which IP addresses you can reach and which networks you can peer.

Google creates a "default" VPC network, with randomly generated subnets for each region. Some subnets may overlap with another VPC's subnet (such as the default VPC network in another Google Cloud project), which will prevent peering.

VPC networks support peering and shared VPC configuration. Peering a VPC network allows the VPC in one project to route to the VPC in another, placing them on the same L3 network. You cannot peer with any overlapping VPC network, as some IP addresses exist in both networks. A shared VPC allows another project to use specific subnets, such as creating machines that are part of that subnet. The VPC documentation (*https://oreil.ly/98Wav*) has more information.

Peering VPC networks is standard, as organizations often assign different teams, applications, or components to their project in Google Cloud. Peering has upsides for access control, quota, and reporting. Some admins may also create multiple VPC networks within a project for similar reasons.

Subnet

Subnets are portions within a VPC network with one primary IP range with the ability to have zero or more secondary ranges. Subnets are regional resources, and each subnet defines a range of IP addresses. A region can have more than one subnet. There are two modes of subnet formulation when you create them: auto or custom. When you create an auto-mode VPC network, one subnet from each region is automatically created within it using predefined IP ranges. When you define a custom-mode VPC network, GCP does not provision any subnets, giving administrators control over the ranges. Custom-mode VPC networks are suited for enterprises and production environments for network engineers to use.

Google Cloud allows you to "reserve" static IP addresses for internal and external IP addresses. Users can utilize reserved IP addresses for GCE instances, load balancers, and other products beyond our scope. Reserved internal IP addresses have a name and can be generated automatically or assigned manually. Reserving an internal static IP address prevents it from being randomly automatically assigned while not in use.

Reserving external IP addresses is similar; although you can request an automatically assigned IP address, you cannot choose what IP address to reserve. Because you are reserving a globally routable IP address, charges apply in some circumstances. You cannot secure an external IP address that you were assigned automatically as an ephemeral IP address.

Routes and firewall rules

When deploying a VPC, you can use firewall rules to allow or deny connections to and from your application instances based on the rules you deploy. Each firewall rule can apply to ingress or egress connections, but not both. The instance level is where GCP enforces rules, but the configuration pairs with the VPC network, and you cannot share firewall rules among VPC networks, peered networks included. VPC firewall rules are stateful, so when a TCP session starts, firewall rules allow bidirectional traffic similar to an AWS security group.

Cloud load balancing

Google Cloud Load Balancer (GCLB) offers a fully distributed, high-performance, scalable load balancing service across GCP, with various load balancer options. With GCLB, you get a single Anycast IP that fronts all your backend instances across the globe, including multiregion failover. In addition, software-defined load balancing services enable you to apply load balancing to your HTTP(S), TCP/SSL, and UDP traffic. You can also terminate your SSL traffic with an SSL proxy and HTTPS load balancing. Internal load balancing enables you to build highly available internal services for your internal instances without requiring any load balancers to be exposed to the internet.

The vast majority of GCP users make use of GCP's load balancers with Kubernetes ingress. GCP has internal-facing and external-facing load balancers, with L4 and L7 support. GKE clusters default to creating a GCP load balancer for ingresses and `type: LoadBalancer` services.

To expose applications outside a GKE cluster, GKE provides a built-in GKE ingress controller and GKE service controller, which deploys a Google Cloud load balancer on behalf of GKE users. GKE provides three different load balancers to control access and spread incoming traffic across your cluster as evenly as possible. You can configure one service to use multiple types of load balancers simultaneously:

External load balancers
> Manage traffic from outside the cluster and outside the VPC network. External load balancers use forwarding rules associated with the Google Cloud network to route traffic to a Kubernetes node.

Internal load balancers
> Manage traffic coming from within the same VPC network. Like external load balancers, internal ones use forwarding rules associated with the Google Cloud network to route traffic to a Kubernetes node.

HTTP load balancers
> Specialized external load balancers used for HTTP traffic. They use an ingress resource rather than a forwarding rule to route traffic to a Kubernetes node.

When you create an ingress object, the GKE ingress controller configures a Google Cloud HTTP(S) load balancer according to the ingress manifest and the associated Kubernetes service rules manifest. The client sends a request to the load balancer. The load balancer is a proxy; it chooses a node and forwards the request to that node's NodeIP:NodePort combination. The node uses its `iptables` NAT table to select a pod. As we learned in earlier chapters, `kube-proxy` manages the `iptables` rules on that node.

When an ingress creates a load balancer, the load balancer is "pod aware" instead of routing to all nodes (and relying on the service to route requests to a pod), and the load balancer routes to individual pods. It does this by tracking the underlying `End points/EndpointSlice` object (as covered in Chapter 5) and using individual pod IP addresses as target addresses.

Cluster administrators can use an in-cluster ingress provider, such as ingress-Nginx or Contour. A load balancer points to applicable nodes running the ingress proxy in such a setup, which routes requests to the applicable pods from there. This setup is cheaper for clusters that have many ingresses but incurs performance overhead.

GCE instances

GCE instances have one or more network interfaces. A network interface has a network and subnetwork, a private IP address, and a public IP address. The private IP address must be part of the subnetwork. Private IP addresses can be automatic and ephemeral, custom and ephemeral, or static. External IP addresses can be automatic and ephemeral, or static. You can add more network interfaces to a GCE instance. Additional network interfaces don't need to be in the same VPC network. For example, you may have an instance that bridges two VPCs with varying levels of security. Let's discuss how GKE uses these instances and manages the network services that empower GKE.

GKE

Google Kubernetes Engine (GKE) is Google's managed Kubernetes service. GKE runs a hidden control plane, which cannot be directly viewed or accessed. You can only access specific control plane configurations and the Kubernetes API.

GKE exposes broad cluster config around things like machine types and cluster scaling. It reveals only some network-related settings. At the time of writing, NetworkPolicy support (via Calico), max pods per node (`maxPods` in the kubelet, `--node-CIDR-mask-size` in `kube-controller-manager`), and the pod address range (`--cluster-CIDR` in `kube-controller-manager`) are the customizable options. It is not possible to directly set `apiserver`/`kube-controller-manager` flags.

GKE supports public and private clusters. Private clusters don't issue public IP addresses to nodes, which means nodes are accessible only within your private network. Private clusters also allow you to restrict access to the Kubernetes API to specific IP addresses. GKE runs worker nodes using automatically managed GCE instances by creating creates *node pools*.

GCP GKE nodes

Networking for GKE nodes is comparable to networking for self-managed Kubernetes clusters on GKE. GKE clusters define *node pools,* which are a set of nodes with an identical configuration. This configuration contains GCE-specific settings as well as general Kubernetes settings. Node pools define (virtual) machine type, autoscaling, and the GCE service account. You can also set custom taints and labels per node pool.

A cluster exists on exactly one VPC network. Individual nodes can have their network tags for crafting specific firewall rules. Any GKE cluster running 1.16 or later will have a kube-proxy DaemonSet so that all new nodes in the cluster will automatically have the kube-proxy start. The size of the subnet allows will affect the size of the cluster. So, pay attention to the size of that when you deploy clusters that scale. There is a formula you can use to calculate the maximum number of nodes, N, that a given netmask can support. Use S for the netmask size, whose valid range is between 8 and 29:

```
N = 2(32 -S) - 4
```

Calculate the size of the netmask, S, required to support a maximum of N nodes:

```
S = 32 - ⌈log2(N + 4)⌉
```

Table 6-2 also outlines cluster node and how it scales with subnet size.

Table 6-2. Cluster node scale with subnet size

Subnet primary IP range	Maximum nodes
/29	Minimum size for a subnet's primary IP range: 4 nodes
/28	12 nodes
/27	28 nodes
/26	60 nodes
/25	124 nodes
/24	252 nodes
/23	508 nodes
/22	1,020 nodes
/21	2,044 nodes
/20	The default size of a subnet's primary IP range in auto mode networks: 4,092 nodes
/19	8,188 nodes
/8	Maximum size for a subnet's primary IP range: 16,777,212 nodes

If you use GKE's CNI, one end of the veth pair is attached to the pod in its namespace and connects the other side to the Linux bridge device cbr0.1, exactly how we outlined it in Chapters 2 and 3.

Clusters span either the zone or region boundary; zonal clusters have only a single control plane. Regional clusters have multiple replicas of the control plane. Also, when you deploy clusters, there are two cluster modes with GKE: VPC-native and routes based. A cluster that uses alias IP address ranges is considered a VPC-native cluster. A cluster that uses custom static routes in a VPC network is called a *routes-based cluster*. Table 6-3 outlines how the creation method maps with the cluster mode.

Table 6-3. Cluster mode with cluster creation method

Cluster creation method	Cluster network mode
Google Cloud Console	VPC-native
REST API	Routes-based
gcloud v256.0.0 and higher or v250.0.0 and lower	Routes-based
gcloud v251.0.0–255.0.0	VPC-native

When using VPC-native, administrators can also take advantage of network endpoint groups (NEG), which represent a group of backends served by a load balancer. NEGs are lists of IP addresses managed by an NEG controller and are used by Google Cloud load balancers. IP addresses in an NEG can be primary or secondary IP addresses of a VM, which means they can be pod IPs. This enables container-native load balancing that sends traffic directly to pods from a Google Cloud load balancer.

VPC-native clusters have several benefits:

- Pod IP addresses are natively routable inside the cluster's VPC network.
- Pod IP addresses are reserved in network before pod creation.
- Pod IP address ranges are dependent on custom static routes.
- Firewall rules apply to just pod IP address ranges instead of any IP address on the cluster's nodes.
- GCP cloud network connectivity to on-premise extends to pod IP address ranges.

Figure 6-15 shows the mapping of GKE to GCE components.

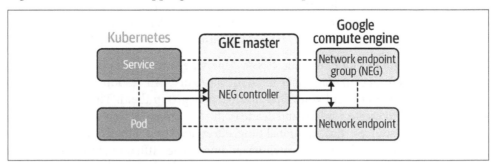

Figure 6-15. NEG to GCE components

Here is a list of improvements that NEGs bring to the GKE network:

Improved network performance
> The container-native load balancer talks directly with the pods, and connections have fewer network hops; both latency and throughput are improved.

Increased visibility

With container-native load balancing, you have visibility into the latency from the HTTP load balancer to the pods. The latency from the HTTP load balancer to each pod is visible, which was aggregated with node IP-based container-native load balancing. This increased visibility makes troubleshooting your services at the NEG level easier.

Support for advanced load balancing

Container-native load balancing offers native support in GKE for several HTTP load-balancing features, such as integration with Google Cloud services like Google Cloud Armor, Cloud CDN, and Identity-Aware Proxy. It also features load-balancing algorithms for accurate traffic distribution.

Like most managed Kubernetes offerings from major providers, GKE is tightly integrated with Google Cloud offerings. Although much of the software driving GKE is opaque, it uses standard resources such as GCE instances that can be inspected and debugged like any other GCP resources. If you really need to manage your own clusters, you will lose out on some functionality, such as container-aware load balancing.

It's worth noting that GCP does not yet support IPv6, unlike AWS and Azure.

Finally, we'll look at Kubernetes networking on Azure.

Azure

Microsoft Azure, like other cloud providers, offers an assortment of enterprise-ready network solutions and services. Before we can discuss how Azure AKS networking works, we should discuss Azure deployment models. Azure has gone through some significant iterations and improvements over the years, resulting in two different deployment models that can encounter Azure. These models differ in how resources are deployed and managed and may impact how users leverage the resources.

The first deployment model was the classic deployment model. This model was the initial deployment and management method for Azure. All resources existed independently of each other, and you could not logically group them. This was cumbersome; users had to create, update, and delete each component of a solution, leading to errors, missed resources, and additional time, effort, and cost. Finally, these resources could not even be tagged for easy searching, adding to the difficulty of the solution.

In 2014, Microsoft introduced the Azure Resource Manager as the second model. This new model is the recommended model from Microsoft, with the recommendation going so far as to say that you should redeploy your resources using the Azure Resource Manager (ARM). The primary change with this model was the introduction of the resource group. Resource groups are a logical grouping of resources that allows for tracking, tagging, and configuring the resources as a group rather than individually.

Now that we understand the basics of how resources are deployed and managed in Azure, we can discuss the Azure network service offerings and how they interact with the Azure Kubernetes Service (AKS) and non-Azure Kubernetes offerings.

Azure Networking Services

The core of Azure networking services is the virtual network, also known as an Azure Vnet. The Vnet establishes an isolated virtual network infrastructure to connect your deployed Azure resources such as virtual machines and AKS clusters. Through additional resources, Vnets connect your deployed resources to the public internet as well as your on-premise infrastructure. Unless the configuration is changed, all Azure Vnets can communicate with the internet through a default route.

In Figure 6-16, an Azure Vnet has a single CIDR of `192.168.0.0/16`. Vnets, like other Azure resources, require a subscription to place the Vnet into a resource group for the Vnet. The security of the Vnet can be configured while some options, such as IAM permissions, are inherited from the resource group and the subscription. The Vnet is confined to a specified region. Multiple Vnets can exist within a single region, but a Vnet can exist within only one region.

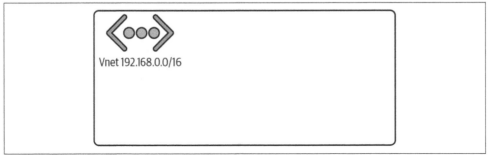

Figure 6-16. Azure Vnet

Azure backbone infrastructure

Microsoft Azure leverages a globally dispersed network of data centers and zones. The foundation of this dispersal is the Azure region, which comprises a set of data centers within a latency-defined area, connected by a low-latency, dedicated network infrastructure. A region can contain any number of data centers that meet these criteria, but two to three are often present per region. Any area of the world containing at least one Azure region is known as Azure geography.

Availability zones further divide a region. Availability zones are physical locations that can consist of one or more data centers maintained by independent power, cooling, and networking infrastructure. The relationship of a region to its availability zones is architected so that a single availability zone failure cannot bring down an entire region of services. Each availability zone in a region is connected to the other availability zones in the region but not dependent on the different zones. Availability zones allow Azure to offer 99.99% uptime for supported services. A region can consist of multiple availability zones, as shown in Figure 6-17, which can, in turn, consist of numerous data centers.

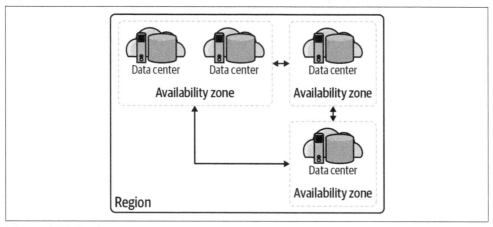

Figure 6-17. Region

Since a Vnet is within a region and regions are divided into availability zones, Vnets are also available across the availability zones of the region they are deployed. As shown in Figure 6-18, it is a best practice when deploying infrastructure for high availability to leverage multiple availability zones for redundancy. Availability zones allow Azure to offer 99.99% uptime for supported services. Azure allows for the use of load balancers for networking across redundant systems such as these.

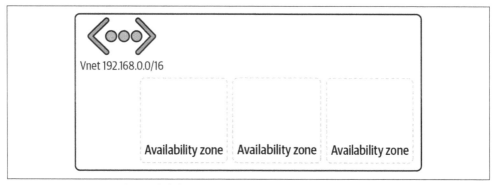

Figure 6-18. Vnet with availability zones

The Azure documentation (*https://oreil.ly/Pv0iq*) has an up-to-date list of Azure geographies, regions, and availability zones.

Subnets

Resource IPs are not assigned directly from the Vnet. Instead, subnets divide and define a Vnet. The subnets receive their address space from the Vnet. Then, private IPs are allocated to provisioned resources within each subnet. This is where the IP addressing AKS clusters and pods will come. Like Vnets, Azure subnets span availability zones, as depicted in Figure 6-19.

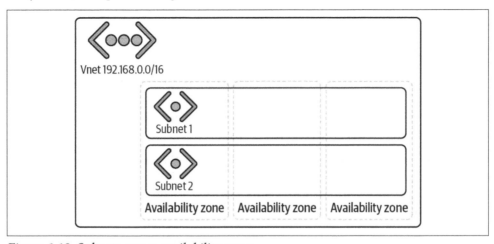

Figure 6-19. Subnets across availability zones

Route tables

As mentioned in previous sections, a route table governs subnet communication or an array of directions on where to send network traffic. Each newly provisioned subnet comes equipped with a default route table populated with some default system routes. This route cannot be deleted or changed. The system routes include a route to the Vnet the subnet is defined within, routes for 10.0.0.0/8 and 192.168.0.0/16 that are by default set to go nowhere, and most importantly a default route to the internet. The default route to the internet allows any newly provisioned resource with an Azure IP to communicate out to the internet by default. This default route is an essential difference between Azure and some other cloud service providers and requires adequate security measures to protect each Azure Vnet.

Figure 6-20 shows a standard route table for a newly provisioned AKS setup. There are routes for the agent pools with their CIDRs as well as their next-hop IP. The next-hop IP is the route the table has defined for the path, and the next-hop type is set for a virtual appliance, which would be the load balancer in this case. What is not present are those default system routes. The default routes are still in the configuration, just not viewable in the route table. Understanding Azure's default networking behavior is critical from a security perspective and from troubleshooting and planning perspectives.

Figure 6-20. Route table

Some system routes, known as optional default routes, affect only if the capabilities, such as Vnet peering, are enabled. Vnet peering allows Vnets anywhere globally to establish a private connection across the Azure global infrastructure backbone to communicate.

Custom routes can also populate route tables, which the Border Gateway Protocol either creates if leveraged or uses user-defined routes. User-defined routes are essential because they allow the network administrators to define routes beyond what Azure establishes by default, such as proxies or firewall routes. Custom routes also impact the system default routes. While you cannot alter the default routes, a customer route with a higher priority can overrule it. An example of this is to use a user-defined route to send traffic bound for the internet to a next-hop of a virtual firewall appliance rather than the internet directly. Figure 6-21 defines a custom route called Google with a next-hop type of internet. As long as the priorities are set up correctly, this custom route will send that traffic out the default system route for the internet, even if another rule redirects the remaining internet traffic.

Figure 6-21. Route table with custom route

Route tables can also be created on their own and then used to configure a subnet. This is useful for maintaining a single route table for multiple subnets, especially when there are many user-defined routes involved. A subnet can have only one route table associated with it, but a route table can be associated with multiple subnets. The rules of configuring a user-created route table and a route table created as part of the subnet's default creation are the same. They have the same default system routes and will update with the same optional default routes as they come into effect.

While most routes within a route table will use an IP range as the source address, Azure has begun to introduce the concept of using service tags for sources. A service tag is a phrase that represents a collection of service IPs within the Azure backend, such as SQL.EastUs, which is a service tag that describes the IP address range for the Microsoft SQL Platform service offering in the eastern US. With this feature, it could be possible to define a route from one Azure service, such as AzureDevOps, as the source, and another service, such as Azure AppService, as the destination without knowing the IP ranges for either.

 The Azure documentation (*https://oreil.ly/CDedn*) has a list of available service tags.

Public and private IPs

Azure allocates IP addresses as independent resources themselves, which means that a user can create a public IP or private IP without attaching it to anything. These IP addresses can be named and built in a resource group that allows for future allocation. This is a crucial step when preparing for AKS cluster scaling as you want to make sure that enough private IP addresses have been reserved for the possible pods if you decide to leverage Azure CNI for networking. Azure CNI will be discussed in a later section.

IP address resources, both public and private, are also defined as either dynamic or static. A static IP address is reserved to not change, while a dynamic IP address can change if it is not allocated to a resource, such as a virtual machine or AKS pod.

Network security groups

NSGs are used to configure Vnets, subnets, and network interface cards (NICs) with inbound and outbound security rules. The rules filter traffic and determine whether the traffic will be allowed to proceed or be dropped. NSG rules are flexible to filter traffic based on source and destination IP addresses, network ports, and network protocols. An NSG rule can use one or multiple of these filter items and can apply many NSGs.

An NSG rule can have any of the following components to define its filtering:

Priority
This is a number between 100 and 4096. The lowest numbers are evaluated first, and the first match is the rule that is used. Once a match is found, no further rules are evaluated.

Source/destination
Source (inbound rules) or destination (outbound rules) of the traffic inspected. The source/destination can be any of the following:

- Individual IP address
- CIDR block (i.e., 10.2.0.0/24)
- Microsoft Azure service tag
- Application security groups

Protocol
TCP, UDP, ICMP, ESP, AH, or Any.

Direction
The rule for inbound or outbound traffic.

Port range
Single ports or ranges can be specified here.

Action
Allow or deny the traffic.

Figure 6-22 shows an example of an NSG.

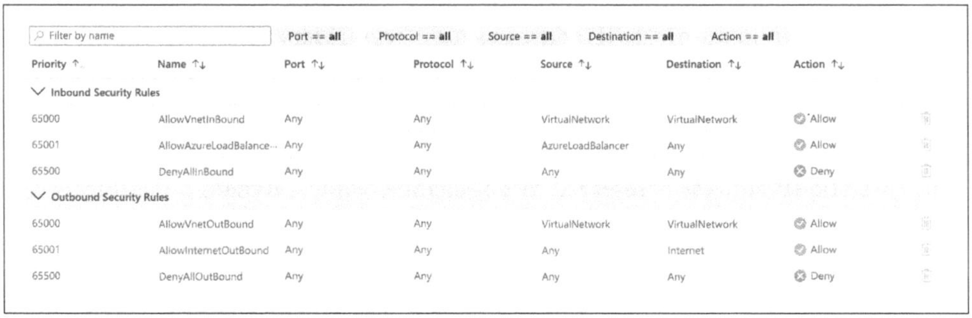

Priority ↑	Name ↑↓	Port ↑↓	Protocol ↑↓	Source ↑↓	Destination ↑↓	Action ↑↓
∨ Inbound Security Rules						
65000	AllowVnetInBound	Any	Any	VirtualNetwork	VirtualNetwork	✓ Allow
65001	AllowAzureLoadBalance…	Any	Any	AzureLoadBalancer	Any	✓ Allow
65500	DenyAllInBound	Any	Any	Any	Any	✗ Deny
∨ Outbound Security Rules						
65000	AllowVnetOutBound	Any	Any	VirtualNetwork	VirtualNetwork	✓ Allow
65001	AllowInternetOutBound	Any	Any	Any	Internet	✓ Allow
65500	DenyAllOutBound	Any	Any	Any	Any	✗ Deny

Figure 6-22. Azure NSG

There are some considerations to keep in mind when configuring Azure network security groups. First, two or more rules cannot exist with the same priority and direction. The priority or direction can match as long as the other does not. Second, port ranges can be used only in the Resource Manager deployment model, not the classic deployment model. This limitation also applies to IP address ranges and service tags for the source/destination. Third, when specifying the IP address for an Azure resource as the source/destination, if the resource has both a public and private IP address, use the private IP address. Azure performs the translation from public to private IP addressing outside this process, and the private IP address will be the right choice at the time of processing.

Communication outside the virtual network

The concepts described so far have mainly pertained to Azure networking within a single Vnet. This type of communication is vital in Azure networking but far from the only type. Most Azure implementations will require communication outside the virtual network to other networks, including, but not limited to, on-premise networks, other Azure virtual networks, and the internet. These communication paths require many of the same considerations as the internal networking processes and use many of the same resources, with a few differences. This section will expand on some of those differences.

Vnet peering can connect Vnets in different regions using global virtual network peering, but there are constraints with certain services such as load balancers.

For a list of these constraints, see the Azure documentation (*https:// oreil.ly/wnaEi*).

Communication outside of Azure to the internet uses a different set of resources. Public IPs, as discussed earlier, can be created and assigned to a resource in Azure. The resource uses its private IP address for all networking internal to Azure. When the traffic from the resource needs to exit the internal networks to the internet, Azure translates the private IP address into the resource's assigned public IP. At this point, the traffic can leave to the internet. Incoming traffic bound for the public IP address of an Azure resource translates to the resource's assigned private IP address at the Vnet boundary, and the private IP is used from then on for the rest of the traffic's trip to its destination. This traffic path is why all subnet rules for things like NSGs are defined using private IP addresses.

NAT can also be configured on a subnet. If configured, resources on a subnet with NAT enabled do not need a public IP address to communicate with the internet. NAT is enabled on a subnet to allow outbound-only internet traffic with a public IP from a pool of provisioned public IP addresses. NAT will enable resources to route traffic to the internet for requests such as updates or installs and return with the requested traffic but prevents the resources from being accessible on the internet. It is important to note that, when configured, NAT takes priority over all other outbound rules and replaces the default internet destination for the subnet. NAT also uses port address translation (PAT) by default.

Azure load balancer

Now that you have a method of communicating outside the network and communication to flow back into the Vnet, a way to keep those lines of communication available is needed. Azure load balancers are often used to accomplish this by distributing traffic across backend pools of resources rather than a single resource to handle the request. There are two primary load balancer types in Azure: the standard load balancer and the application gateway.

Azure standard load balancers are layer 4 systems that distribute incoming traffic based on layer 4 protocols such as TCP and UDP, meaning traffic is routed based on IP address and port. These load balancers filter incoming traffic from the internet, but they can also load balance traffic from one Azure resource to a set of other Azure resources. The standard load balancer uses a zero-trust network model. This model requires an NSG to "open" traffic to be inspected by the load balancer. If the attached NSG does not permit the traffic, the load balancer will not attempt to route it.

Azure application gateways are similar to standard load balancers in that they distribute incoming traffic but differently in that they do so at layer 7. This allows for the inspection of incoming HTTP requests to filter based on URI or host headers. Application gateways can also be used as web application firewalls to further secure and filter traffic. Additionally, the application gateway can also be used as the ingress controller for AKS clusters.

Load balancers, whether standard or application gateways, have some basic concepts that sound be considered:

Frontend IP address
Either public or private depending on the use, this is the IP address used to target the load balancer and, by extension, the backend resources it is balancing.

SKU
Like other Azure resources, this defines the "type" of the load balancer and, therefore, the different configuration options available.

Backend pool
This is the collection of resources that the load balancer is distributing traffic to, such as a collection of virtual machines or the pods within an AKS cluster.

Health probes

These are methods used by the load balancer to ensure the backend resource is available for traffic, such as a health endpoint that returns an OK status:

Listener

A configuration that tells the load balancer what type of traffic to expect, such as HTTP requests.

Rules

Determines how to route the incoming traffic for that listener.

Figure 6-23 illustrates some of these primary components within the Azure load balancer architecture. Traffic comes into the load balancer and is compared to the listeners to determine if the load balancer balances the traffic. Then the traffic is evaluated against the rules and finally sent on to the backend pool. Backend pool resources with appropriately responding health probes will process the traffic.

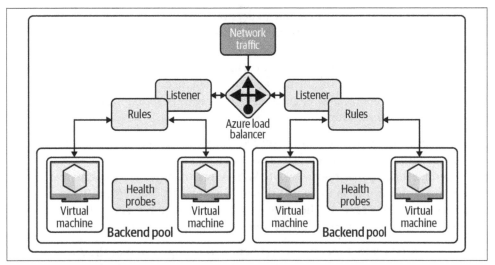

Figure 6-23. Azure load balancer components

Figure 6-24 shows how AKS would use the load balancer.

Now that we have a basic knowledge of the Azure network, we can discuss how Azure uses these constructs in its managed Kubernetes offering, Azure Kubernetes Service.

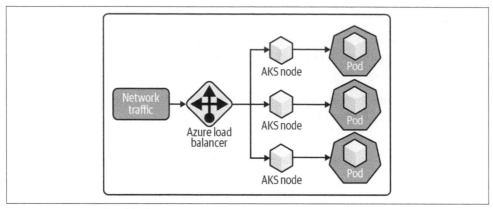

Figure 6-24. AKS load balancing

Azure Kubernetes Service

Like other cloud providers, Microsoft understood the need to leverage the power of Kubernetes and therefore introduced the Azure Kubernetes Service as the Azure Kubernetes offering. AKS is a hosted service offering from Azure and therefore handles a large portion of the overhead of managing Kubernetes. Azure handles components such as health monitoring and maintenance, leaving more time for development and operations engineers to leverage the scalability and power of Kubernetes for their solutions.

AKS can have clusters created and managed using the Azure CLI, Azure PowerShell, the Azure Portal, and other template-based deployment options such as ARM templates and HashiCorp's Terraform. With AKS, Azure manages the Kubernetes masters so that the user only needs to handle the node agents. This allows Azure to offer the core of AKS as a free service where the only payment required is for the agent nodes and peripheral services such as storage and networking.

The Azure Portal allows for easy management and configuration of the AKS environment. Figure 6-25 shows the overview page of a newly provisioned AKS environment. On this page, you can see information and links to many of the crucial integrations and properties. The cluster's resource group, DNS address, Kubernetes version, networking type, and a link to the node pools are visible in the Essentials section.

Figure 6-26 zooms in on the Properties section of the overview page, where users can find additional information and links to corresponding components. Most of the data is the same as the information in the Essentials section. However, the various subnet CIDRs for the AKS environment components can be viewed here for things such as the Docker bridge and the pod subnet.

Figure 6-25. Azure Portal AKS overview

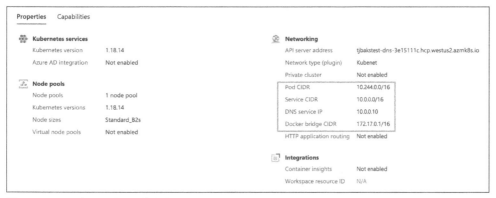

Figure 6-26. Azure Portal AKS properties

Kubernetes pods created within AKS are attached to virtual networks and can access network resources through abstraction. The kube-proxy on each AKS node creates this abstraction, and this component allows for inbound and outbound traffic. Additionally, AKS seeks to make Kubernetes management even more streamlined by simplifying how to roll changes to virtual network changes. Network services in AKS are autoconfigured when specific changes occur. For example, opening a network port to a pod will also trigger relevant changes to the attached NSGs to open those ports.

By default, AKS will create an Azure DNS record that has a public IP. However, the default network rules prevent public access. The private mode can create the cluster to use no public IPs and block public access for only internal use of the cluster. This mode will cause the cluster access to be available only from within the Vnet. By default, the standard SKU will create an AKS load balancer. This configuration can be changed during deployment if deploying via the CLI. Resources not included in the cluster are made in a separate, auto-generated resource group.

When leveraging the kubenet networking model for AKS, the following rules are true:

- Nodes receive an IP address from the Azure virtual network subnet.
- Pods receive an IP address from a logically different address space than the nodes.
- The source IP address of the traffic switches to the node's primary address.
- NAT is configured for the pods to reach Azure resources on the Vnet.

It is important to note that only the nodes receive a routable IP; the pods do not.

While kubenet is an easy way to administer Kubernetes networking within the Azure Kubernetes Service, it is not the only way. Like other cloud providers, Azure also allows for the use the CNI when managing Kubernetes infrastructure. Let's discuss CNI in the next section.

Azure CNI

Microsoft has provided its own CNI plugin for Azure and AKS, Azure CNI. The first significant difference between this and kubenet is that the pods receive routable IP information and can be accessed directly. This difference places additional importance on the need for IP address space planning. Each node has a maximum number of pods it can use, and many IP addresses are reserved for that use.

More information can be found on the Azure Container Networking GitHub (*https://oreil.ly/G2zyC*).

With Azure CNI, traffic inside the Vnet is no longer NAT'd to the node's IP address but to the pod's IP itself, as illustrated in Figure 6-27. Outside traffic, such as to the internet, is still NAT'd to the node's IP address. Azure CNI still performs the backend IP address management and routing for these items, though, as all resources on the same Azure Vnet can communicate with each other by default.

The Azure CNI can also be used for Kubernetes deployments outside AKS. While there is additional work to be done on the cluster that Azure would typically handle, this allows you to leverage Azure networking and other resources while maintaining more control over the customarily managed aspects of Kubernetes under AKS.

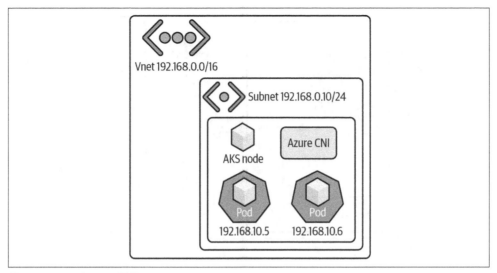

Vnet 192.168.0.0/16

Subnet 192.168.0.10/24

AKS node

Azure CNI

Pod
192.168.10.5

Pod
192.168.10.6

Figure 6-27. Azure CNI

Azure CNI also provides the added benefit of allowing for the separation of duties while maintaining the AKS infrastructure. The Azure CNI creates the networking resources in a separate resource group. Being in a different resource group allows for more control over permissions at the resource group level within the Azure Resource Management deployment model. Different teams can access some components of AKS, such as the networking, without needing access to others, such as the application deployments.

Azure CNI is not the only way to leverage additional Azure services to enhance your Kubernetes network infrastructure. The next section will discuss the use of an Azure application gateway as a means of controlling ingress into your Kubernetes cluster.

Application gateway ingress controller

Azure allows for the deployment of an application gateway inside the AKS cluster deployment to serve as the application gateway ingress controller (AGIC). This deployment model eliminates the need for maintaining a secondary load balancer outside the AKS infrastructure, thereby reducing maintenance overhead and error points. AGIC deploys its pods in the cluster. It then monitors other aspects of the cluster for configuration changes. When a change is detected, AGIC updates the Azure Resource Manager template that configures the load balancer and then applies the updated configuration. Figure 6-28 illustrates this.

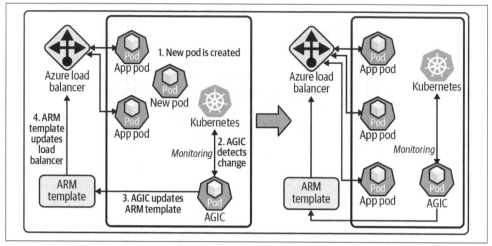

Figure 6-28. Azure AGIC

There are AKS SKU limitations for the use of the AGIC, only supporting Standard_v2 and WAF_v2, but those SKUs also have autoscaling capabilities. Use cases for using such a form of ingress, such as the need for high scalability, have the potential for the AKS environment to scale. Microsoft supports the use of both Helm and the AKS add-on as deployment options for the AGIC. These are the critical differences between the two options:

- Helm deployment values cannot be edited when using the AKS add-on.
- Helm supports Prohibited Target configuration. An AGIC can configure the application gateway to target only the AKS instances without impacting other backend components.
- The AKS add-on, as a managed service, will be automatically updated to its current and more secure versions. Helm deployments will need manual updating.

Even though AGIC is configured as the Kubernetes ingress resource, it still carries the full benefit of the cluster's standard layer 7 application gateway. Application gateway services such as TLS termination, URL routing, and the web application firewall capability are all configurable for the cluster as part of the AGIC.

While many Kubernetes and networking fundamentals are universal across cloud providers, Azure offers its own spin on Kubernetes networking through its enterprise-focused resource design and management. Whether you have a need for a single cluster using basic settings and kubenet or a large-scale deployment with advanced networking through the use of deployed load balancers and application gateways, Microsoft's Azure Kubernetes Service can be leveraged to deliver a reliable, managed Kubernetes infrastructure.

Deploying an Application to Azure Kubernetes Service

Standing up an Azure Kubernetes Service cluster is one of the basic skills needed to begin exploring AKS networking. This section will go through the steps of standing up a sample cluster and deploying the Golang web server example from Chapter 1 to that cluster. We will be using a combination of the Azure Portal, the Azure CLI, and kubectl to perform these actions.

Before we begin with the cluster deployment and configuration, we should discuss the Azure Container Registry (ACR). The ACR is where you store container images in Azure. For this example, we will use the ACR as the location for the container image we will be deploying. To import an image to the ACR, you will need to have the image locally available on your computer. Once you have the image available, we have to prep it for the ACR.

First, identify the ACR repository you want to store the image in and log in from the Docker CLI with `docker login <acr_repository>.azurecr.io`. For this example, we will use the ACR repository `tjbakstestcr`, so the command would be `docker login tjbakstestcr.azurecr.io`. Next, tag the local image you wish to import to the ACR with `<acr_repository>.azurecr.io\<imagetag>`. For this example, we will use an image currently tagged `aksdemo`. Therefore, the tag would be `tjbak stestcr.azure.io/aksdemo`. To tag the image, use the command `docker tag <local_image_tag> <acr_image_tag>`. This example would use the command `docker tag aksdemo tjbakstestcr.azure.io/aksdem`. Finally, we push the image to the ACR with `docker push tjbakstestcr.azure.io/aksdem`.

> You can find additional information on Docker and the Azure Container Registry in the official documentation (*https://oreil.ly/ 5swhT*).

Once the image is in the ACR, the final prerequisite is to set up a service principal. This is easier to set up before you begin, but you can do this during the AKS cluster creation. An Azure service principal is a representation of an Azure Active Directory Application object. Service principals are generally used to interact with Azure through application automation. We will be using a service principal to allow the AKS cluster to pull the `aksdemo` image from the ACR. The service principal needs to have access to the ACR repository that you store the image in. You will need to record the client ID and secret of the service principal you want to use.

You can find additional information on Azure Active Directory service principals in the documentation (*https://oreil.ly/pnZTw*).

Now that we have our image in the ACR and our service principal client ID and secret, we can begin deploying the AKS cluster.

Deploying an Azure Kubernetes Service cluster

The time has come to deploy our cluster. We are going to start in the Azure Portal. Go to *portal.azure.com* (*https://oreil.ly/Wx4Ny*) to log in. Once logged in, you should see a dashboard with a search bar at the top that will be used to locate services. From the search bar, we will be typing **kubernetes** and selecting the Kubernetes Service option from the drop-down menu, which is outlined in Figure 6-29.

Figure 6-29. Azure Kubernetes search

Now we are on the Azure Kubernetes Services blade. Deployed AKS clusters are viewed from this screen using filters and queries. This is also the screen for creating new AKS clusters. Near the top of the screen, we are going to select Create as shown in Figure 6-30. This will cause a drop-down menu to appear, where we will select "Create a Kubernetes cluster."

Figure 6-30. Creating an Azure Kubernetes cluster

Next we will define the properties of the AKS cluster from the "Create Kubernetes cluster" screen. First, we will populate the Project Details section by selecting the subscription that the cluster will be deployed to. There is a drop-down menu that allows for easier searching and selection. For this example, we are using the tjb_azure_test_2 subscription, but any subscription can work as long as you have access to it. Next, we have to define the resource group we will use to group the AKS cluster. This can be an existing resource group or a new one can be created. For this example, we will create a new resource group named go-web.

After the Project Details section is complete, we move on to the Cluster Details section. Here, we will define the name of the cluster, which will be "go-web" for this example. The region, availability zones, and Kubernetes version fields are also defined in this section and will have predefined defaults that can be changed. For this example, however, we will use the default "(US) West 2" region with no availability zones and the default Kubernetes version of 1.19.11.

Not all Azure regions have availability zones that can be selected. If availability zones are part of the AKS architecture that is being deployed, the appropriate regions should be considered. You can find more information on AKS regions in the availability zones documentation (*https://oreil.ly/enxii*).

Finally, we will complete the Primary Node Pool section of the "Create Kubernetes cluster" screen by selecting the node size and node count. For this example, we are going to keep the default node size of DS2 v2 and the default node count of 3. While most virtual machines, sizes are available for use within AKS, there are some restrictions. Figure 6-31 shows the options we have selected filled in.

You can find more information on AKS restrictions, including restricted node sizes, in the documentation (*https://oreil.ly/A4bHq*).

Click the "Next: Node pools" button to move to the Node Pools tab. This page allows for the configuration of additional node pools for the AKS cluster. For this example, we are going to leave the defaults on this page and move on to the Authentication page by clicking the "Next: Authentication" button at the bottom of the screen.

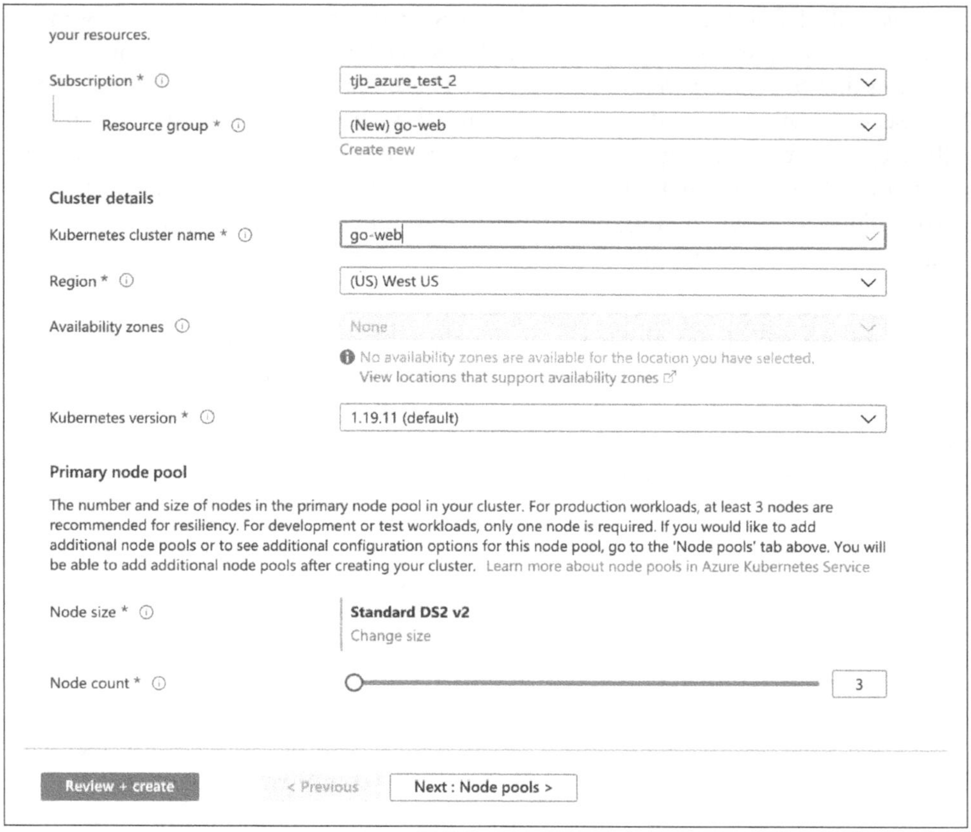

your resources.

Subscription * ⓘ	tjb_azure_test_2 ⌄
└── Resource group * ⓘ	(New) go-web ⌄
	Create new

Cluster details

Kubernetes cluster name * ⓘ	go-web ✓
Region * ⓘ	(US) West US ⌄
Availability zones ⓘ	None ⌄
	ⓘ No availability zones are available for the location you have selected. View locations that support availability zones ↗
Kubernetes version * ⓘ	1.19.11 (default) ⌄

Primary node pool

The number and size of nodes in the primary node pool in your cluster. For production workloads, at least 3 nodes are recommended for resiliency. For development or test workloads, only one node is required. If you would like to add additional node pools or to see additional configuration options for this node pool, go to the 'Node pools' tab above. You will be able to add additional node pools after creating your cluster. Learn more about node pools in Azure Kubernetes Service

Node size * ⓘ	**Standard DS2 v2** Change size
Node count * ⓘ	○────────────────── 3

Review + create	< Previous	Next : Node pools >

Figure 6-31. Azure Kubernetes create page

Figure 6-32 shows the Authentication page, where we will define the authentication method that the AKS cluster will use to connect to attached Azure services such as the ACR we discussed previously in this chapter. "System-Assigned Managed Identity" is the default authentication method, but we are going to select the "Service principal" radio button.

If you did not create a service principal at the beginning of this section, you can create a new one here. If you create a service principal at this stage, you will have to go back and grant that service principal permissions to access the ACR. However, since we will use a previously created service principal, we are going to click the "Configure service principal" link and enter the client ID and secret.

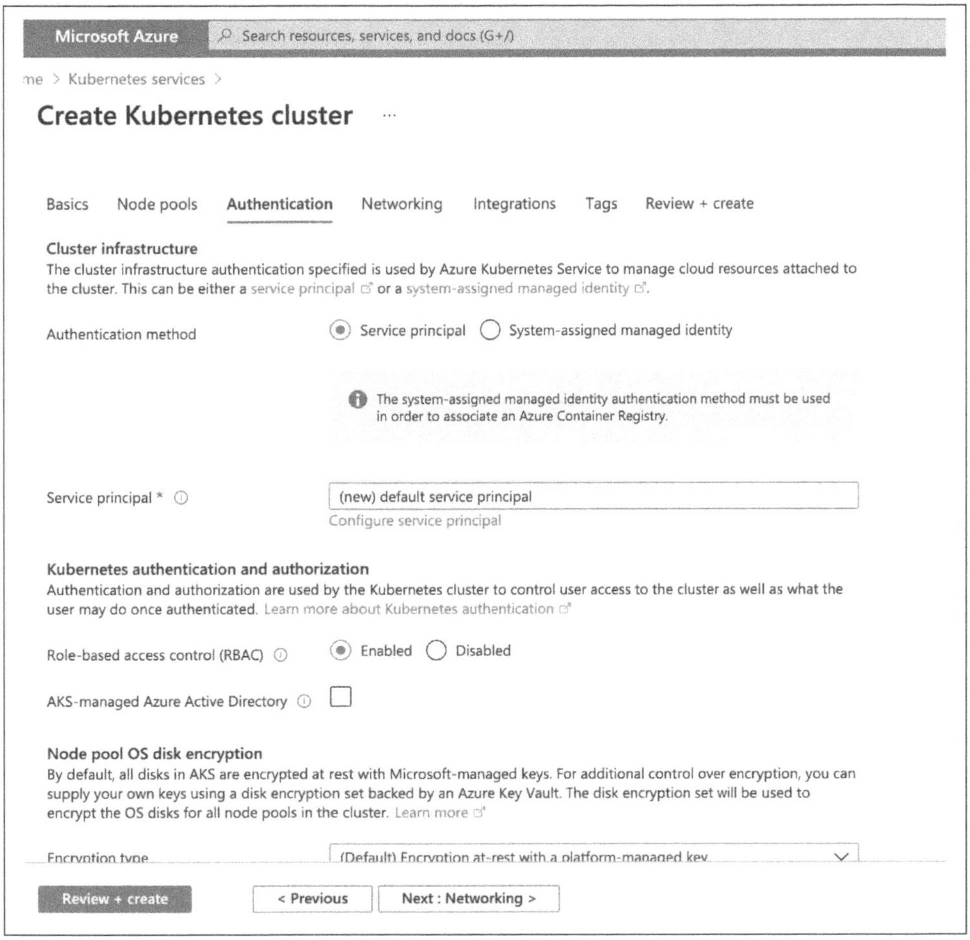

Figure 6-32. Azure Kubernetes Authentication page

The remaining configurations will remain at the defaults at this time. To complete the AKS cluster creation, we are going to click the "Review + create" button. This will take us to the validation page. As shown in Figure 6-33, if everything is defined appropriately, the validation will return a "Validation Passed" message at the top of the screen. If something is misconfigured, a "Validation Failed" message will be there instead. As long as validation passes, we will review the settings and click Create.

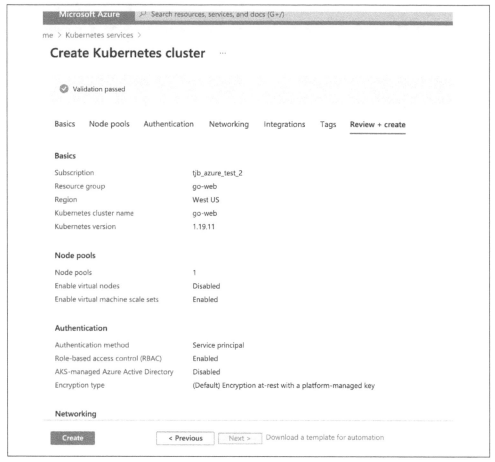

Figure 6-33. Azure Kubernetes validation page

You can view the deployment status from the notification bell on the top of the Azure screen. Figure 6-34 shows our example deployment in progress. This page has information that can be used to troubleshoot with Microsoft should an issue arise such as the deployment name, start time, and correlation ID.

Our example deployed completely without issue, as shown in Figure 6-35. Now that the AKS cluster is deployed, we need to connect to it and configure it for use with our example web server.

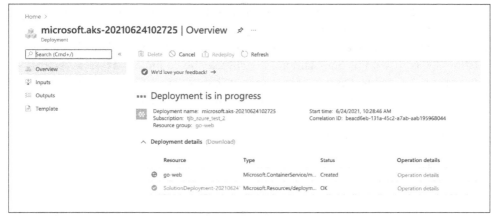

Figure 6-34. Azure Kubernetes deployment progress

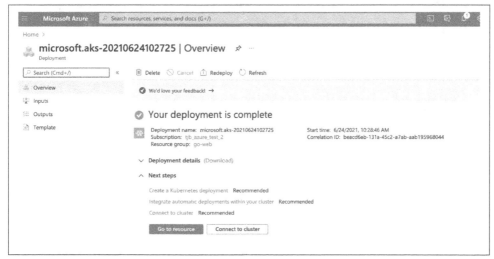

Figure 6-35. Azure Kubernetes deployment complete

Connecting to and configuring AKS

We will now shift to working with the example go-web AKS cluster from the command line. To manage AKS clusters from the command line, we will primarily use the kubectl command. Azure CLI has a simple command, az aks install-cli, to install the kubectl program for use. Before we can use kubectl, though, we need to gain access to the cluster. The command az aks get-credentials --resource-group <resource_group_name> --name <aks_cluster_name> is used to gain access to the AKS cluster. For our example, we will use az aks get-credentials --resource-group go-web --name go-web to access our go-web cluster in the go-web resource group.

Next we will attach the Azure container registry that has our `aksdemo` image. The command `az aks update -n <aks_cluster_name> -g <cluster_resource_group_name> --attach-acr <acr_repo_name>` will attach a named ACR repo to an existing AKS cluster. For our example, we will use the command `az aks update -n tjbakstest -g tjbakstest --attach-acr tjbakstestcr`. Our example runs for a few moments and then produces the output shown in Example 6-1.

Example 6-1. AttachACR output

```
{- Finished ..
  "aadProfile": null,
  "addonProfiles": {
    "azurepolicy": {
      "config": null,
      "enabled": false,
      "identity": null
    },
    "httpApplicationRouting": {
      "config": null,
      "enabled": false,
      "identity": null
    },
    "omsAgent": {
      "config": {
        "logAnalyticsWorkspaceResourceID":
        "/subscriptions/7a0e265a-c0e4-4081-8d76-aafbca9db45e/
        resourcegroups/defaultresourcegroup-wus2/providers/
        microsoft.operationalinsights/
        workspaces/defaultworkspace-7a0e265a-c0e4-4081-8d76-aafbca9db45e-wus2"
      },
      "enabled": true,
      "identity": null
    }
  },
  "agentPoolProfiles": [
    {
      "availabilityZones": null,
      "count": 3,
      "enableAutoScaling": false,
      "enableNodePublicIp": null,
      "maxCount": null,
      "maxPods": 110,
      "minCount": null,
      "mode": "System",
      "name": "agentpool",
      "nodeImageVersion": "AKSUbuntu-1804gen2containerd-2021.06.02",
      "nodeLabels": {},
      "nodeTaints": null,
      "orchestratorVersion": "1.19.11",
      "osDiskSizeGb": 128,
```

```
    "osDiskType": "Managed",
    "osType": "Linux",
    "powerState": {
      "code": "Running"
    },
    "provisioningState": "Succeeded",
    "proximityPlacementGroupId": null,
    "scaleSetEvictionPolicy": null,
    "scaleSetPriority": null,
    "spotMaxPrice": null,
    "tags": null,
    "type": "VirtualMachineScaleSets",
    "upgradeSettings": null,
    "vmSize": "Standard_DS2_v2",
    "vnetSubnetId": null
  }
],
"apiServerAccessProfile": {
  "authorizedIpRanges": null,
  "enablePrivateCluster": false
},
"autoScalerProfile": null,
"diskEncryptionSetId": null,
"dnsPrefix": "go-web-dns",
"enablePodSecurityPolicy": null,
"enableRbac": true,
"fqdn": "go-web-dns-a59354e4.hcp.westus.azmk8s.io",
"id":
"/subscriptions/7a0e265a-c0e4-4081-8d76-aafbca9db45e/
resourcegroups/go-web/providers/Microsoft.ContainerService/managedClusters/go-web",
"identity": null,
"identityProfile": null,
"kubernetesVersion": "1.19.11",
"linuxProfile": null,
"location": "westus",
"maxAgentPools": 100,
"name": "go-web",
"networkProfile": {
  "dnsServiceIp": "10.0.0.10",
  "dockerBridgeCidr": "172.17.0.1/16",
  "loadBalancerProfile": {
    "allocatedOutboundPorts": null,
    "effectiveOutboundIps": [
      {
        "id":
        "/subscriptions/7a0e265a-c0e4-4081-8d76-aafbca9db45e/
        resourceGroups/MC_go-web_go-web_westus/providers/Microsoft.Network/
        publicIPAddresses/eb67f61d-7370-4a38-a237-a95e9393b294",
        "resourceGroup": "MC_go-web_go-web_westus"
      }
    ],
    "idleTimeoutInMinutes": null,
```

```
      "managedOutboundIps": {
        "count": 1
      },
      "outboundIpPrefixes": null,
      "outboundIps": null
    },
    "loadBalancerSku": "Standard",
    "networkMode": null,
    "networkPlugin": "kubenet",
    "networkPolicy": null,
    "outboundType": "loadBalancer",
    "podCidr": "10.244.0.0/16",
    "serviceCidr": "10.0.0.0/16"
  },
  "nodeResourceGroup": "MC_go-web_go-web_westus",
  "powerState": {
    "code": "Running"
  },
  "privateFqdn": null,
  "provisioningState": "Succeeded",
  "resourceGroup": "go-web",
  "servicePrincipalProfile": {
    "clientId": "bbd3ac10-5c0c-4084-a1b8-39dd1097ec1c",
    "secret": null
  },
  "sku": {
    "name": "Basic",
    "tier": "Free"
  },
  "tags": {
    "createdby": "tjb"
  },
  "type": "Microsoft.ContainerService/ManagedClusters",
  "windowsProfile": null
}
```

This output is the CLI representation of the AKS cluster information. This means that the attachment was successful. Now that we have access to the AKS cluster and the ACR is attached, we can deploy the example Go web server to the AKS cluster.

Deploying the Go web server

We are going to deploy the Golang code shown in Example 6-2. As mentioned earlier in this chapter, this code has been built into a Docker image and now is stored in the ACR in the tjbakstestcr repository. We will be using the following deployment YAML file to deploy the application.

Example 6-2. Kubernetes Podspec for Golang minimal webserver

```
apiVersion: v1
kind: Pod
metadata:
  labels:
    test: liveness
  name: go-web
spec:
  containers:
  - name: go-web
    image: go-web:v0.0.1
    ports:
    - containerPort: 8080
    livenessProbe:
      httpGet:
        path: /healthz
        port: 8080
      initialDelaySeconds: 5
      periodSeconds: 5
    readinessProbe:
      httpGet:
        path: /
        port: 8080
      initialDelaySeconds: 5
      periodSeconds: 5
```

Breaking down this YAML file, we see that we are creating two AKS resources: a deployment and a service. The deployment is configured for the creation of a container named go-web and a container port 8080. The deployment also references the aksdemo ACR image with the line image: tjbakstestcr.azurecr.io/aksdemo as the image that will be deployed to the container. The service is also configured with the name go-web. The YAML specifies the service is a load balancer listening on port 8080 and targeting the go-web app.

Now we need to publish the application to the AKS cluster. The command kubectl apply -f <yaml_file_name>.yaml will publish the application to the cluster. We will see from the output that two things are created: deployment.apps/go-web and service/go-web. When we run the command kubectl get pods, we can see an output like that shown here:

```
○ → kubectl get pods
NAME                         READY   STATUS    RESTARTS   AGE
go-web-574dd4c94d-2z5lp      1/1     Running   0          5h29m
```

Now that the application is deployed, we will connect to it to verify it is up and running. When a default AKS cluster is stood up, a load balancer is deployed with it with a public IP address. We could go through the portal and locate that load balancer and public IP address, but kubectl offers an easier path. The command kubectl get [.keep-together]#service go-web produces this output:

```
○ → kubectl get service go-web
NAME      TYPE           CLUSTER-IP    EXTERNAL-IP    PORT(S)          AGE
go-web    LoadBalancer   10.0.3.75     13.88.96.117   8080:31728/TCP   21h
```

In this output, we see the external IP address of 13.88.96.117. Therefore, if everything deployed correctly, we should be able to cURL 13.88.96.117 at port 8080 with the command curl 13.88.96.117:8080. As we can see from this output, we have a successful deployment:

```
○ → curl 13.88.96.117:8080 -vvv
*   Trying 13.88.96.117...
* TCP_NODELAY set
* Connected to 13.88.96.117 (13.88.96.117) port 8080 (#0)
> GET / HTTP/1.1
> Host: 13.88.96.117:8080
> User-Agent: curl/7.64.1
> Accept: */*
>
< HTTP/1.1 200 OK
< Date: Fri, 25 Jun 2021 20:12:48 GMT
< Content-Length: 5
< Content-Type: text/plain; charset=utf-8
<
* Connection #0 to host 13.88.96.117 left intact
Hello* Closing connection 0
```

Going to a web browser and navigating to http://13.88.96.117:8080 will also be available, as shown in Figure 6-36.

Figure 6-36. Azure Kubernetes Hello app

AKS conclusion

In this section, we deployed an example Golang web server to an Azure Kubernetes Service cluster. We used the Azure Portal, the az cli, and kubectl to deploy and configure the cluster and then deploy the application. We leveraged the Azure container registry to host our web server image. We also used a YAML file to deploy the application and tested it with cURL and web browsing.

Conclusion

Each cloud provider has its nuanced differences when it comes to network services provided for Kubernetes clusters. Table 6-4 highlights some of those differences. There are lots of factors to choose from when picking a cloud service provider, and even more when selecting the managed Kubernetes platform to run. Our aim in this chapter was to educate administrators and developers on the choices you will have to make when managing workloads on Kubernetes.

Table 6-4. Cloud network and Kubernetes summary

	AWS	Azure	GCP
Virtual network	VPC	Vnet	VPC
Network scope	Region	Region	Global
Subnet boundary	Zone	Region	Region
Routing scope	Subnet	Subnet	VPC
Security controls	NACL/SecGroups	Network security groups/Application SecGroup	Firewall
IPv6	Yes	Yes	No
Kubernetes managed	eks	aks	gke
ingress	AWS ALB controller	Nginx-Ingress	GKE ingress controller
Cloud custom CNI	AWS VPC CNI	Azure CNI	GKE CNI
Load Balancer support	ALB L7, L4 w/NLB, and Nginx	L4 Azure Load Balancer, L7 w/Nginx	L7, HTTP(S)
Network policies	Yes (Calico/Cilium)	Yes (Calico/Cilium)	Yes (Calico/Cilium)

We have covered many layers, from the OSI foundation to running networks in the cloud for our clusters. Cluster administrators, network engineers, and developers alike have many decisions to make, such as the subnet size, the CNI to choose, and the load balancer type, to name a few. Understanding all of those and how they will affect the cluster network was the basis for this book. This is just the beginning of your journey for managing your clusters at scale. We have managed to cover only the networking options available for managing Kubernetes clusters. Storage, compute, and even how to deploy workloads onto those clusters are decisions you will have to make now. The O'Reilly library has an extensive number of books to help, such as *Production Kubernetes* (*https://oreil.ly/Xx12u*) (Rosso et al.), where you learn what the path to production looks like when using Kubernetes, and *Hacking Kubernetes* (*https://oreil.ly/FcU8C*) (Martin and Hausenblas), on how to harden Kubernetes and how to review Kubernetes clusters for security weaknesses.

We hope this guide has helped make those networking choices easy for you. We were inspired to see what the Kubernetes community has done and are excited to see what you build on top of the abstractions Kubernetes provides for you.

Index

container host, 97
container ID, 121, 130, 132
container networking model (CNM), 122-125
container orchestration, 97
container runtime, 96, 146, 152
container-native cluster, GKE, 280-282
containerd service, 99, 101
containerd-shim, 99, 101
containers
    as abstraction, 93
    addresses for, 122
    benefits of, 95, 112, 122
    cgroups (control groups) and, 97, 103-104,
        105
    creating, 106-112
    CRI-O runtime with, 101
    defined, 96
    Docker (see Docker networking model)
    functionality of, 97-98
    on global systems, 124-125, 134
    history of, 93-96
    initiatives for, 99-102
    layers in, 129
    on local systems, 123, 132-134
    namespaces and (see namespaces, network)
    network modes with, 112-114, 123
    networking scenarios with, 127-135
    OCI specifications for, 98
    runC routines for, 97, 98, 101, 103, 104
    runtimes of, 97-98, 99-102
    terminology for, 96-97
Content-Length header, HTTP request, 11-13
Content-Type header, HTTP request, 11-13
control plane, Kubernetes
    of Amazon EKS, 257, 260, 262
    defined, 144
    with service meshes, 230
control-plane-version, 234
CoreDNS
    components of, 180
    dnsPolicy and, 181-183
    monitoring, 183
    plugins with, 184-185
CoreOS CNI, 125
corporate networks with ENIs, 248
CRDs (custom resource definitions), 138, 140,
    272
create page, AKS, 298-299
CRI runtime, 101, 146, 152

CRI-O runtime, 101
cURL/curl tool
    client requests with, 11, 24, 47, 90, 308
    commands with, 90-92
    for data transfer, 90-92
    for debugging TLS, 91
    localhost command with, 12, 169, 228
    for service meshes, 231
    for testing ingresses, 228
custom container network mode, 114, 123
custom resource definitions (CRDs), 138, 140,
    272
custom route table, VPC, 246, 254
custom routes, Azure, 286
customer VPC, Amazon EKS, 257-260, 263

D
data
    host-to-host transfer of, 7, 9, 14, 124-125
    HTTP content types of, 13
    TCP header field, 16
    tcpdump transmissions of, 24
data flow of TCP/IP, 16
Data Link layer (see Link layer (L2))
data offset, TCP, 15
data plane, 144
database, Postgres, 168, 170, 191, 268
Date header, HTTP request, 11-13
debugging, 25, 52, 81-92, 220
deployment resource, Kubernetes, 138
    endpoint controller and, 195
    pods and, 147
    versus StatefulSets, 191
destination address, IP header, 32
destination hashing (dh), IPVS mode, 76
destination port identification, 14, 28
destination values, routing, 62, 63
developers, 93-95, 101, 112, 135, 231, 240, 249,
    252, 256
Differentiated Services Code Point (DSCP), 30
dig DNS lookup tool, 84-86
DNAT (destination NAT), 60, 68, 72, 74
DNS (Domain Name System)
    dig lookup tool for, 84-86
    ExternalService with, 212-214
    headless services with, 211, 214
    in Kubernetes, 180-185
    StatefulSets and, 191
dnsPolicy, Kubernetes, 181-183

Fargate, AWS, 257
fault testing, service meshes for, 231
Filter table, iptables, 64, 65, 67-70, 72
filtering
    with eBPF, 78-80
    with NSGs, 287-289
firewalls
    and Conntrack, 60
    IP addresses and, 144
    with iptables chain, 70
    NetworkPolicy and, 165, 173
    rules with GCP/GKE for, 277, 281
flags
    in IP header, 31
    with iptable match types, 71
    with kube-controller-manager, 145
    in TCP header, 15
    in tcpdump output, 22
Flannel CNI plugin, 126, 156, 165
flat CNI network model, 155
flat networks layout, 142-144
flows, Conntrack, 61
footers, Ethernet, 40
forwarding
    with IPVS, 77
    kube-dns service rules for, 163
    with Linux IP, 108
    load balancers and, 278
fragment offset, IP header, 31
frontend IP address, 290

G

gateway load balancers, 254
gateway route table, VPC, 247
GCE (Google Compute Engine) instances, 275, 279, 282
GCLB (Google Cloud Load Balancer), 277-279
GCP (Google Compute Cloud), 275-282
    firewall rules in, 281
    Kubernetes Engine (GKE) in, 279-282
    load balancing in, 277-279
    network services in, 275-279
    network tiers in, 275
    regions in, 276-277, 280
    subnets in, 276-277, 280
    VPCs in, 275-277, 280
genmask values, routing, 63
Get HTTP command, 11-13
GKE (Google Kubernetes Engine), 279-282

global drivers, 123
global resources, GCP, 275
Golang (Go) web server
    with AKS cluster example, 306
    with AWS EKS cluster example, 267-275
    with Cilium, 157-161
    with ClusterIP service example, 206
    with container connectivity example, 127-135
    HTTP request to, 10-13
    with Linux networking, 49, 51-53
    with LoadBalance service example, 215-219
    with NetworkPolicy example, 168-173
    overview of TCP/IP layers with, 46-48
    podspec for, 149
    StatefulSets on, 191
Google Cloud Load Balancer (GCLB), 277-279
Google Compute Cloud (GCP) (see GCP (Google Compute Cloud))
Google Compute Engine (GCE) instances, 275, 279
Google Kubernetes Engine (GKE), 279-282
Gore, Al, 3
grep tool for Conntrack, 63
gRPC service, 75, 152, 226

H

Hacking Kubernetes (O'Reilly book), 309
HAProxy ingress, 226
hash table, Conntrack, 61
header checksum, IP header, 31
headers
    for Ethernet, 40
    for ICMP, 38
    for IPv4, 30-32
    for TCP, 14-17
    for UDP, 28
headless services, Kubernetes, 192, 211-212, 214
health checks/probes
    with CoreDNS, 180, 183
    for load balancers, 255, 291
    on pods by Kubelet, 148-153, 240
Helm deployment, 157, 158, 272, 296
high-level container runtimes and functionality, 97-98, 102
Horizontal Pod Autoscaler service, 219
host container network mode, Linux, 113
host headers (URI), 290

IP tunneling, IPVS mode, 77
IP wildcard addresses, 50
ip6tables, 73
IPAM (IP Address Management) interface, 155
IPAMD, AWS VPC CNI, 263, 264
ipBlock, NetworkPolicy, 176
IPC namespace, Linux, 104
ipFamilyPolicy, 186-187
iptables -L command, 68, 73
iptables, Linux, 64-75
    chains of, 57, 65, 66-70, 73, 208-210
    with ClusterIP service, 206, 208-210
    Docker and, 122
    flow of packets through, 66-70
    as kube-proxy mode, 162
    load balancing by, 74-78, 77
    Netfilter and, 57, 65, 66
    versus nftables, 64
    random routing with, 74, 162
    rules of, 65, 71-74, 80, 220
    tables of, 64-66, 67
    target actions and types of, 71-73
iptables-sync-period setting, 220
IPv4
    addresses, 32-35, 50, 248
    and ENIs, 248
    Ethertype of, 42
    header format for, 30-32
    in ICMP error messages, 39
    iptables with, 73
    as wildcard addresses, 50
IPv4 versus IPv6, 34
IPv4/IPv6 dual stack, Kubernetes, 185-187
IPv6
    addresses, 34, 50, 248
    and ENIs, 248
    Ethertype of, 42
    ip6tables with, 73
    as wildcard addresses, 50
Ipvlan container network mode, 114
IPVS (IP Virtual Server), Linux, 75-78
    as kube-proxy mode, 164
    Kubernetes-supported modes of, 76, 164
    packet forwarding modes of, 77
    response time with, 220
    routing packets with, 75
    session affinity and, 77
ipvs-sync-period duration setting, 220
ipvsadm commands, 77

island networks layout, 144
ISO 7498, OSI model, 3, 8
isolated networks layout, 141-142
Istio Ingress, 226
Istio service mesh, 126, 156, 231

K
keepalive options, server, 53
KEPs (Kubernetes enhancement proposals), 185
kernel, cgroups in Linux, 103
kernelspace mode, kube-proxy, 164
key-value store (libkv), 123
keys for encryption, 25-26
KIND (Kubernetes in Docker) cluster, 157-158, 189, 207, 216, 232
Kong ingress controller for Kubernetes, 226
kprobes, eBPF, 79
kube-apiserver, 186
kube-controller-manager, 145-146, 186
kube-dns service cluster, 163, 180
kube-proxy, Kubernetes, 161-164
    bottleneck with, 77, 196
    Cilium as replacement for, 80
    with ClusterIP, 205
    for dual-stack clusters, 186
    endpoints/endpointslices and, 196, 203
    iptable routing rules of, 203
    iptables mode, 162-164
    IPVS mode, 164
    kernelspace mode, 164
    userspace mode, 162
kubectl commands
    Azure installation of, 303
    guide to, 189
    with Network Policy example, 168-173
Kubelet, Kubernetes, 146-153
    with Amazon EKS, 257
    configurable options for probes in, 150
    configuration file of, 125
    CRI interface and, 101
    for dual-stack clusters, 186
    functionality of, 140
    with probes for health of pods, 148-153, 176, 220, 240
    for status of pod readiness, 148
    worker nodes in, 147
kubenet networking model, 294
Kubernetes

types of, 60
NAT GW (AWS Managed Service NAT gateway), 252, 257
nc (netcat) tool, 88
NCP (Network Control Protocol), 3
NEG (network endpoint groups), 281
netcat (nc) tool, 88
Netfilter, Linux
    Conntrack in, 60-63
    hooks of, 57-60, 65, 66
netmask (subnet mask), 32, 63, 280
netns command, 121, 189
netns list, 120, 208
netns, namespaces and, 109
netshoot image, Docker, 218, 220, 239
netstat, 37, 87-88
netstat -a and -l flags, 88
Network (Internet) layer of OSI model, 5, 6, 8
Network (Internet) layer, TCP/IP (L3), 29-39
    CNI plug-ins at, 156
    IP addresses and, 32-35, 48, 141
    IP header and, 29-32
    IPvlan mode at, 114
    overview of, 9, 47
    routing protocols in, 35-39
    testing connectivity in, 38-39
network access control lists (NACL), 250-252
network address translation (see NAT (network address translation))
network administrators, 35, 45, 127, 231, 240, 256
Network Control Protocol (NCP), 3
network endpoint groups (NEG), 281
network engineers, 25, 94, 135, 249, 250, 252, 262, 275
network interface card (NIC), 21, 22, 41, 47
network interfaces, 53-56, 106-112, 279
network load balancers, 254
network namespaces (see namespaces, network)
network security groups (NSGs), 287-289, 290
network, Libnetwork CNM, 122
network-plugin=cni, Kubernetes, 154
networking, 48
    (see also TCP/IP)
    history of, 1-4
    issues in, 137, 140
    OSI model and, 4-8
    overview of basics, 46-48

NetworkPolicies, Kubernetes
    examples of, 168-173, 178-179
    overview of, 165-168, 179, 220
    pods and, 173-176
    rules and, 167, 176-179
    security with, 165
NetworkPolicyPeer rules, 176
never queue (nq), IPVS mode, 76, 164
nftables, Linux, 64
NGINX ingress controller, 226, 226-229
NIC (network interface card)
    and MAC addresses, 41, 47
    and tcpdump packet capture, 21, 22
nicolaka/netshoot image, Docker, 218, 239
nmap port scanner, 86
node pools, 279, 299
node-CIDR-mask-size flag, Kubernetes, 145
nodeName field, Kubernetes, 147
NodePort services, Kubernetes, 201-204, 264, 266, 278
nodeports, dnsutils for checking, 271
nodes
    in AKS, 294, 299
    cluster network layout options for, 141-144
    in EKS, 256, 262, 263-265
    in GCP/GKE, 278-280
    ingress restrictions and, 226
    scheduling of pod and, 147
    worker nodes as, 147, 157, 204, 206-209, 263
none (null) container network mode, 113, 123
nonterminating targets, iptables, 71-73
NSGs (network security groups), 287-289, 290

O

ObjectMeta type, Kubernetes, 174
observability, service meshes for, 230
OCI specifications for containers, 98
offset field, tcpdump, 22
OIDC provider, 271
open source projects, 94, 100, 114, 126, 156, 184, 263
OpenSSL, 89-90
    certificates and keys with, 89-90
    subcommands in, 89
operating systems and networking stack issues, 94-96
operator, Cilium, 159
options
    IP header, 32

TCP header field, 16
tcpdump output, 22
organization unit identifier (OUI), 41
OSI (Open Systems Interconnection) model
    ISO 7498 standards for, 3, 4, 8
    layers of, 4-8
    versus TCP/IP, 8
OUI (organization unit identifier), 41
OUTPUT, iptables chain, 57, 66-70
overlay CNI network model, 155
overlay container network mode, 114, 123-125

P

packets
    defined, 5
    inbound/outbound, 67-70
    IP (Internet Protocol) and, 29
    iptables processing of, 67-75
    Linux kernel management of, 57-63,
        106-112
    Martian and spoofed sources for, 58
    MTUs of, 9, 29, 264
    Netfilter hooks and, 57-60, 65, 66
    in OSI model, 5
    overview of client request with, 47
    tcpdump capture of, 21-25
padding, TCP, 16
pause container, Kubernetes, 200, 208
PDU (Protocol Data Unit), 5, 46
peering, VPC network, 276, 286, 289
performance, improving, 70, 80, 275, 281
perf_events, eBPF, 79
Physical layer
    of OSI model, 7
    of TCP/IP, 10
PID namespace, Linux, 104, 120
ping network utility
    defined, 82
    failure of Kubernetes with, 82
    ICMP echo requests with, 38
    options for, 83
    ping <address> command, 82
    routing for, 111
pod selector, 165-167, 173-176, 177, 200
pods
    and Amazon eksctl, 262
    and AWS ALB, 270
    and Azure/AKS, 293-296
    bridge interface with, 54

cluster network layout options for, 141-144
CoreDNS/dnsPolicy and, 181-185
and endpoints/endpointslices, 193-200
and GCP/GKE/GCE, 278, 279, 281
with kube-proxy, 161-164
maximum number of, 262, 279, 294
overview of, 138-192
readiness of, 147-153
restriction of communication between (see
    NetworkPolicies, Kubernetes)
and services, 200-201, 205-210
worker nodes with, 147
podSelector, NetworkPolicy, 177
port 80, 9, 14, 132-134, 215
ports
    communication problems between, 137, 139
    container connections to, 122, 132-134
    endpoints and, 193
    HTTP 80 and 443, 9, 14
    identification of, 9, 28
    nmap scanning for, 86
    with NodePort Service, 201-204
    privileged versus nonprivileged, 50
    in shared systems, 94
Postgres database, 168, 170, 191, 268
Presentation layer, OSI model, 6, 8
primitives, Linux, 97, 103-112
    cgroups (control groups), 97, 103-104, 105
    namespaces, 97, 103, 104-112
private subnets, 144, 245, 252, 258, 262, 264,
    268
privileged ports, 50
process id, 121, 208
Production Kubernetes (O'Reilly book), 309
proposed standards (IETF RFCs), 3
proto field, tcpdump, 22
Protocol Data Unit (PDU), 5, 46
protocol numbers, IP header, 31
proxies, 141, 143-144
public subnets, 245, 247, 252, 258, 262, 264, 268

R

Raw table, iptables, 65, 67-70
readiness probes, Kubelet, 148-150
readinessGates, Kubernetes, 151
regions in VPC networking
    with AWS, 244, 249
    with Azure, 283-285, 289, 299
    with GCP, 276-277, 280

About the Authors

James Strong began his career in networking, first attending Cisco Networking Academy in high school. He then went on to be a network engineer at the University of Dayton and GE Appliances. While attending GE's Information Technology Leadership program, James was able to see many of the problems that face system administrators and developers in an enterprise environment. As the cloud native director at Contino, James leads many large-scale enterprises and financial institutions through their cloud and DevOps journeys. He is deeply involved in his local cloud native community, running local meetups, both AWS User Group and Cloud Native Louisville. He holds a master of science degree in computer science from the University of Louisville; six AWS certifications, including the Certified Advanced Networking Specialty; and the CNCF's CKA.

Vallery Lancey is a software engineer who specializes in reliability, infrastructure, and distributed systems. Vallery began using Kubernetes in 2017, living through many of the early-adopter challenges and rapidly evolving features. She has built Kubernetes platforms and operated Kubernetes at massive scale at companies such as Lyft. Vallery is a part-time Kubernetes contributor to SIG-Network. There, she has contributed to kube-proxy and early IPv4/IPv6 dual-stack support.

Colophon

The animal on the cover of *Networking and Kubernetes* is a black-throated loon (*Gavia arctica*), an aquatic bird found in the northern hemisphere.

The black-throated loon is about 28 inches long and can weigh between 3 and 7.5 pounds. Adults are mostly black with white patches, white stripes, and white underparts. The loon usually lays a clutch of two eggs, which they incubate for 27 to 29 days. They make their nests on the ground and due to predation and flooding, it is common for only one chick to survive.

Although the overall population of the loon is declining, its conservation staus is considered of least concern due to its large population over an extremely large range. Many of the animals on O'Reilly covers are endangered; all of them are important to the world.

The cover illustration is by Susan Thompson, based on a black-and white-engraving from *British Birds*. The cover fonts are Gilroy Semibold and Guardian Sans. The text font is Adobe Minion Pro; the heading font is Adobe Myriad Condensed; and the code font is Dalton Maag's Ubuntu Mono.

Lightning Source UK Ltd.
Milton Keynes UK
UKHW032054061021
391778UK00007B/9

9 781492 081654